# The Complete Magician

# The

BY

Illustrated by

# Complete Magician

GREER MARÉCHAL, JR.

the Author and Joseph R. Wardlow

LONDON
*Thomas Yoseloff Ltd*
SOUTH BRUNSWICK AND NEW YORK
*A. S. Barnes and Company*

Library of Congress Catalogue Card Number: 57-6894

A. S. Barnes and Co.
Cranbury, New Jersey 08512

Thomas Yoseloff Ltd
Magdalen House
136–148 Tooley Street
London SE1 2TT, England

*Reissued 1977*
*First Paperback Edition 1977*

ISBN 0-498-01985-3 (hard cover)
ISBN 0-498-01974-8 (paperback)

Printed in the United States of America

To

My Mother

# Foreword

by

## BRUCE ELLIOTT

*Editor of* THE PHOENIX

*Author of* MAGIC AS A HOBBY, CLASSIC SECRETS OF MAGIC,
and THE BEST OF MAGIC

From the time a skinny-shanked old man huddled in front of a twig fire and stirred the evil-smelling contents of a primitive pot in order to make mighty black magic, to the day when a man could walk out on a stage and seemingly defy the dictates of natural law without being harmed, covers almost all of man's history.

We will never know how *magick* with a "k" came into being; what fears, what tangled, fuzzy motivations made man invent *magick*. We know that it served its purpose, and now, but for cults and odd people on the lunatic fringe, magic has lost its final consonant and has become a thing of fun, a minor art in the sense that anything that gives pleasure is an art.

It is of course magic and not *magick* that this book you hold in your hands is about. This introduction to a noble and ancient kind of amusement will lead you as a primer should, from the easy to the more difficult. It stops short of the really difficult, again as a primer should. It helps you on the road to becoming, for better or worse, a magician.

For the better? Yes, for a way to enjoy yourself, to get a kick out of performing something that is out of the ordinary. For the worse? If this book serves its purpose, you will have set your faltering feet on the rocky road to magical hobbyism —and a thorny road it is. You will never be satisfied unless you are trying constantly to improve yourself and your technique.

Your technique can cover anything from sleight of hand to stage presence, from patter to the construction of stage illusions. In other words, once the magic bug has really bitten you, a whole new world opens for you.

We know, for we've been riding our magical hobby horse for thirty years, and, although it has thrown us once in a while, we've always gotten back into the saddle.

From our own experience we can promise you that magic is one of the most enjoyable of all avocations. And if you want to make it your vocation? Then the field is wide open for you to become one of the immortals along with Robert Houdin, Thurston, Kellar, and other wand-wielders who have made both children and adults for a little while live in a world of fantasy where anything is more than likely to happen.

If the names of those giants of the magical firmament mean nothing to you, then perhaps this generation of magicians has entranced you. Perhaps you have seen Blackstone make a pretty girl float high in the air while all the time he is passing a hoop over her to prove to your disbelieving eyes that nothing is holding her aloft but the magic of his wand.

Or perhaps you have seen Cardini, a mad, slightly off-balance creature, cloaked and top-hatted, who reaches into the air and finds to his infinite boredom that a billiard ball has attached itself to his world-weary fingers . . . perhaps you have watched as he tried to disconnect his hands from fans of cards which for some inexplicable reason keep appearing from the circumambient ether.

Or, if you are very lucky, you may have seen Dai Vernon, clothed as a Harlequin, do feats that made seasoned magicians rub their eyes and say incredulously that no one could do the things this Harlequin did.

If magic is to be your vocation these are the men for you to keep in mind, to emulate but not to copy. You will find as you learn magic that there are many tricks—some think too many—but that there are comparatively few ways to present these same tricks.

Presentation is rarely covered in books on magic. This book, by a talented performer, tells you about presentation. Tells you in a way that will teach you much, if you will but learn.

However, whether magic is to be your business or your hobby, we can truly say this book will make the learning easy. Much thought has gone into the description of the various effects that Greer Maréchal has written for you. Try them the way he has described them. See if you can reason out why he places the emphasis on what he does.

If you learn that, then the rest of magic, the presentation of it, the performing of it, the joy of it, will follow easily. We hope that you get half as much fun out of reading this book as we did in listening to the author expound his theories.

We know that when you have finished you will be well grounded in magic and in possession of the secrets of some of the best tricks in magic.

On with the show . . . shine up your wand, polish up your props . . . you're on!

# Contents

FOREWORD                                                      7


PART ONE. THE "WHY" OF MAGIC

I. An Introduction to the Theory of Magic          15
Principles of showmanship as applied to magic.
The important tools of deception and entertain-
ment.


PART TWO. IMPROMPTU MAGIC

II. Tricks with Playing Cards                      35
Simple yet effective tricks that can be mastered
within a few minutes and performed anywhere
at any time.

III. Tricks without Playing Cards                  90
Other varieties of "spur-of-the-moment" magic.

IV. When Conversation Lags                         135
Impromptu opening effects to help the magician
turn the conversation to magic as a preface to his
demonstration.

V. Handle with Gloves                              154
How to execute and utilize seven simple and
easily mastered moves with a deck of playing
cards.


PART THREE. PREPARED MAGIC

VI. Prepared Playing Cards                         183
The most useful methods of preparing a deck of

playing cards and how to use them most effectively.

VII. Tricks Using Prepared Cards                    197
Representative effects illustrating the proper way
to use prepared cards. The masterpieces of playing card magic.

VIII. Tricks with Silks and Handkerchiefs           232
The colorful spectacle of the amateur magician's
program. Easy but effective tricks with one of the
most useful of magical items.

IX. Mental and Spirit Effects                       272
The magician as a mind-reader or spirit medium
instead of merely a conjurer.

X. Miscellaneous Tricks                             314
The masterpieces of the amateur magician's repertoire. Effects using nonmagical-looking apparatus that can be made or collected at home.

L'Envoi                                             389

Index                                               393

# PART ONE

# The "Why" of Magic

*An Introduction to the Theory of the Art of Magic—Showmanship, Presentation, and the Tools of the Magician*

# I

## An Introduction to the Theory of Magic

"It's fun to be fooled—but it's more fun to know!" The maxim is often repeated. Perhaps it would be more accurate to say that everyone likes to have a magician try to fool him. Even the complete cynic really enjoys trying to fathom the magician's secrets. Who indeed can resist the pleasure of assuring his partner that he knows the correct explanation of the magician's art?

There is the converse, too. The magician enjoys trying to fool his audience. His recompense for his devotion to the art of magic—perhaps the very motivation of such devotion—is the thrill he experiences from pitting his own wits against those of the audience. Who would deny the pleasure of being able to mystify and entertain friends? Who would not enjoy the feeling of outwitting, even in jest, a brother or an acquaintance—yes, or the boss?

Indeed, this must be so. Every year there are new books

written about magic. Every year more and more people, young and old, try their hands at the magical art. But every year only a few of those people succeed in experiencing even modest enjoyment or proficiency in the hobby of magic.

And yet magic is one of the easiest and most readily satisfying of all the entertainment arts. It demands none of the absolute and inflexible natural talents required of a singer or musician. Neither is magic limited to a specific situation or occasion, in the sense that the impromptu magician needs neither stage, orchestra, assistants, nor supporting cast.

Well-performed magic is a completely satisfying hobby. With the thrill that comes from complete mastery of an audience, the magician gains added grace and poise and self-confidence so helpful in everyday relations with others. With the gratification of being able to entertain and bring enjoyment to a group of people, the magician gains the knowledge that he has become that much more a part of his society. With the satisfaction of being able to outwit his audience, the magician has gained a further insight into the thinking and desires and idiosyncrasies of those with whom he must live and work.

And yet magic is easy to perform well.

But there is a warning. With magic, as with other fields of endeavor, true success and satisfaction go only to those who really comprehend the underlying principles of why a trick succeeds or fails. To reap the fullest of enjoyment and worth from magic as a hobby the magician must fully understand the "whys" of magic. It is not enough just to know how to do tricks.

The amateur or professional, the student or the hobbyist, and particularly the instructor of magic must concern himself not only with tricks and how to do them, but also with the magical art itself and the principles behind it. If the reader can here discover not only how to do tricks successfully but also *why* magic succeeds or fails, he will have paved the way for a proper and fruitful enjoyment of a fascinating hobby, as well as learned a few tricks with which to entertain his friends.

So let us consider here some of the fundamentals of the theory of magical entertainment.

## II

First of all we must dispense with the notion that magic is difficult or time-consuming. It is not, or, at least, it does not have to be.

How many times have people said, while watching a magician, "I'd love to be able to do that, but it must take years!" That is a little fiction fostered by all magicians. It is quite natural: if the public thinks magic is difficult, it will be that much more ready to respect one accomplished in magic.

Not many years ago, of course, the word "magic" was synonymous with sleight of hand. No one could call himself a magician until he had accomplished the years of arduous practice necessary to become proficient as a sleight-of-hand performer. Today, however, the trend is more to fooling the spectators' minds, rather than to fooling their eyes. Of course, an audience will still applaud and appreciate a good demonstration of difficult sleight of hand as such, but it does not demand sleight of hand for good magic.

For instance, anyone can master the mechanics of any of the tricks in this volume in a few minutes. Hours of arduous practice are not needed, since these tricks depend on subtlety rather than sleight. But, although the magician need not practice with his fingers, he must think—and understand his audience.

When we substitute subtlety for sleight of hand, we substitute a complete understanding of why the trick succeeds and *why* the audience is fooled for the reliance that the sleight-of-hand performer places in practice. That is the reason magic now can be so interesting—and so helpful.

Tricks that are mechanically easy to do, however, are not the whole story. It is easy to fool people—everyone deceives someone else sometime or other—but it is a rather exacting job to *entertain* them.

One has only to watch the effect of one trick in the hands of two different performers to realize immediately that the mechanism or working of a certain trick is really a tiny part of the magician's job. One magician may succeed only in boring his spectators, *although he may fool them completely,* while the other, using the identical trick, will succeed in entertaining in the extreme.

Why the difference? Not that one man had actually fooled the audience more than the other. The difference lies in the way in which the trick was performed—what magicians call the "presentation" of the trick. One magician spoke properly and forcefully, without embarrassment. He paused at the proper moments to let what he had said impress itself on the spectators' minds. He utilized every trick of showmanship to build up his effect; he worked toward a theatrical climax by using suspense, hints of grandeur to come, and all the devices of the showman. The other magician merely did a trick.

For this reason considerable pains have been taken to discuss in detail the presentation of each of the tricks in the following pages. As will readily become apparent, the *modus operandi* or bare mechanical working of the various tricks in the following chapters could be published within much less compass. The reader would then have to work out his own presentation. That is not the object of this book.

It is hoped to give the beginner in magic some tricks which he may effectively perform at once so that, having at his command a number of effective and practical tricks, he may then go ahead and develop his hobby as he likes.

Eventually, of course, every performer must work out his own style of presentation of magic as in all other branches of the entertainment arts. This the magician will want to do, *but not until after he has become a magician.* The beginner will find in the following pages not only the bare mechanical essentials of the tricks but also a discussion of how to present them so as to gain a maximum of effect.

Suffice it to mention at the moment just a few general maxims of the showman's technique as applied to magic, leaving the details until later.

1. *Tell the audience that it is going to be astonished and tell it when.* This is the primary maxim of all showmanship. When the acrobat says "Allez-oop!"—when the drums begin to roll at the circus—the audience knows that something is about to happen. The audience does not know, however, *what* is going to happen. As we shall see in a moment, the magician's greatest weapon is that the audience is ignorant of just what will come next. The audience must, however, know that *something* is going to happen in order to focus its attention.

The magician who hesitantly offers the information that "You are thinking of number three" robs himself of his effect. Compare the bombastic performer who looks his spectator straight in the eye, points his finger menacingly and booms, "I shall now read your mind! You are thinking of the number three!" in a voice that implies he is revealing the end of the world.

The amateur magician does not have the benefit of a full orchestra to heighten the climaxes of his program. He must supply the drum rolls and cymbal crashes himself. He must convey by his manner and his voice and his conduct these three successive ideas to the audience: I am about to perform a miracle! I am now performing a miracle! I have just performed a miracle! He must by his conduct tell the spectators that a climax is coming so they will look forward to it; that a climax is here so they will appreciate it; and that a climax has just passed so they will applaud it.

Furthermore, audiences by and large appreciate a performer who gets a lot of applause more than one who gets a little, completely regardless of whether the performer earned the applause. The magician must make it perfectly clear, therefore, at what point the trick is finished. In that way all the spectators will have the desire to applaud at the same moment (whether by clapping their hands as in a theater or merely saying "Ah!" in the living room).

A clear-cut climax and definite finale are the standard prerequisites for success in any branch of showmanship. They apply particularly to the art of magic.

2. *Acting, poise, and personality, so important to any entertainer, are essential to the magician.* A colorless performer has little to hope for in any of the entertainment arts. But in magic, the performer must make himself colorful. A magician is made, not born. The normally acknowledged assets of a pleasing personality or a vigorous, humorous manner must be cultivated by the magician. They are more than just showmanship with him. They are among the tools of his trade.

The performer who chooses to play the part of a Mephistophelean man of mystery acquires dominion over his audience by overawing the spectators. The magician who chooses to play a smiling, open-faced friend acquires his control over the spectators by making fun of himself, by smiling and convincing them that he wouldn't fool them for the world! The performer with a flair for comedy will gain his audience's confidence and attention—regardless of his magic—in the same way that a stage or television comedian does.

Whether the character portrayed is a man of mystery, a comedian, or just a jovial, smiling friend, the audience must be won before the magic begins. *If the audience does not like the performer's personality, it cannot possibly like his magic.*

In this regard, as will be seen in more detail later, the character and personality represented by the magician play an important part in the *modus operandi* of the magician's tricks. The jovial friend can kid a spectator into helping him against that spectator's will. The nonchalant performer can pass over the weak point of a trick without the audience's attaching importance to it. The man of mystery can arouse with interest and awe a desire on the spectator's part to help him with the trick. The comedian can cause the audience to laugh at his wit (or groan at his lack thereof) at just the right moment to make some hidden movement which the audience misses because it is laughing. A pleasing performer lulls the audience with enjoyment to a point where the spectators are not so able to fathom the performer's tricks.

All these devices—awe, exoticism, mystery, comedy, satire, jovial friendliness, nonchalance, self-ridicule—all these are devices that any entertainer must consider in order to hold the attention and interest of his audience. But they are essential devices for the magician, not only to hold his audience but also to aid his magic.

It is easy to fool an audience; the trick will do that. But it is the performer's presentation that entertains, impresses, astonishes, and mystifies the audience. It is the little subtleties of manner, personality, and character that allow the performer to captivate his audience.


III


The art of magic today can be roughly divided into two main categories: visual deception and psychological misdirection.

The first of these concerns us but little here. Among the tricks comprising the visual deception class of magic we include the mirrors, false-bottomed boxes, mechanical tables, trap doors, and all the various gadgets of magical paraphernalia. Such apparatus achieves its effectiveness from the simple fact that it is constructed so as to make any visual detection of its working impossible. The audience is fooled when a girl disappears from a box for the simple reason that the box is so constructed that it is just impossible for anyone in the audience, whether he be magician or layman, to see where the girl went. Such tricks are an indispensable part of the stage magician's lore. But as far as this book goes, we are not stage magicians.

There are, of course, many smaller tricks that depend entirely upon visual deception for their effect. The reader has probably seen them. It is unfortunate that, for the most part, such tricks approach mere puzzles rather than magic. They are usually clever little gadgets that function by themselves.

As puzzles they are wonderful, but as magic they leave a great deal to be desired. The gadget takes the credit, not the magician. The spectator knows that it is not skill or cunning that has fooled him but merely a clever contraption. Such tricks do not concern us, for the amateur who simply wants to know a few effects with which he can entertain his friends is not interested in carrying a lot of apparatus around with him.

Also in this class of the magic of visual deception we must include to some extent sleight of hand. When the magician apparently puts a coin in his closed fist and causes it to disappear, the audience is deceived because the magician was able to fool the spectators' eyes. The magician was able to remove the coin from his hand secretly in such a way that the spectators simply could not see him do it. As has been noted above, we are not here concerned with sleight-of-hand magic either.

As might be assumed, however, we shall borrow occasionally from the visual deception class of magic in order to accomplish our ends in this book. But the tricks herein described do not depend principally upon fooling the audience's eyes with apparatus so constructed that the audience cannot see what the secret is or with quick and long-rehearsed fingers.

We are here primarily concerned with tricks of the second class, psychological misdirection—with tricks that fool the audience's mind. Many persons find this class of magic the more interesting. They enjoy using this second type of magic to gain an insight into the thought processes and the perspicacity of their fellows, whether merely as a hobby or as a means of learning how better to understand and get along with their friends and acquaintances.

To be proficient in this second class of magic, it is necessary to think—and to understand. Here the magician meets his audience barehanded, so to speak. He understands that certain lack of logic and perception common to us all. He depends upon his knowledge of the way most persons think to lead the thoughts of his audience into the channels he chooses. Here the magician deceives his audience with its own weaknesses and idiosyncracies.

Let us look, then, at this psychological misdirection.

## IV

What, for instance, is misdirection? In the magician's vocabulary, misdirecting means directing the attention of the audience away from the correct solution of a trick. When the sleight-of-hand artist attracts the audience's eyes by a gesture with his right just as his left hand makes some secret move, that is misdirection. When the magician, by what he says, makes the audience overlook some important fact, that too is misdirection.

In analysis, the misdirection for the type of magic with which we are here concerned consists of just one thing: selling the audience on a false premise. At the beginning of a trick we convince the audience that certain circumstances exist when they really do not. We make the audience start its thinking from the wrong place. After that, no matter how intelligent or how observant the audience may be, it can never deduce the correct solution because all its deductions start from the wrong spot.

The magician proposes a problem to the audience: How is it done? Then he withholds certain facts from the audience. It is as though the audience were trying to put a jigsaw puzzle together without some of the key pieces. That is our misdirection.

But how is this accomplished? What tools does the magician use thus to manipulate the thoughts of his audience?

The first and most important is never to let the audience know what is about to happen. The magician picks up a hat. The spectators know something is about to happen, but they do not know whether the magician intends to pull a rabbit out of the hat or bake a cake in the hat. Consequently the audience does not know whether to watch for him to sneak something into the hat or to watch for him to sneak something out of it. The magician is going to do just one thing, but the audience must try to catch him in an infinitude of possibilities.

It is to preserve this weapon that the magician refrains from repeating tricks before the same audience. For example, in "Spirit Calling Card" on page 91, the audience is shown a calling card that is apparently blank. Actually, it is not blank; there is writing on it hidden by another piece of card. Should the audience want to examine the card, it would be readily apparent to the spectator that something was wrong with it.

Since the audience has no idea, however, of what is about

to happen to the card, there is no desire to look at it more closely. So long as the card remains merely an unexplained incidental, it is accepted at face value. The audience is awaiting the climax of the trick. The card appears to be blank and, as far as the audience is concerned, there is no reason why it should not be blank.

Had the magician said that writing would appear upon the blank calling card, the audience naturally would want to inspect the card more closely. Or had the magician said that the card was blank, the question would have been raised in the spectator's minds. Once the audience knew in advance that the card was important, and that something would happen to the card, it would no longer be ready to accept the card when shown at its face value.

In the course of the trick, the audience sees that writing has mysteriously appeared on the card. Now the audience knows *what* was supposed to happen. If the magician were to repeat the trick immediately before the same audience, the audience would demand to inspect the card before he started. That, of course, would be fatal to the trick.

The magician in this trick sold the audience on a false premise: he convinced the audience that a card was blank when in reality it was not. Once the audience accepted the card as blank, it could not then go back and decide it was not. Very, very few persons have the ability, once they have accepted a proposition, to go back in their thought processes alone and reject it.

So the first rule for successful misdirection magic is: *never let the audience know exactly what is about to happen.* As well as being an indispensable tool of deception, this rule is also an aid to proper presentation. Equivalent to the suspense of a mystery story, the lack of foreknowledge in the audience keeps its attention focused to see what is about to happen. The ultimate climax of an effect is heightened by the surprise of an unexpected result. Thus is the magician enabled to fool his audience—and to entertain it.

There is another important tool that the magician uses to help him start the audience off on a false premise. It is visual proof, or inspection. An illustration is afforded by the "Linking Rings" on page 344. This startling and pleasing trick is based upon the simple fact that one of the metal rings involved has an opening in it by means of which it can be linked and unlinked with the other rings.

Here, of course, the false premise of which we wish to convince the audience is that the ring with the opening does not have an opening. Once the audience is convinced that all the rings are solid, the trick becomes insoluble. Without such a conviction on the part of the audience, the trick would be nothing.

To accomplish the seemingly impossible feat of convincing the audience that a steel ring with an opening in it does not have an opening, the magician simply substitutes a solid ring for the open one and lets the audience inspect the solid ring to its heart's desire. After everyone is convinced that the ring is solid, the magician secretly exchanges the solid ring for the open one and proceeds with the trick. Naturally the audience is fooled. How could any audience be expected to fathom the explanation of a trick done with an open ring when the audience has been convinced by inspection of the rings that they are all solid?

This second tool is the most direct and convincing, so let us add another rule to our list: *whenever possible, convince the audience of the necessary false premise by apparently direct proof; let the spectators convince themselves by inspecting the articles used.*

There is a third principal tool in the magician's kit. This one is, perhaps, the most interesting of the three from a standpoint of psychological appreciation of the way the human mind works. It is: whenever possible, accomplish the desired trick by the simplest and most obvious means. Indeed, such a suggestion must seem strangely anomalous in this connection, but experience has proved that it is correct.

It is a natural reaction for all persons to believe that deceiving others is difficult and complicated, since it is not very flattering to one's intelligence to believe that one may be deceived by some means neither difficult nor complicated. It seems logical to suppose that the explanation of a very simple trick would immediately be obvious to the spectators and that the magician must devise some very intricate and complicated means whereby to deceive his audience.

The interesting thing is, however, that the simple explanation for a trick *is* immediately obvious to the audience and *that is the very reason the trick succeeds.* The audience immediately discounts the simple explanation as being too obvious. It would be difficult to stress this aspect of audience thinking too greatly.

Take the trick on page 317, "Lucky Lemon," as an illustration. This trick succeeds because the audience is quite understandably convinced that there are no two dollar bills with the same serial number on them. In trying to fathom the secret of the trick, the spectators continually say, "It would be easy if you had two bills with the same number, but of course that is impossible." In reality it is not impossible, for that is how the trick works.

The audience immediately hits upon the correct solution but just as immediately discounts the solution as being impossible. After dismissing from the mind as impossible the only correct explanation of the trick, who could be expected to figure it out correctly?

So our third rule is: *accomplish the desired trick by the simplest and most obvious means.* The simplest stratagems are the most easily disguised.

From the standpoint of showmanship and presentation, too, this is important: not only keep the *modus operandi* simple so the audience will be fooled, but also keep the effect or plot of the trick simple so the audience can follow easily what the magician is trying to do.

The fourth general tool of the magician for misdirection is rather a corollary to the other three: there should be an innocent and logical explanation for everything that must be done. There must be no jagged spots in the logic of what the magician says to attract the spectator's attention and keep him from glossing over an important point.

If it is necessary for the magician to put his hand in his pocket in order to accomplish a certain trick, he is careful to have some logical excuse for doing so. In the "Spirit Calling Card," for example, there is a rubber band around a small stack of calling cards. Apparently it is there to hold the cards together. That is the *excuse* for the rubber band. Its *purpose*, however, is to hide the edge of a little piece of card essential to the trick, but this real use and purpose of the rubber band is not suspected since there is a natural and logical explanation for having the rubber band there.

In "Lucky Lemon," a search for a pencil is the *excuse* for putting first one hand and then the other into a pocket for the secret *purpose* of exchanging a borrowed dollar for a prepared bill. In "Linking Rings," picking up a silk handkerchief is the *excuse* for laying down one of the rings for the *purpose* of exchanging it secretly for another.

Thus the secret exchange of a bill or a ring is not *invisible* to the audience—it is simply *unnoticed* by the audience because the magician has given it a logical excuse for happening.

If everything that is done has a reasonable explanation, the audience will not be inclined to attach any more importance to one happening than to another. If the audience attaches no importance to some happening, it will not remember that happening. For instance, the audience will attach no importance to the magician's search for a pencil in the "Lucky

Lemon" trick if it is done naturally. Consequently it will not remember, along with everything that happens, that the magician stopped to search for a pencil, and hence that there was a time when the magician might have exchanged the borrowed dollar bill for a prepared one. So for the fourth rule, then, *each essential "secret" movement or device must have an innocent and logical excuse for happening.*

With the proper use of these four tools the magician is able to prevent his audience from correctly deducing the proper explanation of his tricks. How these tools are used and when, of course, depends both upon the requirements of the trick and the demands of its proper presentation.

## V

If the general statements given above are kept well in mind, their specific application to the various tricks discussed in the following pages will be much more easily understood. Consequently, the tricks themselves will be more readily learned and more effectively performed because the reader will understand *how* and *why* the audience is deceived. The reader will then see the reason for each move—no matter how immaterial it may seem—described in the following tricks.

One more advantage which the magician has over his audience should be mentioned, although it is an advantage over which the magician has no control. It is the plain fact that an audience has a very poor memory for details.

In the discussion of each of the tricks that follow there will be found a description of what is known as the "effect." The effect is nothing more than what the audience is supposed to see; it is a description of what would actually happen if the magician were in fact endowed with magical powers and did not have to rely upon skulduggery for his tricks.

It behooves the magician, if he will be a successful entertainer, to make an effort to perform his tricks as nearly as possible as he would if he really did have magic powers.

Just as the dancer who visibly counts with the music ruins his performance by reminding his audience of the more mechanical and less beautiful aspects of his art, so the magician who is visibly concerned with the mechanical intricacies of his tricks reminds his audience that there really is some logical device with which the deception is being accomplished and robs his trick of any magical effect it may have.

Fortunately for the magician, his audience will help him here if given half a chance. With proper emphasis and enthusiasm, the climax of a trick can be made so startling that all memory of the details of what went before will be wiped out. As the spectators think back over what has happened and try to reconstruct in their minds the motions that the magician went through, they will be unable to remember sufficient of them to fathom the trick.

This should be obvious from our consideration of the four rules mentioned above. The audience does not know what is coming and so it must analyze each occurrence as it comes along without knowing whether it is important to the trick or not. This no one—magician or layman—can do efficiently. Consequently the audience forgets many important moves and events that took place during the trick.

This aspect of audience thinking will become apparent the first time the reader hears one of his spectators trying to describe a trick he has witnessed. The description will be a miracle defying all explanation. Once the spectator is deceived, his memory of the trick will be even more mystifying than the magician could hope for. He will forget the necessary mechanical details and remember only the effect, once he is fooled.

We have considered up to here some of the general aspects of the art of magic. Now let us go on to a discussion of specific tricks that we can do. Here we have been discussing the theory of magic. Now let us turn to the practical side . . . to the tricks themselves.

# PART TWO

# Impromptu Magic

*A Score of Simple Yet Effective Tricks to Learn Within a Few Minutes and Perform Anywhere*

The effects that follow in this part are simple enough to learn in a few minutes. Yet each is a practical bit of magic that the reader will use over and over, regardless of his advancement in the art.

All the effects here described are completely impromptu; they can be performed anywhere at any time. They may, therefore, have no place in the planned magic show. That subject is treated in Part Three of this volume.

Here are tricks that are simple enough to learn quickly, effective enough to entertain those not learned in the art of magic, and so devised as to be performed quite on the spur of the moment.

There is, however, yet another reason for choosing these particular effects for publication here: to learn to do magic—not just tricks. The accomplishment of each trick in this section not only adds another effect to the reader's repertoire, it also adds another general principle to his magical thought. With each new principle the reader is better able to think magically and to devise and perform his own effects.

# II

## Tricks with Playing Cards

This first section deals with impromptu tricks using ordinary playing cards. There is no difficult sleight of hand, nor any faked or gimmicked cards involved. Such tricks with playing cards provide a natural introduction to the hobby of magic. There are no objects in everyday use that lend themselves more perfectly to impromptu magic than do playing cards.

Everyone is familiar with a pack of cards. When a magician brings forth his deck, everyone immediately knows that it is (or should be) made up of fifty-two different cards—and the spectators start their thinking from that point. If the magician's deck should, for example, contain an extra ace of hearts, the idea will not immediately occur to the spectators. The spectators will continue to think that there is only one ace of hearts in a deck of cards until something happens to make them change their minds.

If the magician merely used a packet of various pictures,

for example, the spectators would have no preconceived notions about it and the magician would have to convince the spectators that the pictures were all legitimate, etc. Obviously it is much easier to prevent spectators from thinking that there might be an extra card in what appears to be an ordinary pack than it is to prove to the spectators that in fact the extra card does not exist. The burden of proof, as it were, is on the spectators.

Furthermore, the fifty-two cards in a pack are perfect for the magician's purposes since their primary purpose is to deceive—that is, the backs of the cards are made exactly alike so that only the person holding them can see their values. Cards in magic serve the same purposes as they do in card games: as a means whereby one person knows the value of the card and another person tries to guess what it is. Playing cards are thus magical objects without the curse of appearing to be especially made for a magician as some other of the magician's apparatus does.

It is not surprising, then, to realize that most of modern impromptu magic stems from the use of playing cards and, indeed, that virtually all the basic principles of sleight of hand with cards had their birth at the gaming tables with gamblers whose motives had nothing to do with entertainment.

Of course, many persons look with disfavor upon card tricks. Obviously, such categoric disapproval has sprung from the widespread use by inexperienced performers of tricks which create an effect that is, to say the least, unexciting if not downright boring. It gets back to the question of presentation discussed earlier. No one will get very excited about nothing more than a magician's ability to find a presumably lost card. Every magician is supposed to be able to do that.

The performer in selling his trick must remove it from the type of card magic that has given the term "card tricks" an unwholesome connotation in many circles. He must keep his card tricks short, direct, uncomplicated, and snappy—tricks that derive their main entertainment value from something other than the performer's ability merely to run through the deck and pick out a selected card.

## LOOK, NO HANDS!

EFFECT: The magician is able to divine a card selected by the spectator without so much as touching the cards at all. This is a very fine opening effect for an impromptu demonstration that has been prefaced by a discussion of magic or by some such remark as, "Oh, I didn't know you were a magician!"

The trick is baffling in the extreme, but it derives its main effect from a very specialized context: it is the magician's demonstration that he can do "real magic," an illustration of his ability to perform his miracles without recourse to such "ordinary" methods of deception as sleight of hand or apparatus. If the trick is presented specifically in this light, its effect on the spectators and on the spectators' opinions of the magician's ability is invaluable.

Furthermore, as an illustration of the proper application of magical principles to gain a desired result, "Look, No Hands!" is unequaled. The pure mechanics of the trick as disclosed below are the simplest and most obvious in the world. The magician is able to discover the chosen card simply because he has made the spectator replace the card in the deck right above a card which the magician knows. The magician merely has to find his known key card in the deck and he knows that the next card is the one the spectator chose.

But don't stop reading now just because the principle seems both simple and widely known. That is its main virtue. The reader is admonished to study in the presentation below exactly what weaknesses of audience thinking are exploited in order to get the spectator to replace his card precisely where the magician wants him to and to afford the magician the opportunity to look through the cards without appearing to do so, all without the magician's ever touching the cards. This is the magic of "Look, No Hands!"

PRESENTATION: While idly though continuously and ostentatiously shuffling a pack of cards, the magician remarks that he admires very much the ability of some performers to do difficult sleight-of-hand manipulation. That in itself, he says, is an art. But, he continues, what he is really interested in is something more than "digital dexterity." The magician wants to do real magic—and sometimes it appears that he has almost approached the point where he is actually endowed with magical powers.

(It seems hardly necessary to mention that the sort of presentation suggested here should be accomplished in a barefaced, exaggeratedly serious manner. Generally speaking, the most fatal blunder a magician can ever make is to let his audience think that he actually takes himself seriously!)

While he has been talking and shuffling the cards, the magician has noted and remembered the top card.* This is the magician's key card.

The noting of this top card is simple. The magician, while he is toying with the cards, simply glances over their faces, and then, as he shuffles the deck—preferably using a riffle or interlacing shuffle—he is careful to let the noted top card fall last, so that it will always remain the top card. Many persons habitually and unconsciously shuffle cards without disarranging the top few cards. A moment with a deck of cards will show that this is no problem. Be sure, however, to shuffle the cards several times after the top card has been noted, and be sure to remember that top card.

* Here and elsewhere in this volume, the top and bottom of the deck refer to the position of the deck when it is lying face down on the table. Thus, the "bottom" card is the card whose face is against the table and the "top" card is the card whose back is showing.

For instance, the magician continues, he will do a trick without even touching the cards, just to eliminate the possibility that he might be using sleight of hand. So saying, he places the deck on the table or floor, directly in front of one of the spectators, and tells the spectator to cut the deck into as many little piles of cards as he pleases.

It makes no difference into how many piles the spectator divides the cards. The only thing the magician has to do is to *watch where the spectator puts the top card of the deck.* That top card must always be on top of a pile. If the spectator tries to cover it up by some erratic method of cutting the cards, stop him with a casual but firm admonition to cut the cards in a straightforward manner, or any such statement that will interrupt his actions. It will be noted with experience that, when a spectator is about to do something undesirable, a firm direction to change his tactics will have the effect of embarrassing him for making a blunder, whereas an embarrassed plea on the part of the magician will only cost him prestige and mastery over the audience by revealing a weak spot in his art.

Figure 1

From here on it will be convenient to visualize the trick in terms of the drawing in Figure 1. No matter how many piles the spectator cuts, the magician must always keep track of the pile with the known key card on top throughout the following procedure.

SELECTING THE CARD. It is desirable to allow the spectator as much freedom of choice as possible. He is invited to point to—but *not* "pick up"—any pile he wants. If he points to the key card pile, he is asked to remove any card from that pile and look at it. If, as is more probable, he points to another pile, he is asked to shuffle that pile and then remove any card he chooses. He is to replace the pile and retain his card which he memorizes and shows to other spectators if he chooses. The magician should never forget to admonish the spectator to remember his card since there is nothing so fatal to the climax of a trick as the spectator who has forgotten what card he picked.

REPLACING THE SELECTED CARD. The spectator must now be made unwittingly to replace his card in the deck directly above the known key card. If the magician simply told the spectator to replace his card on the key card pile, it would probably be rather obvious to the audience what the magician was trying to do. Therefore the magician manages to accomplish the same thing while making it appear that the spectator is assembling the deck just the way he wants to.

The spectator is asked to point to "another" pile. Since the spectator has no idea what is coming, he will do so. If he points to the key card pile, the magician tells him to place his selected card on top of that pile and then to reassemble the rest of the piles in any way he chooses. That, of course, is the easiest possibility.

It is more probable that he will point to some pile other than the key card pile. In that case, the magician asks the spectator to place his card face down on the table and place the pile to which he is pointing on top of his card. Again the spectator is asked to point to another pile, and, if he again misses the key card pile, this second pointed-to pile also goes on top of the first pointed-to pile.

In other words, *the spectator is asked to point to one pile after another, until he finally points to the pile with the key card on top.* All the piles other than the key card pile go on top of his selected card. He may be invited to shuffle some of these piles before adding them to the deck.

When the spectator does finally point to the key card pile (and, as will be seen, it makes no difference *when* he does so), the magician stops and asks the spectator—in a manner that should suggest what the magazine writers call "disarming candor"—where his selected card is. The spectator will say that it is resting on the table at the bottom of the partially assembled deck. That's right, says the magician, but it would be very easy to find it there, so just bury it completely by putting that pile (the key card pile) underneath the selected card so it will be completely hidden above and below.

The effect of this procedure is that the spectator is directing by his pointing just how the deck is to be reassembled, and, in the process, has buried the selected card so that it is completely lost. The magician emphasizes this aspect by remarking that the card is lost since the spectator has chosen pile after pile according to his own desire.

It must be noted that the magician said "point to another pile" each time and only after he saw which pile was selected did he tell the spectator what to do with it. The spectator, however, does not know that fact. If the spectator pointed to two piles, for example, before he hit the key card pile, he will assume that each time the magician does the trick the first two piles are placed on top of the selected card and the third pile underneath it. If someone suggests that the magician is using a key card, the assisting spectator will be the first to say, "But suppose I had pointed to a different pile!" as if that were a complete answer.

Indeed, strange as it may seem, even if one of the spectators happens to follow the top card's movements sufficiently to realize that it ends up next to the selected card, he will attach no importance to that fact. It appears that such a situation is mere coincidence and if the spectator had pointed to a different pile, the top card would not have ended up next to the selected card. Besides, there is little need to worry that anyone in the audience will follow which card is the top card originally, since there is no reason to suppose that it might be important. As a matter of fact, unless the magician watches what he is doing, he too may lose his key card in the process!

IDENTIFYING THE SELECTED CARD. Having got the selected card in a position immediately above the key card that the magician knows, some way must be devised to afford the magician an opportunity to look through the cards without appearing to do so and especially without the magician's having to touch the cards at all.

When the deck is completely assembled, the magician suggests that the spectator cut the deck and complete the cut. "Just a regular cut to confuse the issue," the magician says, holding himself ready to add "nothing fancy!" in case the spectator starts to show off with some weird method of mixing the cards. As will be seen upon a moment's reflection, the deck can now be cut an infinite number of times without in any way affecting the fact that the selected card is immediately above the key card. The worst that can happen is that the spectator will cut exactly between the key and selected cards so that one will be on top of the deck and one on the bottom; but that is really no problem since the magician knows, if he finds his key card on the top of the deck, that the selected card is at the bottom.

Notwithstanding the truth of this statement, most laymen believe that a cut will materially mix the cards in the deck. Obviously, this is a carry-over from the gaming table. If in a poker game, of course, someone set up some cards in a sequence so as to give certain cards to certain players, a cut would completely disrupt such a sequence. But a cut, or any number of single cuts, will never separate the magician's key card from a selected card.

After the spectator has "mixed" the cards by cutting, the magician asks him if he remembers what his card was. Perhaps the spectator would like to look at it again or make sure it is still in the deck. Sometimes, the magician says, people accuse him of sneaking the selected card out of the deck under their very noses, and he insists that the spectator make sure that did not happen here. Would the spectator turn the deck face up and spread it out on the table so that he can assure himself his card is still there? But he must be sure— again the disarming candor—to give no indication of recognition when he sees the selected card, not even the twitch of an eyelash. The magician makes a great show of gesturing to show what he means, and of having to restrain himself from touching the cards.

As the spectator spreads the cards on the table to look for his selected one, the magician begins to recapitulate what has happened. He points out that the spectator took a shuffled deck and cut it into as many piles as he pleased. He then selected any one pile, and from that pile selected any one card. The deck was reassembled "completely as the spectator directed, shuffling as he went along," and finally the deck was cut so that the spectator's selected card was completely lost in the pack. Had the cards been in any special order, that order would, of course, have been upset, etc., etc. And at no time has the magician so much as touched the deck of cards.

While saying this, the magician is casually watching the spectator spread the cards to look for his own. The performer is careful not to appear to study the cards—just a glance now and then to see that what the spectator is doing is enough. *As soon as the spectator can see his own card in the spread, the magician can, of course, see his key card, the original top card of the pack.* The magician knows that the selected card is the one above or behind the key card, and so the magician knows what card the spectator selected as soon as the spectator finds it in the spread.

Thus, as the spectator spreads the cards to look for his selected card, the magician glances at the spread and sees, for example, something like Figure 2. Assume that the queen

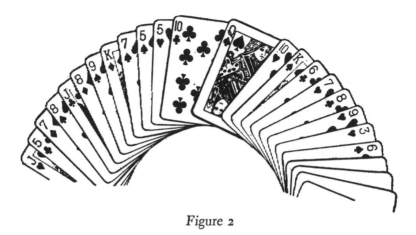

Figure 2

of spades was the original top card of the deck that the magician noted at the start of the trick. As soon as the spectator can see his card in the spread, the magician can see the queen of spades and knows immediately that the card above it in the deck—the ten of clubs—is the card the spectator selected.

As soon as the spectator himself has been assured that his card is still in the deck (and the fact, by the way, that it would be completely impossible by any means for the card not to be in the deck does not lessen the effectiveness of insisting that the spectator assure himself it still is) the magician suggests that the spectator shuffle the deck. That, of course, is pure flimflam, but afterward, everyone will remember that the spectator did shuffle the deck himself, even if they do not remember exactly when he did so. Also, it helps separate the looking through the deck from the magician's disclosure of the selected card, so that the former will not appear to be a necessary prerequisite to the latter.

Now, says the magician, rising beautifully toward his climax, if everyone will concentrate on the selected card, he will try—without ever having touched the deck, indeed, without the deck's ever having left the spectator's control—to divine the selected card by means of real magic, not sleight of hand. The magician frowns and thinks and gradually the impression of the selected card comes to him, so that, with a final flourish, he announces triumphantly the name of the card.

NOTE: It has taken much longer to describe this trick than to perform it. The author has indulged himself in so detailed a description in the hope that the reader will recognize and become interested not only in the trick itself but also in the theoretical application of magical principles illustrated by "Look, No Hands!" The reader should try this trick as described and then again, making whatever changes may suit his fancy, trying all the while to discover in how many ways the extremely simple requirements of the working of the trick can be disguised. In what other ways could the spectator be forced to replace his card next to the magician's key card without the magician's touching the deck? What other explanation could be given as an excuse for the magician's having a chance to look through the deck?

There are many words and many acts suggested in the above description. Each of those words and each of those acts has its purpose, and its contribution to make toward the ultimate effect of the trick and of the reader as a magical performer. One who understands the purpose and the contribution of the various parts of the trick will become an artist in magic. One who does not will be merely doing tricks which will not entertain and sometimes not even deceive an audience.

## BACKWARD GLANCE

EFFECT: A spectator finds his own card in the deck while holding it behind his back.

PRESENTATION: The magician shuffles the cards thoroughly and then, placing the deck on his outstretched palm, invites a spectator to cut off about half the deck. The spectator is then instructed to shuffle his half well.

While all eyes are on the spectator's shuffling, the magician quietly and secretly turns the bottom card of his packet face upward. There is no need to hurry about this. Just wait until all are watching the spectator shuffle. If all eyes do not watch him, make some remark about how well or how poorly he handles the cards to direct attention to his shuffling.

When the spectator has his packet shuffled, the magician instructs him to reach into the middle thereof and extract one card, which he is to memorize and show to the others present. After all (except the magician) have noted the selected card, the magician instructs the spectator to place his card on the top of his packet. The magician then buries the selected card by placing his own packet on top, holding it level so that the audience will not see the bottom card is face up. This procedure, of course, places the face-up card secretly right on top of the selected card in the face-down deck. The situation now is indicated by the exploded diagram of Figure 3A.

The magician, after calling attention to the fact that the selected card is buried in the deck, says he wants the spectator to find the card for himself. To this end the magician takes the deck from the spectator in his left hand. He asks the spectator to come stand in front of the audience and places him facing the other spectators in such a way that no one can see behind the assisting spectator's back.

Asking the spectator to place his hands behind his back, the magician's left hand carries the deck behind the spectator and places it in his hands. As soon as the deck is out of sight behind the spectator, but before giving it to him, the magician turns the top card of the deck face up. (This is quite simply accomplished with one hand, by pushing the

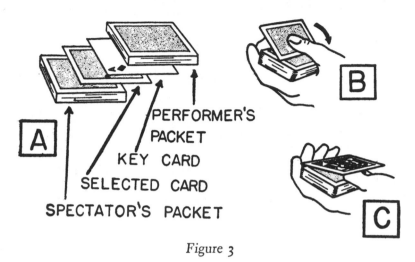

PERFORMER'S
PACKET
KEY CARD
SELECTED CARD
SPECTATOR'S PACKET

Figure 3

top card off one side of the deck with the thumb and flipping it over with the fingers, as in Figures 3B and 3C.)

Now, explains the magician, the spectator is to take the top card of the deck, turn it face up, and insert it in the deck at any point he chooses. He is then to square up the deck and bring it forward. When he has done this, the magician tells him that he unwittingly inserted the face-up card directly above his own selected card. The deck is spread out and the magician is found to be correct.

Obviously, what happened was that the spectator took the already face-up top card (believing it to be face down) and turned it face down before inserting it into the deck. The reversed card visible at the finale is the original bottom card of the deck secretly reversed by the magician himself.

## SPELLBOUND

EFFECT: Although the magician himself is unable to discover a selected card, the card announces itself by spelling out its name. This is one of the many effects disclosed to the author by Dr. F. V. Taylor.

PRESENTATION: While handling the cards, the magician secretly notes and remembers the top card of the deck and then shuffles the cards thoroughly, being careful not to disturb the top card. Suggesting that he will try a very difficult feat in card magic, the magician offers a spectator a free choice of a card from the deck by spreading it between his hands.

While the spectator is looking at his card and memorizing its name, the magician squares up the deck and, holding it in his left hand, pulls out the bottom half of the deck with

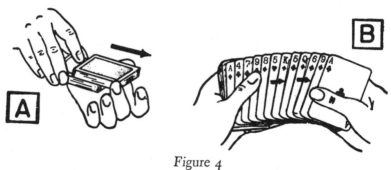

Figure 4

his right thumb and second finger, as in Figure 4A. When the spectator has noted his selected card, the magician extends his left-hand packet toward the spectator and requests that he place his card "right on there," indicating the top of the left-hand packet. This, of course, puts the selected card directly on top of the original top card of the deck—the magician's key card. Immediately the magician slaps the right-hand packet down on top of the selected card, thus, to all intents and purposes, burying it in the middle of the deck. The effect of this move is that the magician merely cut the deck for the return of the selected card. Because the bottom half of the deck is withdrawn, the cut seems backward and none of the spectators will be aware that the selected card was returned on top of the original top card instead of in the middle of the deck.

The magician places the deck immediately on the table and says that nothing disturbs the order of cards more, or makes a selected card harder to find, than three successive cuts. The magician then asks the spectator to cut the deck three times (or asks three spectators each to cut the deck once) making sure that each is a single, complete cut. As has already been noted, no amount of cuts will ever change the fact that the selected card is immediately above the magician's key card, but the emphasis on just three cuts and no more will tend to distract the spectators' attention from a desire to shuffle the deck at this point.

Although the deck has been cut three times by the spectators themselves before the magician handled the cards, the performer says, he will attempt the very difficult feat of finding the selected card. He picks the deck up and, starting at the face of the deck, runs the cards rapidly, one at a time, from hand to hand (left to right) without reversing their order as in Figure 4B. He frowns and gives the impression that it is harder to find the selected card than he thought it would be.

As he studies the faces of the cards, he looks for his key card. Assume it to be the queen of spades. As soon as he sees it, he knows that the selected card is the one next above (to the left of) the queen. As soon as he knows the identity of the selected card, the magician begins spelling its name to himself and running one card for each letter from his left hand to his right. Thus, assuming the selected card to be the ten of clubs, the magician spells to himself T-E-N-O-F-

C-L-U-B-S, and he runs one card for each letter from his left hand to his right, beginning with the ten of clubs for the first letter.

When the magician has reached the card corresponding to the last letter, he looks up and says that this is more difficult than he thought. He can't seem to get an impression of the cards. Would the spectators mind concentrating a little more energetically?

As he spoke, the magician stopped running the cards from hand to hand so that he could keep his place in the deck. Now he again studies the cards and notes the name of the card just to the left of the card last spelled off—that is, the card to the left of the one corresponding to the final "s" in "Clubs." Let us say that this card is the six of spades. Imme-

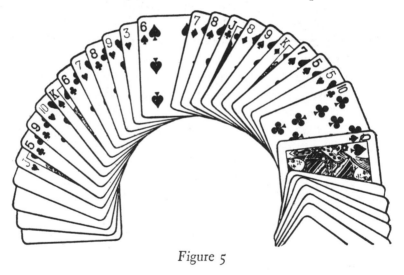

Figure 5

diately the magician begins running cards from hand to hand again, this time spelling S-I-X-O-F-S-P-A-D-E-S and running one card for each letter as before.

Reference to Figure 5 may make this clearer. In looking through the deck starting with the face, the magician thumbs the cards from hand to hand (without reversing their order) until he comes to the key card he noted at the start of the trick—the queen of spades. Because the selected card was replaced in the deck on top of the queen, the magician knows that the next card (the ten of clubs) must be the selected card. Beginning with the ten, then, he spells off "ten of clubs," one card for each letter, silently to himself. This brings him to the seven of diamonds, which falls on the "s" of "Clubs." The next card is the six of spades so the magician, after pausing to speak to the audience, spells off "six of spades" silently, one card for each letter, while appearing merely to be studying the cards.

Now the magician stops studying the cards and shakes his head disappointedly. At the same time he separates in his left hand any cards remaining after he has finished spelling the six—that is, all the cards to the left of the jack of hearts in Figure 5. These he nonchalantly moves to the face of the deck, so that the last card spelled (the jack of hearts in the illustration) becomes the top card of the deck. Should there not be enough cards to spell out the second name, the magician continues his spelling by going back to the face of the deck. When he is finished, he cuts the deck so that the card that corresponds to the last letter of the second name will be the top card of the deck.

Obviously the situation now is that the magician has set up the top few cards of the deck so that if he were to deal off one card for each letter in S-I-X-O-F-S-P-A-D-E-S, the six would turn up on the last letter. Similarly, if he were then to deal off one card for each letter in the name of the selected card (ten of clubs), that card would turn up on the last letter. What is more, the magician has been able to accomplish this right under the spectators' very noses while he was apparently merely studying the faces of the cards while hunting for the selected one. The only reason for stopping between the two setups and speaking to the spectators is to cut down the length of time the magician must be silent while counting the cards.

The magician now tells the spectators that he has failed. The three cuts fooled him and he cannot find the card. But, he says, he will "snap" the deck (which he does by running his thumb across the edges of the cards so that they make a snapping or tearing noise), and that will cause the cards all to arrange themselves in such order that, when the name of any card is spelled, it will turn up on the last letter.

Thus, illustrates the magician, if the spectator's selected card were the six of spades (the magician speaks as if he were naming a card at random) he would spell the name of the card dealing one card for each letter, from the top of the deck. The magician does so and the six turns up on the last letter.

Now, asks the magician, what was the selected card? The spectator tells him it was the ten of clubs, and the magician then spells its name, one card for each letter, and the selected ten turns up on the last letter.

NOTE: It is difficult to overestimate the effectiveness of this trick in the hands of the good-natured and casual performer. The natural tendency to hurry through the setup, almost with a guilty conscience, must be curbed. Take all the time needed; there's no rush. The performer should grimace and frown as if he were really trying to discern the selected card with brain power alone. The more he acts, the better. The audience, of course, realizes that he is acting. No one realizes, however, why he is acting, and the idea of being able to set the deck up without picking cards out and replacing them in the deck never seems to occur to the audience.

At the climax of the trick the spectators, of course, realize that somehow or other the magician succeeded in setting up the deck so that the selected card would spell out in the right spot. The reason the trick is impressive is because the spectators cannot for the life of them conceive when the magician set up the deck, since apparently all he did was to look through the cards.

This is just another example of the lack of audience logic. The spectators—if they think about it at all—have the idea that the only way to get a certain card tenth from the top of the deck is to count down ten cards and put the desired card there. The idea of counting up from the desired card and removing any excess cards seems never to occur to the spectators. And the idea of setting up *two* cards to spell out properly while all eyes were focused fixedly on the performer, to say nothing of how the magician discovered the identity of the selected card in the first place, is just beyond most spectators' comprehension.

The magician need strive for but two goals: to count the cards to himself without moving his lips and to run the cards from hand to hand in a uniform manner as if he were merely looking through the deck and not as if he were counting the cards.

## COLOR BLINDING

EFFECT: Two spectators find that they are apparently endowed with magical powers because they can separate all the cards of the deck into black and red piles without ever looking at the faces of the cards.

Little reflection is needed, of course, to realize the entertainment possibilities of the type of trick where the magician apparently does nothing at all but the assisting spectators succeed in accomplishing some result that not only baffles the rest of the audience but the assisting spectators as well. Also, the more the performer praises the psychic powers of his baffled assistants, the more the audience will credit him as a very clever fellow.

PRESENTATION: As might be expected, this trick requires some prearrangement of the order of the cards. Many performers can accomplish this right under their spectators' noses while thumbing through the cards apparently looking for the joker. It is perhaps better, however, for the performer to arrange his setup while he is momentarily out of the room or absently playing with the cards while no one is paying much attention.

The setup itself is rather simple. The cards are simply arranged so that three black cards alternate with a group of three red cards all through the deck. Thus the top three cards will be black, the next three red, the next three black, and so forth. This will leave two black and two red cards left over. These are placed on the face of the deck—first one red, then two black, and lastly the remaining red. As a result all the cards in the deck are arranged three by three in alternate black and red trios except the last four cards on the face of the deck, which are one red, two black, and one red. In this condition, the deck can be fanned (see page 136) or spread between the hands and the faces shown to the audience without any prearrangement of the cards being apparent—especially if the fan or spread is rather uneven.

As with all setup tricks, a false cut (see page 161) or false shuffle (if the performer can do a convincing one) is in order if it can be performed casually. But if the performer cannot accomplish a false cut or shuffle without being so studious and careful with the cards as to call attention to his efforts, they should be avoided completely. Allowing the audience—very casually and without making a point of it at all—to glance at the faces of the cards is sufficient to convince the audience that nothing is amiss.

It must be remembered that fanning the cards with the faces to the audience convinces the spectators that all is fair with the deck, not because they can actually see that the faces look all right, but because they believe that, if the deck were set up in some way, the magician would not dare show the faces of the cards to the audience.

The magician wants to create the impression that he just

does not care whether the audience sees the cards or not, and to do that, he must be casual. If he makes a point of wanting to display the cards so that the audience can see that they are not prearranged, the spectators will really want to look at the pack, shuffle it, etc. If he casually flashes the faces toward the audience without any emphasizing comment, the spectators will see nothing amiss and immediately rule out the possibility of there being anything wrong with the cards.

The magician fans the cards so that the audience can see the faces and says that anyone can separate the cards according to their respective colors by looking at the faces. That, he says, is easy. But some persons are endowed with some sort of unusual sixth sense that lets them separate the cards into red and black piles *without* looking at the faces. And such persons are frequently completely ignorant of their extraordinary ability. Perhaps, he suggests, there are some such psychically endowed persons among the spectators. Anyway, the magician proposes a contest between two spectators to see which one can be most successful in separating the cards according to color without looking at the faces.

As he talks, the magician begins dealing the cards into two face-down piles. He thumbs the cards off the deck three at a time as if to save time in the dealing or as if he were an inveterate pinochle player. He deals rapidly and without calling attention to what he is doing. He is talking all the while, deciding which two spectators shall compete and saying that it is not a race but rather a contest to determine which one possesses the more occult power, or what have you. Obviously, dealing the cards three at a time into two piles means, because of the setup, that one of the piles contains all black cards and the other all red cards. The audience, of course, has no reason to suppose that the colors are not randomly mixed in each pile. The performer explains the dealing by saying he has divided the deck exactly in half so that each contestant has an equal number of cards.

Because the last four cards of the deck (dealt two on each pile) were out of order, the last card dealt onto the black pile was a red card and the last card dealt onto the red pile was a black one. The magician remembers where the two last cards fell so that he can pick them out when desired.

Now, says the magician after the cards are dealt and the contestants chosen, each will take a pile. Mr. A will take that pile (pointing to the all black pile) and Mr. B will take this one (the all red pile). Mr. A (with the black pile) will simply pick out all the cards he thinks are black and slide them to one side and Mr. B, just to be different, will pick out all the cards in his pile that he thinks are red and push them aside—all without ever looking at the faces. Then at the end of the contest the cards will be turned over and the score tallied.

In order to show where who is to put what cards, the magician reaches over to the black pile and picks up any card and looks at it. It is black and so he lays it aside face up. That black card is to indicate where Mr. A is to place the cards he thinks are black. Reaching again into the black pile, the magician picks up another card and looks at it. It also is black and he throws it back face down on the pile and picks up the one red card—the last card he dealt onto the pile. This red card he lays face up near the black pile. This card will indicate where Mr. A is to leave all the cards in his pile he believes to be red.

The effect of all this is that the magician, desiring a red and black card to use as indicators, picked several cards at random from the pile until he got one red and one black. The maneuver also serves to convince the audience even further that the face-down cards are both red and black mixed. The magician then does the same thing with the red pile, picking out first a red card and then the one black card, the whereabouts of which he knows.

MR. "A" TOLD TO
PUSH CARDS HE
THINKS ARE <u>BLACK</u>
OVER HERE

MR. "B" TOLD TO
PUSH CARDS HE
THINKS ARE <u>RED</u>
OVER HERE

MR. "A"

ALL BLACK

ALL RED

MR "B"

R

B

Figure 6

Figure 6 will clarify the above description. The placement of the cards is critical in the success of the trick and so the reader should study the drawing until he understands where the cards are and how they got there. Mr. A (on the left) is told to slide all his black cards from his pile over toward his black indicator without looking at them. Mr. B (on the right) is told to slide all the cards in his pile that he thinks are red over to his red indicator card, leaving the black ones behind.

If the magician has kept a straight face throughout these instructions, both spectators will probably look at him blankly, wondering how they are to tell which cards are red and which black without looking at the faces. The magician explains that they are just to slide whatever cards they feel like sliding and that their psychic powers—if any—will subconsciously guide their hands. Then he coyly adds the hint, that, since each has half of a well-mixed deck, the law of averages indicates that about half of each pile should be red and half black.

Naturally, the spectators will be inclined to feel rather silly, but the magician cajoles them each into sliding about half of each pile toward the two indicators—either one card at a time or in bunches. When about half of each pile has been transferred the magician stops the proceedings. It is immaterial exactly how many cards are pushed around, just so each of the four resulting piles contains more cards than can be counted at a glance.

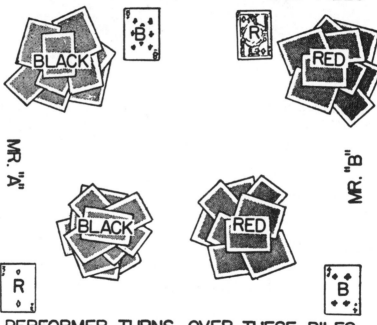

Figure 7

The final result at the end of the "contest" is depicted roughly in Figure 7. Note that each of the piles to which Mr. A and Mr. B slid cards matches its indicator card as to color but that the original piles do not match their indicators.

Now, says the magician, the score will be counted. Mr. A is asked to turn over the pile of cards he picked out as being black and Mr. B is asked to turn over the cards he picked as being red. Naturally each discovers that all the cards he picked are of the proper color. "All black!" cries the magician, and "All red!" as each pile is turned up.

"Wonderful!" says the magician. At least all the cards that each picked were the right color. Now let's see if each picked out all the cards he should have.

So saying, the magician himself scoops up the remains of both the original piles by scooping Mr. B's remaining cards together and using those cards as a shovel to slide under Mr. A's remaining cards and pick them up. He turns the whole batch face up and, taking off the top (all red) half of the pile, he drops it face up beside Mr. A's red indicator and says "All red!" He then drops the remaining cards face up beside Mr. B's black indicator saying ". . . and all black!" A perfect score, proclaims the magician, and the contest is a tie, each spectator apparently possessing the ultimate of color-separating occult power.

Obviously the scooping up of all the remaining cards together and turning them over allows the magician in the most natural manner possible to switch the two piles so that they match their indicators. The surprise occasioned by finding the first two piles to be correctly separated as to color when the magician has not touched them is flabbergasting enough that the audience will not worry that the magician himself turned over the second pair of piles. The repetition by the magician of "All red!" and "All black!" as each pile is shown will aid this idea.

NOTE: 1. As was noted at the start, the locations of the various piles of cards is very important to the working of the effect. Therefore the magician is careful to deal the deck originally into two piles rather close together and directly in front of himself. The two indicator cards he is careful to place at some distance from original piles, as in Figures 6 and 7. Also, he tells the spectators to stand or sit near the farther indicators. Thus, when the trick is completed, the spectators are closest to the piles that correctly match their indicators, whereas the remains of the original piles are directly in front of the magician. Hence it is completely natural for the magician to turn over the original piles, since he is closest to them.

2. Sooner or later the performer will run into the clown who flatly refuses to move any cards from his pile, jokingly maintaining that there are no red cards there, etc. When this occasion arises the magician, depending on his presence of mind, will either manage to get another "contestant" or will say that he knew the spectator would feel that way and so just for his benefit gave him nothing but red cards to play with—thus saving some small measure of effect by taking credit for being able to separate the cards into their respective colors while merely dealing them out.

3. The reader is heartily recommended to another color separation trick to use as an alternate with the above effect. It is called "Out Of This World" and is a product of the exciting magical inventiveness of Mr. Paul Curry. Any magic shop can supply full instructions for around a dollar or so. Mr. Curry's effect is perhaps one of the most startling and effective impromptu effects yet devised and only the fact that it is a currently popular proprietary trick dissuades the author from including it in this volume.


## SYMPATHETIC STUDENT

EFFECT: The magician offers to teach a spectator how to perform one of his tricks. Not only does the magician succeed in finding the student's selected card but, much to his own surprise, the student succeeds in discovering the magician's card. This is another effect which, though simple in itself, derives considerable punch from the fact that the baffled spectator apparently succeeds in accomplishing a trick without having the slightest idea how he did so. Credit for the basis of this amusing effect goes to Mr. Al Baker.

PRESENTATION: The magician offers to show one of the spectators how to do a trick. He will do more than just explain it, says the magician, he will perform it right along with the spectator, just to make sure he gets everything right.

First of all the magician hands the spectator a deck of cards and asks him to shuffle it thoroughly. A would-be magician must always shuffle his cards thoroughly, he explains. Next the student spectator is asked to hand the magician about half of the deck so they will each have some cards with which to work.

From here on out, explains the performer, the student must follow his moves exactly and, presumably, if the two work exactly together and each does a trick, the two tricks should come out with the same result. But first the magician asks the student to look through his half of the deck and remove the joker if it is there. The joker always seems to get in the way in tricks like this. The magician does the same but as he looks through his packet of cards he secretly notes and remembers the top card of his packet as his key card.

Now, says the magician, he will be the student's audience and the student must be the magician's audience. So the magician, acting as the student's audience, shuffles his packet of cards and requests the student to do the same for him. The magician is careful, however, to let the top card (his key card) fall last in the shuffling.

The magician and the student now exchange packets. This increases the difficulty of the experiment, the magician explains, because now each is holding a packet of cards shuffled by the other. Also the student is now holding a packet the top card of which the magician knows.

The magician reaches into the packet he holds and removes one card, looks at it, and places it on top of the packet. He requests the student to do the same with his own packet, move for move. The magician admonishes the student to remember the card he selected but the magician does not bother to remember the card at which he looked. Each now cuts his packet, thus burying the card each selected. But when the student cuts his packet, he is burying his selected card right on top of the magician's key card.

Once more the magician and the student exchange packets. The situation now is, explains the magician, that each is holding a packet of cards in which is hidden one card selected by the other. Since both the magician and the spectator have gone through exactly the same moves, says the magician, they should end with exactly the same result—that is, if the student has been paying attention like a good student.

The student is now asked to look through the cards he holds and to pick out the card that he finds *most resembling his own selected card*. Thus if the student had selected the ten of clubs, he is to pick from the cards he now holds the ten of spades, or, if that card is not there, a red ten, etc., and to lay that card on the table. The magician will do the same, he explains. When both cards are on the table the magician announces that he has found the student's selected card. He turns the card he has just laid on the table face up and it proves to be the one selected by the student. Now, says the magician, he hopes the student was attentive enough to have succeeded in finding the magician's card. It was, he says, the ten of spades. Whereupon the student turns over the card he had placed on the table and, much to his own amazement, it is the ten of spades.

Naturally the magician is hearty in his congratulations to the student on his success and says how happy he is that the student is so quick to learn how to do tricks.

The method by which the foregoing is accomplished is simple. If the above procedure is followed it will be seen that magician is holding the student's packet containing the student's selected card immediately above the magician's key card. In looking through his cards, the magician looks first for his key card. The card immediately behind the key will be the student's card. This is the card the magician will place on the table.

Figure 8

Consider the situation as depicted in Figure 8. Assume the magician's key card to be the queen of spades. The magician finds his key card, the queen, and knows at once that the student's selected card was the ten of clubs, the next card. *Eventually the magician will lay the ten on the table.* But before he does so, he looks through the rest of the packet.

The student has been told to lay on the table the card most resembling his selected card (the ten of clubs). Looking through his cards, the magician finds that the ten of spades (the card most resembling the ten of clubs) is not there. He then knows *that the ten of spades must be in the student's packet* and so that will be the card the student will lay on the table. The ten of spades, then, will be the card that the magician will say he selected.

Thus at the climax of the trick the magician shows the ten of clubs on the table and announces that it is the student's selected card. Saying that he hopes the student has been able to find his card, the magician announces that he had chosen the ten of spades, the card he knows the student has before him on the table.

In other words, by looking at his own cards, the magician is able to deduce what card the student selected as well as what card the student will lay on the table as most resembling the card he originally took. Thus the magician is able to claim that he had selected the card he knows the student has before him on the table.

The only trouble comes in a situation like this: referring again to Figure 8, suppose the magician had discovered from his key card that the student had selected the six of clubs. In looking through his cards, the magician would find that the sixes of both clubs and spades were there but neither of the red sixes. Since the student has both the red sixes, there is no way of knowing which he will lay on the table. In such a case the magician merely asks, before announcing the name of his own "selected" card, if the student laid a heart on the table. If the student says "Yes," the magician says, "Good, because I chose the six of hearts." If the student says "No," the magician says, "That's good, because I chose a diamond—the six!"

NOTE: It might be well to notice here the essentials of the classical precursor of the above effect. The trick is known as "You Do As I Do" and is performed with two decks of cards. The magician and the spectator each takes a deck, shuffles it, etc., and the magician notes the top card of his deck. The two then exchange decks and each removes one card from his deck, places it on top, and cuts his deck essentially the same as with "Sympathetic Student." Once more the decks are exchanged and the magician and spectator each looks for the card that he selected from the other's deck. Using his key card, the magician finds the spectator's card and, of course, the spectator finds the duplicate of his own card. The plot of the presentation is built on the notion that if the two are "psychically in sympathy" each will have selected the same card, since they went through the same motions.

## BETWEEN THE EYES

EFFECT: In order to demonstrate his ability to foretell the future, the magician predicts what two cards the spectator will later select when given a perfectly free choice of the whole fifty-two. Credit for this very startling effect goes to Mr. Paul Curry.

PRESENTATION: Without preamble the magician asks someone to suggest a card with a lot of white space—that is, a deuce or three. The magician wants to write something on it. Assume the deuce of spades is suggested. The magician looks through the deck until he finds the deuce of spades. While doing so, he notes and remembers the top card and the next to the bottom card of the deck.

IIe then moves the deuce of spades to the bottom (face) of the deck without otherwise changing the order of the cards. Without saying what it is that he is writing, the magician writes the initials of the two noted cards on the face of the deuce. Reference to Figure 9 will clarify this procedure. The top card of the deck in the illustration is the queen of hearts and the card originally next to the bottom is the six of diamonds. So, when the performer moves the deuce of spades to the face of the deck, he writes on it "QH" for queen of hearts and "6D" for six of diamonds.

The writing finished, the magician holds the deck in his left hand with his fingers along one side and his thumb at the other and tilts the deck so that the spectators can see the face of the deuce but so the writing is upside down. He moves his hand back and forth to make reading impossible. The spectators can see, explains the magician, that he has written something on the face of the deuce but he does not want them to see *what* he has written just yet.

Figure 9

So saying, the magician turns his hand over so the deck is face down and moves over to the table or squats down on the floor and apparently draws the deuce off the face of the deck and leaves it face down on the table or floor. Actually, what happens is that the magician executes a move known as the "glide" whereby the next-to-the-bottom card is withdrawn although the spectators think it is the bottom card. This maneuver is quite simple, emphasizing naturalness rather than skill, and is described in detail on page 163.

Thus the magician shows that he has written something on the deuce. Then he executes the "glide," apparently withdrawing the deuce from the face of the deck, but actually withdrawing the card above the deuce (the jack of clubs in Figure 9). This leaves the deuce on the face of the deck, the six immediately above it, and the queen still on top of the deck. The spectators, however, believe the deuce to be lying face down on the table.

As he lays the deck aside after having withdrawn the face-down card, the magician says, continuing his same sentence, that in fact it is essential in the working of the trick for the spectators not to know what he has written and so he does not want anyone to look at the deuce (pointing to the card on the table) until the trick is over.

It is essential that the magician time his remarks with his movements. He must convince the audience that turning the deck over and withdrawing the card in the peculiar way required for executing the glide are solely for the purpose of keeping the spectators from seeing what is written on the deuce. Also, there must be no awkward pause in what the magician is saying while he is executing the glide. Neither must there be any hurrying or embarrassment that will call attention to the fact that something untoward has happened. There is no difficulty about the move; it is one of the most perfect in magic because it is easy and completely covered. The spectators can see nothing. Therefore, when the move is used in some such context as this where there is an excuse for handling the cards as required by the move, the illusion is perfect. For this reason there is absolutely no cause for the performer to have a guilty conscience about what he is doing.

Devices of this sort fail more often because the performer telegraphs to the audience by his embarrassment the fact that something unusual is happening than because the performer does not execute them properly. Naturalness is the keynote. If the magician seems to pay no attention to what he is doing, neither will the audience. For this reason the magician keeps chatting about not looking at the face of the deuce as he nonchalantly does the glide and withdraws the next-to-the-bottom card onto the table.

Next the magician spreads the deck ribbonwise across the table or floor, each card overlapping the next just a little. The situation now is as depicted in Figure 10. On top of the deck is the queen. On the bottom is the deuce and imme-

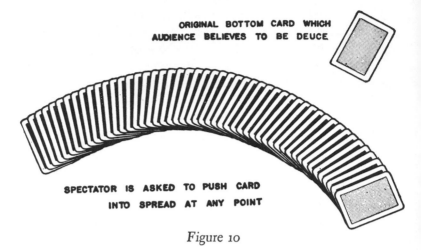

Figure 10

diately above it is the six. An indifferent card (the jack) is lying to one side and the spectators believe that this single card is really the deuce. The magician aids this belief by always referring to this card as the deuce—although he never actually makes a statement that the single card is the deuce since such a statement would raise a question in the spectators' minds.

Now the magician slides the single card that everyone thinks is the deuce toward one of the spectators and invites him to push that card into the deck at any point. He is very careful to insist that the spectator insert the card into the ribbon spread just where he wants to. In order to obviate the possibility that the spectator might look at the card and discover that it is not the deuce, the magician insists that he use just one finger to slide the card into the ribbon spread. After the spectator has decided on a spot in which to insert the card, the magician stops him and wonders if the spectator would not like to change his mind. It must be perfectly clear, the magician insists, that the spectator has a perfectly free choice of where to put the deuce.

When at last the spectator is satisfied and has pushed the card into some spot in the ribbon spread, the magician, using only the tips of his fingers in the most open manner possible, pushes the cards back together and evens up the deck, remarking all the while that the audience should notice the complete absence of any of sleight of hand. When the deck is squared up, the magician says he will give it just one cut "for good measure" and cuts the cards, completing the cut.

Now, says the magician, he will announce what it was he wrote on the face of the deuce of spades. He wrote the names of the very two cards between which the spectator subsequently inserted the deuce, long before the spectator even decided where he would insert it! He pauses a moment to let this pronouncement sink in, and then asks the spectator who did the pushing if he would look through the deck until he comes to the deuce of spades and see if on its face are not written the names of the cards on either side of the deuce in the deck.

Figure 11

When the spectator looks through the deck, he finds a situation like that shown in Figure 11. As will be apparent upon a little reflection, the single card that was pushed into the deck is of course lost among the cards. But, when the magician cut the deck after the spectator had inserted his card, the deuce and six were placed on top of the queen so that now indeed the deuce bears on its face the names of the two cards between which it is lying in the deck.

The cut, of course, serves two purposes. It allows the important cards to remain at the very ends of the spread while the spectator is inserting his card so there is no possibility that he will by chance push the indifferent card in between the crucial cards. Also, the cut after the insertion of the spectator's card makes it impossible for anyone to keep track of the approximate position at which he actually inserted the card.

Needless to say, the effect of the magician's apparent ability to predict in writing the very two cards between which the spectator inserted the deuce long before the spectator even knew what he was supposed to do is indeed a startling one. The effect, of course, depends upon selling the spectators on the fact that it is really the deuce that the magician originally lays on the table. And selling them on this premise, in turn, depends on the casualness with which the magician can execute the "glide." The magician has a perfect excuse to keep the spectators from looking at the card on the table —that is, they must not see what is written on it—but it is his ease and naturalness in handling the "glide" that achieves the primary deception.

NOTE: It is also possible to utilize here the move known as the "double lift" (described on page 171) instead of the glide. In this case the deuce would be brought to a position *second from the top* of the deck. The two top cards are then turned face up as if they were one and the names of the *third* card and the *bottom* card are written on the deuce. The two top cards are then turned face down onto the deck again and only the top card is thumbed face down onto the table. The rest of the effect follows as described.

It is actually immaterial whether the "glide" or the "double lift" is used for the purpose of getting an indifferent card onto the table while apparently placing the deuce there. The choice is up to the performer and should depend solely upon which move he can execute with more ease and naturalness. In this particular trick, where the performer has a good excuse for hiding the face of the card from the audience, either move is adequate and the reader will probably find the "glide" somewhat easier to perform at first try.

## BLACKSTONE'S PENETRATION

EFFECT: A card selected by the audience magically emerges unaided from the deck despite the fact that the deck is enclosed in its box and wrapped in a handkerchief. This impromptu penetration of both a cardboard box and the cloth of a handkerchief is one of the many contributions made to modern magic by the famous and very distinguished contemporary stage magician, Mr. Harry Blackstone.

PRESENTATION: The only requirement for this trick is a pack of cards that comes in the sort of box that opens with a flap at one end (as shown in Figure 12). Boxes such as hold two decks of bridge cards or those that are made in two telescoping portions cannnot be used here. Most varieties of cards, with the exception of the pairs of matching bridge decks, have the type of box necessary.

The magician offers the spectator a perfectly free choice of any card either by fanning the cards face down in front of the spectator, running the cards face down from hand to hand, or letting the spectator reach into the deck and extract the card. The spectator is asked to note and remember the card. While the spectator is noting the card, the magician gets set to have the card returned to the deck and to bring it secretly to the top with the Hindu Shuffle as described on page 165.

Obviously, any method of controlling the selected card to the top of the deck (such as Short Card, page 190, or any of the many methods not included in this volume) would suffice for this trick. The magician could even have the selected card returned on top of a key card which he had previously noted (as has been described before) and then locate it by looking through the deck to remove the joker or some such excuse. The climax of this trick is sufficiently startling to cover up the most blatant method of locating the selected card.

In any case, the card noted by the spectator is secretly brought to the top of the deck by whatever means the magician wishes. Up to this point, the magician has had very little to say about the trick he is performing, except to emphasize the freedom with which the spectator was allowed to make his choice of card and the completeness of the shuffling of the cards.

Once the selected card is secretly on top of the deck, the magician should slow down and start building up his trick. For the magician, the trick starts with the selection of the card, but as far as the audience is concerned, the trick starts when the magician begins to talk about the effect, and that is what is more important.

With the selected card on top of the deck, the magician speaks of how the spectator has, by touching the card, imparted to it some of his own personality. Thus, just as the spectator would object to being imprisoned in a tiny cell, so his card is now no longer content to remain confined with the other cards.

As the magician speaks, he places the whole deck of cards into the card box, so that the selected card is to the front and the face of the deck is next to the back of the box (the side to which is attached the closing flap) as in Figure 12A. The magician then closes the box, but in doing so *he secretly inserts the pointed tongue of the box flap between the selected card and the rest of the deck.* Squeezing the box at the sides and holding the top card back with the left index finger will facilitate this maneuver (see Figure 12A).

Thus the deck is completely enclosed within the card box, but the selected card is simply lying in the box in front of the flap so that it may be withdrawn without opening the box. Actually, part of the back of the selected card shows through the semicircular notch cut in the top of the box in

Figure 12

front to facilitate opening the box. This exposed portion of the selected card the magician covers with his thumb as he grasps the closed box between thumb and index finger of the right hand and exhibits quite openly on all sides to the audience as in Figure 12B.

As a matter of fact, the magician continues, the selected card just won't stay anywhere without trying to escape. Furthermore, since the card is now a magical one, it really has much more success escaping than the spectator who selected it would ever have. That is, not only can the selected card escape from the card box, but it can do even more.

Here the magician, still holding the card box between right thumb and index finger, asks for the loan of a gentleman's handkerchief. Taking the handkerchief with his left hand, he holds his right hand (still with the box of cards) a little below the level of his waist, and drapes the handkerchief over it, as in Figure 13A.

Since the magician has only two hands, and one of those is busy holding the card box, it is quite natural for him to drape the handkerchief over his right hand and then reach under the handkerchief with his left hand, withdraw the card box, and place it on the center of the handkerchief as it is spread over his upturned right palm. When he does this, however, his right thumb presses upon the exposed portion of the selected card and retains it in his right palm under the handkerchief as the left hand withdraws the box of cards and

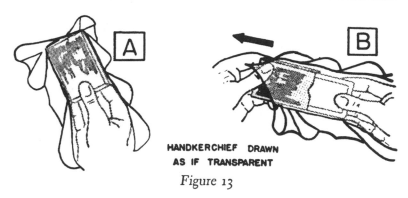

HANDKERCHIEF DRAWN
AS IF TRANSPARENT

Figure 13

places it in the right palm on top of the handkerchief. (See Figure 13B.) The right thumb also draws the selected card back fully onto the extended right palm under the handkerchief.

The situation now is that the magician has the selected card lying on his right palm covered by the handkerchief and the box of cards also on his right palm, but on top of the handkerchief. Being careful that the selected card is perfectly aligned with the box of cards, the magician folds the part of the handkerchief which is hanging down over the tips of the right fingers up over the box of cards toward his right wrist as in Figure 14A.

Then, seizing the box of cards by the sides through the handkerchief with his left hand, he lifts box, handkerchief, and selected card all off his right palm, as in Figure 14B. The right hand, in turn, gathers up the two corners of the handkerchief which hang down on either side of the card box and

 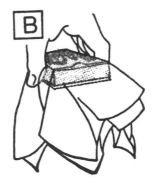 

Figure 14

carries them upward to join the other two corners of the handkerchief, all of which the right hand then grasps, allowing the card box to swing freely in its handkerchief sling.

Figure 14C shows the magician's view of the situation at this point, with the box of cards inside the handkerchief sling, and the selected card nestling in the folds of the handkerchief, visible to the magician but not to the audience.

Asking the spectator to call his card by name, the magician explains that the card will fight its way not only through the bottom of the cardboard box, but also through the fabric of the handkerchief, all so magically that neither the box nor the handkerchief will be the least bit harmed. As the spectator calls upon his card, the magician gently shakes the handkerchief, and the selected card will be seen to emerge slowly from the bottom of the handkerchief-covered bundle, just as if it were penetrating the box and the handkerchief.

Seizing the card and pulling it completely free of the handkerchief, the magician shows that it is the selected card, and then throws both the handkerchief and the box of cards out for the audience to examine to its heart's delight.

It should be unnecessary to remark that the magician has a perfect opportunity here to build up his effect with as much comedy or drama as he chooses. He can pretend that the card is a trifle coy and won't appear until the spectator calls it some foolish names, or he can be completely Mephisto-phelean and command the card to penetrate the cloth with much frowning and glaring as if the magician were pulling the card through the cloth by sheer force of will or what have you.

## THAT'S ALL

EFFECT: While attempting to find two selected cards, the entire deck vanishes from the magician's hands. This effect is suggested as a finale for the magician's extemporaneous demonstration. When the magician has run out of card tricks, he can perform this one, causing the whole deck to vanish, and thus obviate the necessity of having to say, "That's all I know." Again we are indebted to Mr. Al Baker for the basis of this effect.

PRESENTATION: After having done tricks in which just one card was selected, the magician says he will now try one with two selected cards. He offers two spectators a choice of cards. After the second spectator has removed his card from the deck, the magician returns to the first spectator and executes the Hindu Shuffle as described on page 165, thereby bringing the first card secretly to the top of the deck. Approaching the second spectator, he again prepares to execute the Hindu Shuffle. He pulls out about two thirds of the bottom part of the deck with his right hand, letting the top one third fall into the left palm as in Figure 15A. Extending this left-hand packet toward the second spectator, he tells him to place his card "right in here"—that is, directly on top of the first se-lected card—and then brings both selected cards secretly to the top by means of the Hindu Shuffle.

To make it even more difficult, the magician states, he will attempt to find the cards by touch alone—that is, with-out looking at the deck. To this end he borrows a napkin or scarf, which he throws over the deck that he holds in his left

## (SCARF DRAWN AS IF TRANSPARENT)

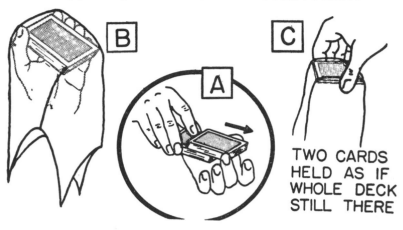

TWO CARDS
HELD AS IF
WHOLE DECK
STILL THERE

Figure 15

hand. The bigger the scarf is, the better. A large kerchief like the ones women are wont to wear over their heads is all right. A large napkin will do. Actually, a man's handkerchief is too small to use. Preferably the scarf should be heavy enough so as to be difficult to see through when held against the light.

The magician is standing with his left hand about waist high, holding the deck of cards which is covered by the scarf as in Figure 15B. His right hand goes under the scarf as he attempts to find the cards "by touch." Actually, the right hand separates the top two cards from the rest of the deck just enough so that the left little finger can get between the top two cards and the rest of the deck to keep them separated.

The right hand now comes out from under the scarf and gestures to accompany what the magician is saying about how really difficult it is, even for his sensitive fingers, to feel the slight difference in the "vibrations," or what have you, of the selected cards, caused by the spectators' handling of them. As a matter of fact, he admits, it is necessary to have something with which to amplify the vibrations so that he can feel them. So saying, the magician reaches with his right hand into his right jacket pocket for his "amplifier," but fails to find it there.

In order to free his left hand of its burden so that he can search for the "amplifier" in his left jacket pocket, the magician's right hand apparently grasps the deck of cards through the scarf from the top, and holds it while the left hand goes to the left jacket pocket. What actually happens is this: the right hand reaches over to grasp the deck of cards through the scarf, but *it takes only the top two cards by the ends through the scarf*, being careful to hold them so that it looks as though the right hand is holding the whole deck through the scarf as in Figure 15C. At the same time, the magician turns with his right side facing the audience, and the right hand lifts the cards and scarf up to eye level. The magician follows the right hand with his eyes to lead the audience to do the same.

Just as the right hand lifts the two selected cards covered by the scarf from the left hand and raises them to eye level, the left hand carries the rest of the deck into the left jacket pocket. This move is covered by the raising of the left hand and by the fact that the magician has turned so that his left side is away from the audience. The left hand then openly emerges from the left jacket pocket, carrying a packet of matches or anything else that is in the pocket. This object, the magician says, is his "amplifier." The left hand places the matches on top of the bundle in the right hand and then goes beneath the scarf and grasps the two cards, the thumb and fingers extended upward at the sides so that it still looks as if the whole deck were under the scarf. With the "amplifier" in place, the magician says, all he need do is touch the various cards and the "amplifier" will tell when he touches the selected card. The right hand goes under the scarf and starts fumbling. Suddenly the matches leap off the scarf, propelled by a flick of the right fingers under the scarf. That is the signal, the magician says, and the right hand comes out holding the bottom card, which proves to be the first spectator's card. The left fingers still maintain the outline of a deck of cards under the scarf.

The magician turns to the second spectator and asks him to name his card. He does so. The magician smiles and says that of course he does not need the "amplifier" to find the second card, because it is the only one left, and he whips the scarf away to show the left hand holding just one card. As the scarf is whipped away, the left hand, of course, moves so that the card is being held at the finger tips and not with the hand still as if it held the whole deck.

NOTE: There is really little reason to worry about the seemingly blatant way in which the deck is disposed of. The audience has no inkling that the cards are going to vanish. As far as the spectators are concerned, they are waiting for the magician to bring on a climax. They assume the business about an "amplifier" is just window dressing and may even be annoyed that the magician does not know where his "amplifier" is.

As a result, the barest amount of cover is sufficient to hide the deck's trip to the left jacket pocket. Therefore the magician's turn to the left and his raising the scarf to eye level should not be exaggerated lest the spectators deduce that the magician is trying to distract them. The turn to the left can accompany some casual remark to a spectator standing at the magician's left. Raising the scarf to eye level should also have some excuse.

Thus the magician might turn to a spectator at his left and say: "It may seem silly, but when the cards are covered with a scarf like this, it is just impossible to find your cards without my amplifier." As he says ". . . like this . . ." he raises his right hand and nods towards the scarf as if illustrating his words. Just at that moment, then, his left hand goes to his left pocket. There is no rush and certainly any rapid movement of the left hand is to be avoided.

As soon as the left hand and the deck are safely inside the left pocket, the magician should turn front again and look at his left pocket saying "Ah, here it is," as the left hand emerges with the "amplifier." In this way the whole crucial process of disposing of the deck will be reduced to an apparently unimportant and incidental occurrence. It is, of course, a help to hold the scarf close to the body so that the left hand has the least possible distance to travel in the open, but overemphasizing this idea will mean that the magician assumes a cramped and unnatural position, which is obviously undesirable.

## A WORD ABOUT IMPROMPTU CARD ROUTINES

It should be apparent that the proper routining or interweaving of the performer's various tricks is an essential contribution to the over-all effect that his performance creates. This is true in all forms of entertainment and no less so in magic.

Many performers, however, make the mistake of relegating their worries about routining and the order in which their effects are presented exclusively to planned magic programs. Presenting tricks in the proper sequence is equally important when the performance is impromptu, however. There is a great tendency for the magician to present his best (or best liked) effects first when asked to do a trick on the spur of the moment and then gradually to go down the scale of effectiveness as he tries to think of additional tricks to perform.

The reader will probably discover after he has learned a great number of tricks that they are like funny stories: one hears a great many but is frequently unable to recall one when wanted. For this reason it is suggested that the performer arrange his favorite tricks in some sort of sequence for impromptu presentation. Additional tricks may be interpolated between the set effects, but he will always be sure of several dependable climactic tricks on which to rely as surefire peaks in his demonstration.

Especially is it important for him to have some effect with which to bring his performance to a close (such as the foregoing "That's All") beyond which he will not go. Thus he can always end even an impromptu demonstration with the proper climax.

This does not mean, however, that there should be no improvising in an impromptu demonstration. Quite the contrary: the impromptu performer spends a great deal of his demonstration "ad libbing" his tricks. Thus the magician may not know when he has a card selected just how he will reveal it for a climax. The spectators believe that each trick the magician performs is a separate and long-rehearsed entity.

But the reader will find from experience that his most startling effects are those that he improvises as he goes along by taking advantage of some lucky break, some twist in the general conversation, or some occurrence that makes possible just once an effect that could never be performed again. After each of these improvised effects, however, the magician should schedule a rehearsed trick on which he can always depend in case something goes wrong with his improvised effect.

In the planned formal magic program, there is no excuse for the performer who does not have the mechanics of all his tricks so well rehearsed that he performs the necessary movements and actions almost without thinking about it and can thus devote himself entirely to "selling" his show enthusiastically to the audience. But the successful impromptu performer must be able to improvise. It is the spontaneity that such improvisation necessarily introduces into his demonstrations that holds the interest of his informal audience.

Such a discussion suggests, of course, that the successful

extemporaneous performer must develop the ability to think about one thing, talk about another, and do still another all at the same time. This is neither an exaggeration nor a simple task. But at the same time, such demands made on the magician are the very things that make the hobby of magic so interesting—especially impromptu magic. It must always be remembered that the fun of performing, the amateur magic hobbyist's main stimulus, is the excitement he gets from matching wits with his audience, and such excitement reaches its peak in the living-room demonstration with no holds barred on either side.

But the impromptu performer still needs a basis of set tricks into which he can weave his extemporaneous ideas. It is hoped that the effects described in the first part of this chapter will provide for the reader such a framework of dependable standard climaxes. As to what tricks might be effectively improvised and interpolated into the basic routine, the reader is referred to the following discussion of miscellaneous discoveries.

## MISCELLANEOUS DISCOVERIES

Any card trick of the take-a-card-and-I'll-find-it variety is divided into three main parts: selection, location, and discovery. The "selection" refers to the manner in which the spectator selects the card, the "location" refers to the way in which the magician himself discovers the identity or location of the selected card. The "discovery" is the method the magician uses to disclose to the audience that he has located the card—that is, the climax of the trick.

As far as the magician is concerned, he must worry about all three parts. The audience, however, is interested only in the discovery. That is the whole trick for the spectators. Thus a magician who can disclose his location of a selected card in a hundred ways is credited with knowing a hundred "tricks" although he may know only one method of finding the selected card after it is returned to the deck.

The reader who can locate a selected card by some such simple means as having it returned to the deck on top of a key card, or by using the Hindu Shuffle as described on page 165, or Short Card as described on page 190, can apply this one magical method of location to a dozen magical discoveries and thus be able to perform a dozen apparently different tricks.

The following suggestions of various discoveries are included here to start the reader on the way to building up a repertoire. Each of the discoveries presupposes the reader's ability to bring the selected card secretly to the top of the deck by using the Hindu Shuffle, or Short Card, or by cutting after the card is located by the use of a known key card next to which the selected card is returned to the deck. The deck should be shuffled without disturbing the top card before the discovery.

### 1. Your Number

Using an overhand shuffle (page 158), the selected card is transferred from the top of the deck to second from the bottom and the audience is given a glimpse of the bottom card. The deck is then held face down in position to do the "glide" (page 163). The performer asks the spectator to suggest a number under ten. Assume that he selects eight.

The performer withdraws the bottom card and throws it face up on the table counting "one." Then, executing the "glide," the performer draws the selected card on the face of the deck backward so that he can withdraw from above it six more cards, one at a time. He finally withdraws the selected card as number eight, thus bringing it up in the exact position that the spectator chose.

## 2. Reversed Card

Although there are many ways of reversing the selected card in the deck by the use of sleight of hand, this simple device is extremely effective.

With the selected card on top of the deck, the magician says that, if he were controlling the cards by sleight of hand, the most logical spot to place the selected card would be on top of the deck. He apparently turns over the top card and shows it is not the selected card. Actually, he executes the "double lift" as described on page 171, turning the two top cards as if they were one and placing the two face-up cards squarely on top of the deck.

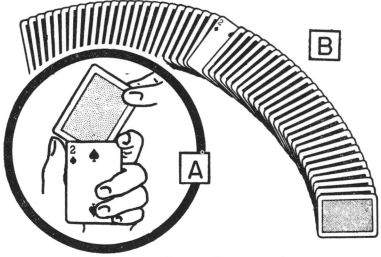

Figure 16

The next most logical place to control a card, says the performer, would be the bottom. He raises the deck so the bottom card is visible and holds it vertically before the spectators. The bottom card is not the selected card either. Without lowering the deck, the magician removes the top face-up card and buries it in the deck as in Figure 16A. This, of course, leaves the selected card face up on top. Still keeping the deck so that the audience cannot see the top, the magician cuts the deck, thus burying the face-up selected card. He points out that since the selected card is neither on the top nor bottom, it must be in the middle. He spreads the deck face down on the table and the selected card is seen to be face up, staring at the spectator from the middle of the deck as in Figure 16B.

### 3. Sleight of Foot

The selected card is reversed in the deck as above described. The deck is placed squared and face down on the floor. The magician says that naturally the selected card was not at the top nor bottom, since he was not using sleight of hand. Instead he is using sleight of foot. Now, if the spectator will name his card, the magician will attempt to make it turn face up in the face-down deck, using his foot alone to accomplish the miracle. The spectator names his card and the magician merely spreads the cards with his foot to disclose that the selected card is face up.

### 4. Gravity Magic

With the selected card on top of the deck, the magician asks the spectator to name his card. As soon as the spectator does so, the magician throws the deck face down on the table and the selected card is seen to pop face up in mid-air. To accomplish this, the top card (selected card) is pushed to one side so that it extends over the top of the deck about half an inch. The deck is then dropped onto the table or floor from a position about eighteen inches away. If the deck is dropped face down and perfectly horizontally, the rush of air will cause the top card to flip over face up as in Figure 17A.

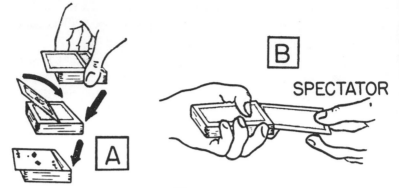

Figure 17

## 5. Ambitious Card

The selected card is brought second from the top with an overhand shuffle (page 158). The spectator is asked to blow upon the shuffled deck and is shown that his selected card has apparently risen to the top: that is, the magician does a "double lift" (page 171) and turns the two top cards face up as if they were one card. To explain that phenomenon, the magician turns both cards face down and apparently places the selected card in the middle of the deck. Another blow by the spectator and the selected card once more rises through the deck to the top. Actually, the magician merely placed the indifferent top card in the middle after turning the two that he held in the "double lift" face down, leaving the selected card on top.

## 6. Mistaken

With the selected card on top the magician does a "double lift," explaining that whatever card is showing will be an indicator card to help find the selected card. Turning the two cards face down onto the deck, he hands the top (selected) card to a spectator face down and miscalls it whatever card was just shown. The spectator is asked to hold the card face down with just two fingers, the magician guiding his hand so that he will not turn the card over prematurely. The spectator is to jab the "indicator" card into the deck at any spot, thereby using the indicator card to find his own selected card as in Figure 17B.

He jabs the card into the deck but fails several times to find his own card. Eventually he realizes that the indicator card has apparently changed into his selected card as he held it in his hand. The "glide" (page 163) might also be used here instead of the "double lift," although it is probably not so effective.

## 7. Turnabout

Here the magician must depend on a little luck. Sometime during his performance he attempts to introduce a card secretly into the jacket pocket of any of the spectators. Since there is no rush, this is quite an easy task while performing some trick with that spectator. The performer merely stands beside him and slips one card into his pocket. The magician remembers that card.

A few moments and at least one trick later, the magician hands the deck to the spectator who has the card in his pocket. He has the spectator shuffle the deck and pretend that he is the magician. The spectator is to offer the magician a card. The magician takes one, replaces it in the deck, and tells the spectator to shuffle the cards just as though he were a magician.

After shuffling, the magician coaches the spectator in the role of being a magician. He has the spectator ask him the name of his card, which the magician miscalls as the card he knows is in the spectator's pocket. Then he suggests that the spectator should act like a real magician and cause the selected card to fly invisibly into the spectator's pocket. The spectator is then asked to withdraw the magician's "selected" card from his pocket.

The effect of this presentation, especially with regard to the completely flabbergasted look on the spectator's face when he finds the "selected" card in his own pocket, is wonderful to behold.

## 8. Pure Luck

The magician should never overlook the aid that Lady Luck may extend to him during an impromptu demonstration. Thus if, before commencing a trick, the magician gives the deck to a spectator to shuffle, the spectator may by chance handle the cards so that the magician can get a glimpse of the bottom card of the deck, especially if the magician is seated and the shuffling spectator is standing.

Such an occurrence is all the magician needs to direct the spectator to offer to another spectator the choice of a card. The card is then returned to the deck by placing it on top and cutting so as to bring the known bottom key card next to the selected card. The spectator who is playing magician is then asked to run the cards from hand to hand before the magician's eyes and the magician, by looking for the known key card, is able to "read" the spectator's mind while lounging in a chair without having touched the cards at all. The effectiveness of such a presentation cannot be overemphasized, especially since the spectator who did all the work as if he were a magician has no idea of how the magician succeeded in his trick.

Naturally, any such chance glimpses the magician gets of the top or bottom card of the deck allow him to go right into any of the tricks in the first part of the chapter that require a key card. In such a case the magician would be careful to emphasize that the spectator shuffled the cards before the trick started and that the magician did not even touch them, etc.

Such bits of luck during an impromptu demonstration should never be overlooked. The reader should learn to utilize not only chance glimpses of possible key cards but also to be on the lookout for chance glimpses of the selected card itself in fortuitously placed mirrors and by virtue of careless handling by the spectators.

After reading the "Fan Force" on page 175, the magician should get into the habit of trying to "force" a card on the spectator each time he offers him a choice of cards. If he is successful, he can hand the deck to the spectator for immediate shuffling, and utilize the freedom of a forced card in reading the spectator's mind, etc., without touching the deck. If he is unsuccessful, he can go on with any other location and discovery at his pleasure.

The alert performer who takes advantage of every such opportunity and never lets his luck pass him by will soon find "truly miraculous" affixed to his reputation, no matter how infrequently he gets such lucky breaks.

# III

## Tricks without Playing Cards

In this, the second section of impromptu magic, are collected several tricks dealing with objects other than playing cards. Here the field is much more limited.

Objects other than cards do not lend themselves as easily to magic—or at least to magic not involving sleight of hand. Coins, rings, bills, etc., have always been an important part of magic, but only because such objects are easily adapted to sleight-of-hand manipulation. Such objects are lacking in the magical attributes of a deck of cards insofar as impromptu magic goes.

Herewith are collected, however, several effective and impromptu tricks using neither playing cards nor difficult sleight of hand, that, it is felt, will be welcome additions to the amateur magician's repertoire.

## SPIRIT CALLING CARD

EFFECT: A question is written to the spirits on the back of a calling card and the spirits answer the question by causing spirit writing to appear on the previously blank calling card.

This clever little idea was shown to the author by Dr. Walter Grote, then of Charleston, W. Va., but whether he invented the effect himself is unknown.

Actually, the trick is something less than completely extemporaneous, because it requires the magician to have a prepared calling card. The card, though, may be carried in a wallet or card case with the magician's regular calling cards and forgotten about until such time as the effect is needed. The author has found very few impromptu tricks that measure up to the effectiveness of this one.

PREPARATION: The following items are needed for this effect: half a dozen calling or business cards, a small drug envelope about two by three inches in size, and a small but wide rubber band. It may become necessary to take a large rubber band (at least a quarter of an inch wide) and cut a two-inch length out of it; then cement the ends of the two-inch piece together with rubber cement, thus making a rubber band about an inch long and a quarter of an inch wide.

Take one of the calling cards and cut off about one-third of its length. Place the rest of the cards in a stack, printed side down, and put the rubber band around them about one-third of the way from one end of the stack, so that the rubber band divides the blank side of the top card of the stack into a large and small portion.

Using a pen or colored pencil, write the name of any color (let us say blue) on the smaller exposed portion of the top card. Now take the one-third cut from the other card and cover what has just been written by placing the piece of card over the writing and slipping its edge under the rubber band. With the cover in position, the top card of the stack should

look as blank as before "blue" was written on it, the extra
piece of card hiding the writing and the rubber band hiding
the edge of the extra piece of card. The final setup is shown
in the exploded diagram of Figure 18.

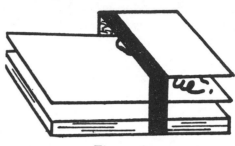

*Figure 18*

With the one card of the stack thus prepared, slip the
whole stack into the envelope and put it in your wallet to
await the time when you will perform the effect.

PRESENTATION: The magician calls the spectators' attention
to the fact that, as they well know, a great many persons still
have a lot of faith in talking with the dead and such things.
So much so, he says, that he felt he should look into the
subject of spiritualism. The magician admits that he is not a
devout spiritualist and certainly not an accomplished medium, but that, by virtue of his experiments, he has been able
to acquire sufficient ability to make contact with the spirits
at certain times and under certain very limited conditions.
So, if the spectators would like, he will try to make a contact now. The magician removes the stack of calling cards
from his wallet.

The reason, says the magician, why so few persons can
make contact with the spirits is that the spirits have a very
difficult time expressing themselves. They seem to object to
being watched and they rarely are able to accomplish vocal
expression. For that reason the magician has found that the
best way to make contact is for him to write questions to the

spirits on his own calling cards. (Do not under any circumstances suggest that the spirits will answer on the calling card!)

Since the spirits are accustomed to his handwriting, the magician will undertake to write a question for one of the spectators. So saying, he takes a pencil and writes on the large exposed portion of the prepared calling card, "What is the color of my suit?" (or tie, or dress, or car, or anything that is blue). Unfortunately, the magician points out, he has not perfected himself to the extent of asking the spirits just anything, but must limit himself to questions about certain very common objects.

Now the magician wonders if one of the spectators would sign the question. He places the stack of cards in front of one of the spectators and has him write his initials under the question. For the purposes of this experiment, says the magician, that spectator will be the questioner. Obviously, the magician picks as his "questioner" the person present with a blue suit, tie, dress, car, etc., to fit the prepared answer.

Picking up the stack of calling cards, the magician asks the "questioner" to initial the other side of the card also, "just for good measure." As he speaks, he takes the unprepared end of the calling card and starts to withdraw it from under the rubber band. Before he does so, however, he turns the entire stack upside down so that the calling card is withdrawn with the written-on side down as in Figure 19.

He places the card in front of the spectator, writing side down, for the spectator's initials on this, the card's other side. The magician keeps his finger, which points out the spot for the spectator's initials, on the card, so that the spectator cannot accidentally turn the card over.

Being careful not to expose the bottom side (with the question and previously prepared answer on it) to the spectator's view, he slips the card in the little envelope, still hold-

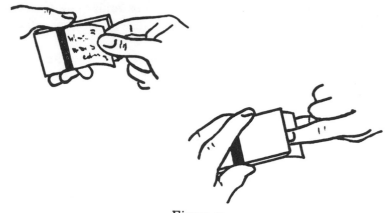

*Figure 19*

ing it writing side down, and lays the envelope aside. He then slips the stack of cards into his pocket as he talks, secretly sliding the little piece of card that covered the prepared writing out from under the rubber band with his thumb.

The magician picks up the envelope and holds it to his ear, listening. The spirits have started to work on the question, he says, but they may take a little time. First the spirits must read the question, then discover who signed it, and then look to see the correct answer and finally answer the question. This, the magician explains, takes time since the spirits are a little bashful occasionally.

For a moment or so, the magician discourses on his ideas of spiritualism, regretting that he must confine his experiments to such very common objects as articles of clothing, etc., etc., but hoping in time to become a more proficient medium. Every once in a while he holds the envelope to his ear to see if the spirits are progressing properly, and acknowledges that things are coming along nicely.

Finally, after building up what suspense he can, the magician suggests that the spirits must have finished by this time.

He hands the envelope to the spectator who initialed the card and requests him to look at the card.

As the spectator removes the card from the envelope, the magician asks if those are not his initials. They are. The magician then asks him to turn the card over and look at the question. The spectator does so, and finds the correct answer to his question written right beside the question and written in ink or colored pencil, whereas the question was written in pencil!

The spectator, of course, keeps the card to remind him of the magician's prowess, and the magician removes the stack of calling cards (minus, of course, the little covering piece of card) from his pocket for all to examine if they choose.

Naturally this device can be used for any sort of question the answer to which can be forced on the spectators. Brands of cigarettes, whisky, radios, watches, and the like, as well as colors, first names, ages, birthdays, and so on, all suggest themselves as possibilities, especially when the magician is attending a party where he personally knows many of the guests and can prepare himself beforehand for the event. As a general rule, the color blue will be found almost universally applicable in the effect, for in every gathering there will be some personal object of wearing apparel or the like of that color.

NOTE: Many performers prefer to use this effect in connection with card magic, and so a variation using playing cards is appended here.

The prepared calling card has written on it the name of any card—say the deuce of spades. While presenting some card tricks, then, the magician looks through the deck until he finds the deuce of spades and cuts it to the top of the deck. As if he had just been struck by a sudden thought, he lays the deck aside, (but where no one will get at it) and removes the prepared stack of calling cards from his wallet.

Utilizing the same patter as above indicated, to the effect

that he must limit his experiments to common objects, the magician writes the question "What card did I select?" on the card and has it initialed and placed in the envelope as before.

As he lays the envelope aside, he invites the "questioner" to cut the deck at any point he chooses, and lay the cut-off top portion beside the bottom half of the deck. The magician remarks that so far, no one knows the correct answer to the question propounded to the spirits, and that thus the experiment is doubly difficult.

The magician picks up the envelope and listens to it. Nothing has happened as yet, he reports. Perhaps it would be easier if the spirits actually knew the correct answer to the question. To that end, the magician lays the envelope across the cut-off *top* portion of the deck directly on the original top card of the deck and places the original *bottom* half of the deck crosswise on top of the envelope. That way, says the magician, the place where the spectator cut the deck will be marked and the spirits will be closer to the cards.

The magician now goes on to expound his ideas of spiritualism "to give the spirits time to work!" He talks for a moment or so in order that the spectators will forget just exactly which half of the deck was the original top half, and hence just which card was the original top card and which was the card to which the spectator actually cut.

Finally, the magician decides that the spirits have had enough time. He reaches over and removes the half of the deck above the envelope and keeps it in his hand. He invites one spectator to remove and hold the envelope and the "questioner" to "take his card and show it around" pointing to the top card of the remaining portion of the deck. The magician seeks to create the impression that this is the card to which the spectator cut, but does not say so for fear of raising the question of the validity of the selection in the spectators' minds. Of course, the card which the spectator takes is the original top card of the deck and is thus the correct answer to the question written to the spirits.

Naturally, any method of forcing the spectator to select a certain card suggested elsewhere in this volume may be used. This very simple force is quite effective here, however. It depends upon the nonchalance the magician can affect in "marking the cut" by placing the envelope in the deck. If the magician does not place any importance on how the card is selected, the audience will not, since this is not a trick, but rather a demonstration of spiritualism. The magician is not seeking to find the card; the spirits are trying to find it.

## DRAWN AND QUARTERED

EFFECT: A length of rope is cut into four parts, which the magician succeeds in restoring into one unbroken length of rope. This effect is presented as being perhaps the easiest and one of the most effective of the many tricks, impromptu and otherwise, involving cutting and restoring a length of rope. In its present form, it is in part the product of the magical inventiveness of Mr. Ted Collins, combined with a move of the brilliant English magician, Edward Victor.

REQUISITES: The only items required for this effect are a length of cord about four feet long and a pair of scissors. The easiest material to use is a soft, hollow, braided cotton rope about three-eighths of an inch in diameter made especially for doing rope tricks, but almost any sort of clothesline or cord can be used. Very flimsy string or very stiff cord is practicable but difficult, and should be avoided.

PRESENTATION: Holding the cord by one end with the thumb and index finger of the left hand at about eye level, the magician allows the cord to dangle toward the floor. "The center should be about here, shouldn't it?" says the magician as he extends his right hand palm downward, and picks up the center of the cord by letting it lie across the backs of his right fingers. He pauses to survey his estimate of the position of the middle of the cord, as it drapes over the backs of the right fingers with the end still held by his left thumb and forefinger, as in Figure 20A.

The magician says that he wants to cut the cord in two at approximately the center. Thereupon he moves his right hand over to his left, carrying the cord still draped across the back of the right fingers. The left hand is held with the palm toward the body.

As the right hand reaches the left, it grasps the part of the cord that is hanging down inside the left palm between the index and second fingers of the right hand, as in Figure 20B. At the same time the right hand tilts so that the right fingers point downward, allowing the loop of cord which has been draped over the right fingers to slide downward and off the right fingers. The right fingers should grasp the cord near the bottom edge of the left palm so that the left hand will hide from the audience the fact that the cord is allowed to slide off the right fingers as in Figure 20C.

Simultaneously, the right hand moves upward, drawing a loop of cord into view above the left index finger as in Figure 20D. It will be seen that this loop is actually formed with only about three inches of the left end of the cord, but it appears that the magician has merely brought the middle of the cord over for the left fingers to hold while the right hand immediately reaches for the scissors (Figure 20E).

The magician takes the scissors and cuts the cord quite openly through the top of the visible loop, (Point X in Figure 20E) allowing the long end to drop so that, from the magician's view, the situation is as in Figure 20F, but as far as the audience is concerned, the left hand appears to be holding two separate pieces of cord hanging down one beside the other.

Remarking that he did (or did not, as the case may be) guess where the middle was with some accuracy, the magician lays the scissors aside and ties the two top ends together in

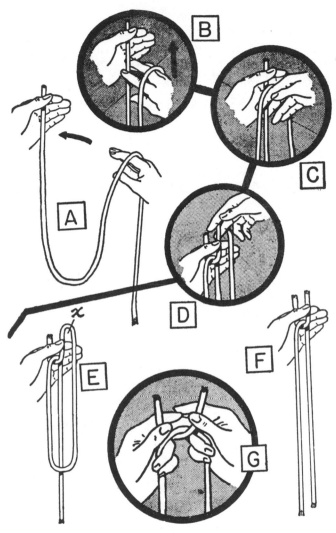

Figure 20

a single knot. This, of course, merely ties the short piece of cord around the long piece, but to the audience, the magician has apparently tied the two halves of the cord together.

The easiest way to accomplish this is as follows: Laying the scissors aside, the right hand takes the right piece of cord so the two hands are holding the cord as in Figure 20G —still hiding from the audience the place where the two pieces join. Using the thumbs and index fingers of both hands, the short ends are given a twisting motion to simulate the first step in tying a double knot, and then a single overhand knot is tied using the two top short ends.

The magician is not content, however. He must do more damage to the cord. He grasps one end in his right hand, and, bending the cord back on itself, ties a square knot about mid-

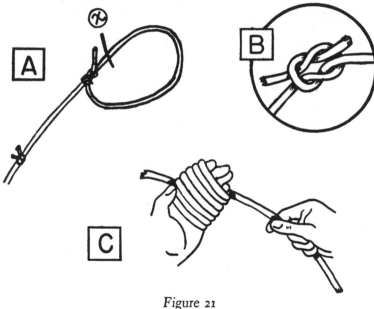

Figure 21

way between the end and center of the cord as in Figure 21A. This must be a true square knot (see Figure 21B) for the trick to work. Taking the scissors, the magician cuts the cord at Point X in Figure 21A—that is, on the side of the knot from which the short end protrudes. The magician then repeats the above moves with the other end of the cord. The knots should not be tied too tightly.

Holding the cord by one end up in front of him, the magician remarks that the cord has thus been cut into four almost equal pieces which he indicated by touching each as he speaks. When he touches the second piece (that is, below the top knot), he gives the cord a little tug until he feels something give. This tug upsets the first knot so that it too, like the center knot is merely a short piece of cord tied loosely around the long piece. This is repeated with the third or bottom knot.

Warning the audience to be sure to keep the ends of the rope in view, so that there can be no possibility of a substitution, the magician grasps the rope above the top knot with his right hand and begins to wind it around his left hand, being sure to keep the top end in view.

As the cord slips through the right fingers during the winding operation, the three knots are retained by the right hand, that is, the right hand slides the knots along the cord as the cord is wound onto the left hand. The left hand remains stationary, palm toward the body, to give the effect that the knots are all being wound on the palm side of the left hand where they are hidden from view (see Figure 21C).

When it reaches the end of the cord, the right hand, still with the knots enclosed within the fist and slipped completely off the cord, extends the end portion of the cord toward one of the spectators to hold. Another spectator is requested to hold the other end as it protrudes from the bundle of cord wound around the left hand.

The right hand, then, still holding the three knots, reaches into the magician's trousers pocket and emerges, having left the knots behind, with a coin or cigarette or pencil or any object at all. This, says the magician, is the magic coin with which his wonders are worked. Waving the coin over the cord-covered left hand, the magician requests the two spectators to pull gently on the ends of the cord which they hold and allows the cord to be pulled off the left hand completely restored.

NOTE: The first reaction of most audiences is that another piece of cord was substituted for the cut one. It is, therefore, important for the magician to emphasize that the cord has never once left the view of the audience, and that, indeed, two spectators were holding it during the restoration. It will soon be discovered just how to handle the cord so that as little as possible will be cut off, both to lessen the necessary shortening of the cord and to decrease the bulk of the knots when hidden in the right hand.

There is no need to worry about "palming" the knots. The right hand is normally closed as the cord is drawn through it to be wound on the left, and it simply continues in this condition as the magician reaches into his pocket. Since we started with a length of cord about four feet long, the fact that the final length of cord is some six or eight inches shorter owing to the three small portions that were cut off will go completely unnoticed.

The main effort in the trick should be directed at making the first move as natural and convincing as possible. All the other moves are completely open and aboveboard, depending for their effectiveness upon the fact that the audience does not realize that the second and third cuts merely sever the knots from the cord rather than, as it appears, actually sever the cord itself into quarters. The importance to the audience of the fact that the ends of the cord are at all times in view during the winding cannot be overemphasized.

## SHOULD NOT KNOT

EFFECT: The following little routine is something more than a trick. It takes on the aspect of a community sing if properly performed, with its effectiveness stemming from the picture of a room full of rational people standing around, all trying to tie knots in their neckties and scarfs—and all failing.

PRESENTATION: While toying with a large scarf or a necktie or a piece of clothesline or cord, the magician points out that it is theoretically impossible to tie a knot in something without letting loose the ends since the essence of a knot is putting an end through a loop and then tightening the loop. Of course, he admits, there are "trick" methods whereby the arms are twisted around before picking up the cord, but the magician means that it is impossible to tie a knot in a "straightforward manner" without letting go the ends of the cord. If the audience will think about this proposition, the magician says, it will discover that it is so.

The magician, however, will endeavor to tie a knot without letting go the ends of the cord, and he proceeds to tie the following knot.

Using cord or a necktie (or a scarf large enough to have a diagonal dimension of at least twenty-five or thirty inches and twisted ropewise) the magician grasps it about six inches from one end with the thumb and index finger only of his left hand, and at the other end with the thumb and index finger only of his right hand. He holds his arms extended before him, the cord stretched between them, the palms of his hands upward.

Moving his right hand only, the magician describes a clockwise circle, carrying the right-hand end of the cord in toward his body, over to the left, over his left arm, downward, and back to the right again, leaving a large loop hanging on the inside of his left forearm as in Figure 22A.

It will be seen that the downwardly extended part of the cord on the outside of the left arm divides the large loop in two as the magician looks through it (marked *a* and *b* in Figure 22A). The right hand now carries its end of the cord downward (away from the body), through the loop *a* as in-

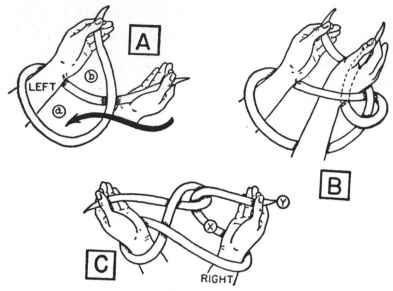

Figure 22

dicated by the arrow in Figure 22A, and immediately upward through the loop b, catching the part of the cord that divides the big loop over the back of the right wrist as it does so. The position of the hands is now as shown in Figure 22B.

The hands are now separated as far as the cord will allow, all portions of the cord being pulled taut as in Figure 22C. Then the hands are turned with the palms down, the cord still held only by its ends between the respective thumbs and index fingers.

Now comes the chicanery. Both hands bend down at the wrists, tossing the loops off the wrists over the hands, the hands twisting as they move and coming up palms upward. As the right wrist bends down, however, the right second, third, and fourth fingers grasp the cord at Point X in Figure 22C against the base of the right thumb, and the right thumb and index finger release their hold upon the cord at Point Y.

When the hands are now separated, a knot will be seen to

have formed in the center of the cord. This move with the right hand may be done rather slowly (as a matter of fact, it should be), since it is completely covered by the motion of both hands in tossing the loops off the wrists. If the positions of the hands before the toss are as described, the right fingers will quite naturally engage the cord at the right spot as the wrist is bent to toss the loops over the hands. There should be no grabbing for the cord, as the move is a completely natural one and should be done exactly as if the tossing were being done without any secret moves.

Having completed the knot as described, emphasizing all the while that he has never let go the ends (and, indeed, so it appears since the tossing motion completely covers the fact that the right hand actually does let go the end and grasp another part), the magician invites one of the spectators to see if he can do the knot.

Giving the spectator another piece of cord (or suggesting that he use his necktie) so that they two may do the knot in concert, the magician leads the spectator step by step through the knot, omitting, of course, to mention anything about the skulduggery of the right hand. The magician comes up again with a knot in his cord, whereas the spectator fails to get a knot although he has followed the magician apparently move by move! (The spectator may get what appears to be a knot but is actually just a slipknot, which can be dissolved by pulling on the ends of the cord.)

The magician appears to be completely at a loss to understand why the spectator has failed while the magician has succeeded. He requests the spectator to try again, directing him move by move as to what to do. When the spectator has reached the point depicted in Figure 22C, just before he is about to toss the loops over his hands, the magician stops him and inspects the knot very carefully, "just to make sure the spectator is correct." Everything looks correct, the magician says, let's see.

The magician takes the ends of the spectator's cord from him and requests the spectator to toss the loops over his hands. A knot forms, much to the magician's apparent satisfaction, and the spectator's confusion, since the transferring of the ends from one person to another has the same effect as letting go the one end, as far as the knot is concerned.

The magician now invites the spectator to try it by himself. The spectator does so, and, of course, fails to get a knot. By this time, the audience will be accusing the magician of all sorts of duplicity. To answer such accusations, the magician takes his cord once more, and, tying the ends to his thumbs (or affixing them there with rubber bands if the material is such that tying is impracticable), he agains executes the knot and moves up to the point where he has reached Figure 22C.

Here he pauses to point out that he certainly has not let go the ends, since they were tied to his thumbs. To further obviate any further duplicity, the magician requests two spectators to untie the ends from his thumbs and each hold one, being sure not to let go while he tosses the loops off his wrists. Naturally, under these circumstances, a knot is formed.

Once more the magician requests the spectator to try. By this time the spectator is feeling rather foolish at not being able to tie a knot that the magician can accomplish with such ease and apparent lack of chicanery. By this time, also, other members of the audience will feel that certainly they will not be as stupid as the spectator who has been trying, and one by one the other spectators will want to attempt so "easy" a feat, if only to show up the unsuccessful spectator.

This sort of thing, of course, the magician encourages, and soon several persons will be trying to accomplish the magician's feat. The magician patiently instructs each one, always omitting to mention the secret move of the right hand. Occasionally with each one, the magician goes through the baiting moves of taking the ends from the spectators and letting a knot be formed.

After most of the spectators are thoroughly tantalized by the challenge which they have accepted, and before the most perspicacious of them succeeds in correctly analyzing the problem, the prudent magician will make his exit, leaving the spectators to struggle with their problem and to remember the magician as a very clever fellow.

## WHERE THERE'S SMOKE . . .

EFFECT: The magician snuffs his lighted cigarette out on a borrowed handkerchief, but the cloth is not burned, and the cigarette butt vanishes completely. Actually this effect is a classic in magic and is widely known not only among magicians but also among many laymen. The presentation given below, however, is so arranged that even someone familiar with the usual method of working the trick will be completely baffled by this version. The effect in its present form was disclosed to the author by Dr. F. V. Taylor, but it is not known whether he devised it himself.

The trick requires a small piece of apparatus, but it is no less impromptu since the gadget can readily be carried in the pocket until needed. The required gimmick is what is known as a thumb tip and is nothing more than a metal shell shaped somewhat like the end of the magician's thumb, painted flesh color, and made so that it will fit the thumb like a thimble (see Figure 23A). Obviously such a thumb tip is quite visible when in place on the thumb if anyone takes the trouble to look, but, surprisingly enough, if the thumb is pointed with its end directly toward the audience so that only the end of the thumb tip can be seen, the gimmick is almost completely invisible.

The magician will have no need to test the truth of that

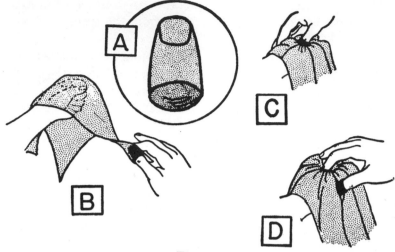

*Figure 23*

assertion in this effect, however, since the audience here is never allowed to get a glimpse of the thumb tip. For that reason, as far as this particular effect is concerned, the magician could just as well use a flesh-colored thimble that will fit over the end of his thumb. The thumb tip is such a useful magic utility item, however, that the reader might well find it worth while to purchase one at any magic store or novelty shop where tricks are sold.

PRESENTATION: The thumb tip is carried in the right trouser or jacket pocket until needed. The only other requirement of the trick is that the magician or some one of his spectators be smoking a cigarette and have it about three fourths smoked.

The magician asks to borrow a handkerchief. As one is handed to him, he takes it with his left hand. His right hand, which has been resting easily in his trouser or jacket pocket, picks up the thumb tip and emerges with the tip on the thumb just as the left hand takes the handkerchief. The right hand goes to the left immediately and takes one corner of the handkerchief with the fingers in front and the thumb behind. The left hand takes the opposite corner and the handkerchief is spread out and displayed to the audience.

So far the audience has not seen the thumb tip because it was hidden by the right fingers as the right hand moved leisurely from the pocket and now it is hidden behind the corner of the handkerchief that the right hand holds.

The left hand releases its corner of the handkerchief and is formed into a loose fist. The right hand drapes the handkerchief over the left fist, still holding one corner so as to hide the thumb tip as in Figure 23B.

Chemists are doing some wonderful things these days, remarks the magician, along the line of flameproofing cloth. All sorts of chemicals are used to make even the flimsiest cloth fireproof. The magician wants to see if this borrowed handkerchief has been so treated.

So saying, he makes a little well in the handkerchief by pushing it down into his left fist using his right thumb as in Figure 23C. The right hand merely drops the corner of the handkerchief it has been holding and moves, perfectly relaxed with the fingers hiding the thumb tip, up to the left fist. When the right thumb pushes the cloth down into the left fist, it leaves the thumb tip behind in the little well, retained by pressure of the left fingers. Now the right hand gestures naturally to show that there is nothing concealed in it.

Taking his own cigarette or borrowing the cigarette that a spectator is smoking, the magician says he will test the flameproof qualities of the cloth. He drops the lighted cigarette just as openly as possible into the well in the handkerchief and, of course, into the thumb tip. Continuing the remarks about flameproofing cloth, the magician lets the cigarette burn away in the thumb tip so the spectators can see smoke rising from the handkerchief. Occasionally he looks inquiringly down into the well in the handkerchief as if to see just how badly things were getting burned.

Finally he decides that the cigarette has burned long enough and says he will snuff it out. He sticks his right thumb down into the well in the handkerchief just as he did when he poked the handkerchief down into the fist. In this one motion he stuffs the cigarette down into the thumb tip and picks the tip up on his right thumb. He jerks his thumb out quickly with some exclamation as if he had burned it on the cigarette and immediately sticks the tip of his index finger down into the well and begins poking around as if trying to get the cigarette snuffed out.

The thumb tip and thumb, of course, are now behind the left hand where they are hidden from the audience. While the magician is poking in the well with his index finger, the right thumb moves so that the tips of the closed left fingers can reach the thumb tip through the cloth of the handkerchief and press it against the base of the left thumb. The right thumb is then withdrawn from the tip, which is held in the folds of the handkerchief by the left hand as in Figure 23D.

The right hand stops its poking and makes some gesture to show that it is completely empty. Spectators who are familiar with the usual working of the trick whereby the thumb tip is simply carried away by the right thumb will be baffled to note that the magician does not have a thumb tip on. In case any of the spectators has already announced that he knows how the trick works, it might be well to wriggle the right thumb meaningfully at him just to dispel any notion that a thumb tip is involved. The magician should not, however remark that his right hand is empty or that he has no thumb tip. Merely a gesture that will show his hand unmistakably empty is necessary. The spectators can see from an apparently casual gesture that the performer's hand is empty, whereas they would never in the world believe him if he tried to tell them it was.

After gesturing, the right hand once more goes back to the left fist and the index finger takes a couple more pokes into the well in the handkerchief. The right thumb picks up the thumb tip from the left fingers with the same movement used to place it there (Figure 23D). The right finger then emerges quite openly from the well and the right hand drops down to take one of the dangling corners of the handkerchief (just as in Figure 23B) and pulls it very slowly off the left fist to show that not only has the handkerchief come through the ordeal unharmed but the cigarette butt has completely vanished.

Once more the handkerchief is displayed by holding it at the two top corners, fingers in front and thumbs behind. The back side of the handkerchief can also be shown by criss-crossing the hands, the thumb tip still remaining hidden.

The left hand then tosses the handkerchief back to its owner as the right hand drops listlessly to the side. Or, if the performer is worried about the thumb tip, he may start to stuff the handkerchief absentmindedly into his own pocket with his right hand. As soon as the right thumb is inside the pocket where it can dispose of the thumb tip the performer stops embarrassedly as he "remembers" that the handkerchief is not his own but a borrowed one.

NOTE: The only advice that one can give in the use of a thumb tip is to forget all about it. As far as the beginner in magic is concerned, this advice goes completely unheeded. It is always difficult to assure oneself that that audience just will not notice a thumb tip, especially when the magician can feel its presence on his thumb even when he cannot see it. As in the well-known simile of a sore thumb, the novice finds it very difficult not to be self-conscious when he is wearing a thumb tip. Self-consciousness, of course, results in holding the hand in such unnatural positions in an effort to hide the tip that the spectators' attention cannot help but be directed at the very place where it is least wanted.

If the reader will endeavor not to think or worry about the thumb tip and to use no movements or positions of his hand when wearing the tip that he would not without the tip, then he will have at his command not only a very effective trick, but also one of magic's most useful tools.

Also it should be obvious that the fewer pokes the magician has to take at the handkerchief in order to steal the thumb tip, deposit it momentarily in the left fingers, and then steal it back again the greater will be the effect. The more the magician has to fuss around poking foolishly at the handkerchief, the more likely are the spectators to think he is up to some sort of chicanery.

## CUTTING WIT

EFFECT: A strip of paper is repeatedly and openly cut in half with scissors and after each cut it restores itself to one piece without the magician's doing anything at all.

The effect as here presented cannot actually be considered as a completely impromptu trick since a prepared piece of paper is needed, which the performer will hardly carry around in his pocket awaiting the opportunity to perform. It is included here, however, because there is no reason why it cannot be done completely on the spur of the moment in the performer's own living room.

Furthermore, this is a type of trick that gains in effect with repetition, contrary to the more usual magic. As such it is the perfect accompaniment for an amusing raconteur's most extended series of anecdotes. The performer who fancies himself capable of the Bob Hope type of endless comic patter will probably find little excuse just to stand up in front of his friends and reel off a long series of gags for no reason at all. Yet if he is supposedly performing a trick, he has a perfect hook on which to hang his comedy endeavors.

"Cutting Wit" is tailor-made for such a situation. The performer may emphasize the mystery of the trick and perform it just as he would any other sort of effect. Or he may use the trick as a sort of running gag, nonchalantly snipping away at the paper every now and then and letting it restore itself each time while he prattles on about something wholly irrelevant to the trick.

PRESENTATION: Since the strip of paper in this effect can be cut and restored as many or as few times as the performer desires and since the trick is virtually self-working so that the performer really does not have to think about what he is doing but only about what he is saying, "Cutting Wit" will fit practically any patter scheme or characterization that the performer desires to supply. For this reason the presentation is suggested here only in a sketchy form.

In contrast to the tricks heretofore presented, there are no definite magical ideas that the performer must get across to the audience to make the deception work. The presentation could be all in pantomime or with comedy patter. The magician could use the trick as an illustration of the trouble he had trying to even up the legs of a table, cutting first one and then the other but always cutting one too short until there was no leg left. He could talk about his tailor's troubles in cutting out a suit of clothes. He could go through the old but effective routine of "Once I saw a magician who cut a piece of paper and put it back together again and so I went to a magic store and asked if they had the trick where you cut a piece of paper and put it back together again but they said they didn't have a trick where you cut a piece of paper and put it back together again . . ." and on and on, cutting and restoring the paper each time he mentions the incident.

As suggested before, the performer could also use the effect merely as an excuse to try out what he believes to be an effective gag patter on his friends. As a matter of fact the performer could perform the trick in almost any context, including standing on his head or dancing a classical ballet, should he so desire. It must be remembered, however, that, although "Cutting Wit" is baffling, it will not stand alone as many tricks will. In the trick a piece of paper is repeatedly cut and restored, but that is all. The paper cannot be inspected by the audience, and, after the second or third restoration, there is nothing to provide a magical climax or finale. The whole success of the trick depends on the performer's presentation, not on the magic of the trick itself.

Unfortunately, all the books in the world are not going to teach the reader how to be a comedian or a ballet dancer. Therefore the author can do no more than offer these very general presentation ideas.

PREPARATION OF THE PAPER. A strip of paper about a foot long and one and one-half or two inches wide is required. A strip cut from the columns of a newspaper is usually used. One side of the strip of paper is coated lightly with the adhesive solution described below and allowed to dry thoroughly.

A suitable adhesive solution is nothing more than diluted rubber cement. Any stationery or office supply store sells rubber cement, an adhesive made by dissolving white latex (or synthetic rubber before it has been vulcanized) in some organic solvent such as benzene. Care must be taken to get white rubber cement made for use in pasting paper and not the black kind made for tire repairmen and cobblers.

As sold, rubber cement is of a rather viscous consistency. A small portion of the cement is diluted slightly with the solvent made for that purpose by the manufacturers of rubber cement (or with cigarette lighter fluid, benzene, carbon tetrachloride, or any such organic solvent that may be handy). This diluted solution is then painted on one side of the paper strip and allowed to dry. Finally white talcum powder is dusted over the rubber cement in order to keep the strip of paper from sticking to itself when folded. It should be noted that suitable strips of prepared paper can be purchased at any magic store under the name of "Clippo," as well as a suitable adhesive solution called "Clippo Fix."

PERFORMING THE EFFECT: The strip of paper is folded across the middle so that the rubber-cemented sides come together. With a regular pair of scissors the magician quite openly cuts off a little strip of paper along the fold (as in Figure 24A). There can be no doubt but that the paper has been cut fairly and completely through the middle. Yet, when the magician unfolds the paper it is seen to be once more in one whole strip. This cutting and restoration can be repeated as often as desired.

The explanation is quite simple. When the scissors cut through the paper, the shearing action of the blades presses the cut edges tightly together so that the rubber cement on one edge adheres to that on the other. When the magician allows the paper to unfold, it is really in two pieces, but there is enough adherence by the rubber cement to hold the slight weight of the bottom half of the strip of paper to the cut edge of the top half as in Figure 24B.

If the faces of the strips stick to each other it means that there is too much cement on the paper and not enough talcum, that is, the rubber cement was not diluted enough before being applied. If, on the other hand, the edges refuse to stick together when cut, it means that there was not enough cement applied, that is, that the cement was diluted too much.

Obviously the joint formed at the cut edges is very weak. Therefore the magician should not try to unfold the paper after the cutting but should merely release one end and let gravity cause the strip to unfold. Otherwise he may pull the two halves apart in handling the paper.

Since the audience cannot be allowed to inspect the prepared paper, the impromptu performer should devise his patter scheme with one of two endings: (a) His patter

PAPER REALLY CUT HERE
BUT RUBBER CEMENT
MAKES CUT·EDGES
HANG TOGETHER

A

B

FOLDED WITH
STICKY SIDES
TOGETHER

Figure 24

should indicate that the strips be burned or completely used up at the finale so that there is nothing left of the strip for the audience to inspect. (b) Or his patter should give some excuse for ending with two pieces of paper—that is, some excuse for the paper not to be restored after the last cutting. In this latter case the magician would apply the adhesive only to the center portion of the strip and then make sure that he cuts all the adhesive-covered parts away so that he ends by holding two perfectly unprepared pieces of paper which the audience can inspect to its heart's delight.

The impromptu performer will also find it convenient to cut the paper so that the cut-off strips fall into a wastebasket or large and well-filled ashtray. Then the spectators will not be tempted to retrieve the cut-off bits for inspection as they might if the scraps were allowed merely to fall to the floor.

As another alternative the magician might burn or crumple into a ball the final bits of paper and produce from the ashes or the crumpled scraps a duplicate strip as if the paper had restored itself one final time after all the cuttings so as to be back to its original size. Such a duplicate strip should be folded in tiny accordion pleats and resting beside the ashtray in which the final scraps are burned or secreted in a thumb tip (see page 107) from which it would be stolen while crumpling up the final cut pieces. The scraps would then be disposed of into the thumb tip which would go back on the thumb as the "restored" strip was displayed.

It should also be noted that there is no reason why the strip need be cut straight across. If a diagonal cut is made, the strip will be in the form of a V when it unfolds; if refolded and cut straight across, it will unfold into a straight strip once more.

## DEMI-TASSE

To conclude the section on impromptu tricks with objects other than playing cards, several intriguing little effects are presented here. They all have one thing in common: the presentation here given is directed to performance at the dinner table either at home or in a restaurant.

Lingering over coffee after dinner makes a perfect setting for the impromptu magician to perform. Not only is the audience amenable to a little entertainment, but also the fact that magician and spectators are sitting at a table can be turned definitely to the magician's advantage.

The several effects herein contained may be readily adapted to other settings than the dinner table, of course, but are perhaps more effective as table stunts than otherwise. It is not presumed that these effects are miracles, but rather little appetizers for things to come for the spectators—little magical jokes, so to speak, with which to titillate the spectators' appetite for magic.

It might be well to emphasize here that the table magician's most potent tool is his lap, which acts as a convenient repository for all sorts of objects and is completely hidden from the audience. Hence table magicians should sit close to the table when performing tricks and learn to use their hands in their laps without moving their upper arms and shoulders.

## 1. Crystal Clear

EFFECT: To win a bet, the magician manages to unwrap a sugar cube by simply slapping it with his hand.

PRESENTATION: During dinner in a restaurant where there are sugar cubes wrapped in paper on the table, the magician finds an opportunity to unwrap one of the cubes very carefully with his hands in his lap. After removing the sugar from the wrapper, he refolds the wrapper so that it still looks as though it contained a lump of sugar.

When he is thus all set, he challenges someone to a race to see who can unwrap a lump of sugar faster. He offers his opponent the sugar bowl to choose his lump. He then brings the bowl over in front of himself with his right hand. Holding the empty wrapper lightly at his left finger tips, he brings his left hand up from his lap and reaches into the sugar bowl, his hand emerging holding the same empty wrapper which he places on the table in front of him. The wrapper will retain its shape and appear to be a regular lump. His right hand, meanwhile, has procured the unwrapped lump from his lap and holds it hidden in his palm.

Someone sets the two contestants off and at the word "Go!" the magician merely bangs his right hand down on the empty wrapper and leaves the unwrapped lump in full view—apparently having unwrapped the lump with a mere lightning stroke of his hand.

## 2. Soda Jerk

EFFECT: The tissue wrapping of two soda straws is torn to bits and then completely restored.

PRESENTATION: The magician prepares for the effect by secretly taking the tissue wrapper off a pair of soda straws in his lap. He does this by tearing the tip off one end of the wrapper and then forcing it down the straws so that the wrapper is squeezed into tiny pleats and is finally compressed into a tight ball. Because of the way it was formed, however, this ball can be pulled out into the full wrapper in one motion.

When the magician is ready, he places the balled-up tissue between the left thumb and index finger and reaches for a new set of straws with his right hand. Placing one end of the straws also between the left thumb and index finger, he tears off the other end of the wrapper and removes the straws. The duplicate wrapper can be compressed so much that it will pass unnoticed in its hiding place.

Moistening his right thumb and index fingers at his lips, he tears the wrapper in half, placing the right half in front of the left half between the left thumb and index finger. Moistening his right fingers once more, he tears the two halves of the wrapper in half, placing the right-hand pieces in front again in the left fingers.

Continuing in this way the magician tears the tissue wrapper into tiny pieces, moistening his right fingers at his lips each time and always placing the right-hand pieces in front of the left.

When the pieces are down to about three quarters of an inch long, the magician begins to crumple them into a ball, moistening his right fingers all the while as if to help him handle the tiny bits of tissue. At this point, of course, the crumpled duplicate in the left fingers will not be discernible from the crumpled pieces of the torn wrapper so the magician need have no fears of what the audience may see and he can invite the spectators to watch his restoration process closely.

As soon as the torn pieces are fairly well crumpled, the magician carries a few of them hidden between his right thumb and index finger and deposits them in his mouth each time he moistens his fingers. Since he has laid the foundation for this finger-moistening gesture all through the tearing, it will go unnoticed.

When all the torn pieces have been carried to the performer's mouth (and it should take but two or three trips at the most), he utters the magic words or what have you and pulls the duplicate tissue wrapper out full length to show the torn tissue apparently completely restored. The torn pieces in the mouth will not bother the performer at all since they are very tiny when wet and crumpled. They are merely allowed to remain there until the magician has an opportunity to remove them secretly, or they may be swallowed without harm if the performer is a perfectionist.

### 3. *Tumbling Tumbler*

EFFECT: While attempting to force a coin through the table, a large water glass is forced through instead.

PRESENTATION: The magician asks for the loan of a coin, and while it is being procured, covers an inverted water tumbler with a napkin. The napkin should be fresh, and the stiffer the better. The magician takes care to mold the napkin around the tumbler so that the napkin assumes the shape of the tumbler.

The magician says he will cover the borrowed coin with the inverted tumbler and force the coin to penetrate the table top. Grasping the tumbler through the napkin, the magician raises it so that the spectator who loaned the coin may place the coin under the inverted tumbler. The magician starts to replace the tumbler and then stops, suddenly draws the tumbler back toward the edge of the table, and remarks that the spectator apparently wants the coin to "go through the table heads first" (or "tails first" as the case may be).

Just as all eyes are directed to the coin by the magician's witticism, the magician carries the glass over the edge of the table and allows it to slip out of the napkin into his lap. If the napkin is properly stiff, it will retain the shape of the tumbler and look as though the tumbler were still under it.

The magician quickly covers the coin with the now empty napkin still in the shape of the glass, and, with his free hand, strikes the napkin a mighty blow. To the astonishment of all, the napkin collapses. Somewhat sheepishly, the magician removes the napkin to show that he failed to drive the coin through the table—but, reaching under the table to get the glass, he did manage to make the tumbler penetrate the solid table top.

As a variant, the magician may use a salt shaker instead of the tumbler. In this case, when the salt shaker is dropped into the lap, the left hand sticks it up under the front edge of the magician's vest or into his shirt. At the finale, then, the magician dramatically unbuttons the second top button of his vest or shirt and reaches down inside it to bring forth the salt shaker. The effect is that the salt shaker somehow or other got from under the napkin on the table to inside the performer's vest. The reaching in at the top of the vest for the shaker completely distracts the audience's thoughts from the magician's lap or anything else under the table.

### 4. *Salt and Pepper Cheat*

EFFECT: The salt shaker vanishes from under a napkin and the pepper shaker takes its place.

This effect is really what might be called cheating since the performer makes use of an impromptu confederate under the circumstances which the baffled spectators would be sure to claim were "unfair." The effect is widely known among both magicians and laymen and, peculiarly enough, it derives its main success from that fact. In every gathering there may be several persons who know or are able to figure out what is happening. These perspicacious spectators will appreciate the stunt all the more, then, because they will enjoy seeing other spectators getting fooled by so simple a trick.

The blatant simplicity of this effect would seem to belie

any notion that it might fool anyone. However, as has been
mentioned before, the most obvious ruse is frequently the
most baffling. Only when the reader has seen a group of intelligent people repeatedly baffled by this method of vanishing any small object will he appreciate just how valid such
a theory is. The use of an impromptu confederate—that is,
one who has been pressed into service on the spur of the
moment without any prearrangement—seems never to occur
to the audience. The spectators are trying to figure out how
the magician himself caused the object to vanish. They seem
to experience some sort of psychic block that prevents their
thinking of a confederate. And the confederate, delighted at
the part he takes in deceiving the others, will never give the
trick away.

PRESENTATION: The magician takes the salt shaker and
covers it with a napkin. He then holds the shaker with both
hands underneath the napkin. He is going to cause the
shaker to vanish, he explains, but he wants to do so in the
fairest manner possible. For this reason he allows several of
the spectators to reach under the napkin and make sure the
shaker is still there in his grasp. The spectators that the magician chooses thus to aid him are the two sitting on his left
and the one on his right. He presents the napkin-covered
shaker first to the left two and has them assure the rest of
the spectators that the shaker is still there.

He then asks the spectator on his right to do the same. As
he proffers the shaker to the right spectator so that he can
reach up under the napkin and feel that the shaker is still
there, he lowers the bundle until the dangling corners of the
napkin are resting on the table. As soon as the spectator's
hand is hidden beneath the napkin, the performer winks at
the spectator, places the shaker in his hand, and closes his
fingers over it. He then pushes the spectator's hand, still
hidden by the napkin, downward toward his lap. All this
while, of course, the magician is asking the spectator to make

sure the shaker is still under the napkin. Naturally the magician holds his left hand so there is still a bulge under the napkin and the audience is not aware that the shaker has departed.

The reader will find that virtually anyone can be thus pressed into service as a confederate. The spectator will at once realize something of what is about to happen and when the performer places the shaker in his hand and pushes his hand toward his lap, the spectator will take the shaker and allow his hand to drop into his lap.

Now the magician, still holding his hands under the napkin so that it appears that the shaker is still there, extends his arms so that the napkin bundle is over the center of the table. He mutters the magic words and asks someone to pull the napkin away to disclose his two empty hands.

REAPPEARANCE OF THE SHAKER. 1. The performer goes through the reverse of the above moves to cause the shaker to reappear under the napkin. He covers his empty hands with the napkin and then allows the two left spectators to feel under the napkin to assure themselves that the shaker has not yet returned. He then asks the spectator on the right to do the same, lowering the napkin so that the spectator can replace the shaker with his hand hidden by the napkin. There is an alternate effect.

2. Before he started the trick, the performer secretly placed the *pepper* shaker in his own lap. After the *salt* shaker has vanished, the performer draws his hands back into his own lap and asks some spectator to pick up the napkin and inspect it closely to make sure that the shaker is not hidden therein. Then the spectator is asked to fold the napkin in some peculiar fashion for the reappearance of the shaker. Or the performer merely patters about how difficult a feat it is to cause the shaker to vanish under these circumstances— anything to stall a minute or so.

The performer tries to keep the audience's attention

focused on the napkin in the center of the table so that he can put both hands in his lap and lean forward with his upper arms against the edge of the table as if frightfully interested in the napkin. While any movement of his arms is thus covered, the magician takes the pepper shaker from his own lap and reaches over to hand it under the table to the spectator on his right. He takes the salt shaker that the spectator is holding and sticks it in his vest or shirt as described in "Tumbling Tumbler" on page 120.

Now when he passes the napkin around, it is the pepper shaker that the spectator replaces and not the salt shaker so the magician appears to be as surprised as anyone else when the pepper shaker and not the salt shaker appears under the cloth. The salt shaker is finally retrieved from the magician's vest or shirt as in "Tumbling Tumbler."

## 5. Watch Out!

EFFECT: Borrowing the spectator's watch and slipping it into a folded napkin, the magician proceeds to crush the watch with some heavy object and then restore the pieces.

PRESENTATION: In preparation for the effect, the magician secretly places several lumps of sugar in his lap sometime during the meal when the spectators' attention is diverted elsewhere. The magician also secretly removes his handkerchief from his pocket. If the napkins in use at the table are rather small, the handkerchief should be folded into quarters. If the napkins are considerably larger than the handkerchief, it need not be so folded.

When almost ready to perform the trick, the magician, always working with his hands beneath the table, places the lumps of sugar in his handkerchief and gathers the four corners thereof together in his left hand. He then asks to borrow a watch. A pocket watch is preferable, although a wrist watch will do if the strap is not too bulky.

As the watch is being proffered, the magician gathers the

four corners of his napkin together in his left hand to form a bag. Hanging inside this napkin bag he holds—also with his left hand—the handkerchief containing the sugar. The napkin bag is mostly formed under the table, the magician raising his hands into view as soon as the handkerchief bag is safely hidden inside the napkin. The handkerchief bag containing the sugar should be hanging so that the sugar is about halfway down in the napkin bag.

Taking the proffered watch, the magician drops it openly into the napkin bag, as in Figure 25A. It will fall completely

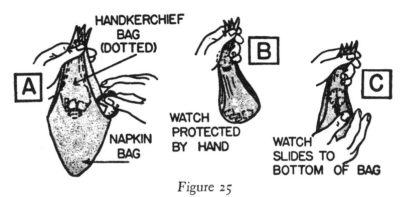

Figure 25

to the bottom without bumping the lumps of sugar since the sugar is suspended away from the bottom. Now the magician grasps the bottom of the napkin bag with his right hand and bends it upward to join the top of the bag held by the left hand. Actually, the watch is grasped through the cloth and also carried upward to the left hand, but the bending of the napkin bag will make the bulk of the sugar visible and will look as though the watch has merely slid to a new position inside the bag. See Figure 25B.

With the watch and the corners of the bag all held by the left hand, the sugar is banged upon the table. The magician then takes a heavy glass tumbler, metal sugar bowl, coffee pot, or the handle of a knife and proceeds to smash the sugar.

The sound of the lumps of sugar being crushed will lend to the effect that the watch itself is being beaten into little pieces. The magician, of course, emphasizes this illusion.

When the contents of the napkin have been completely pulverized, the magician grasps the mass of sugar very gingerly, cradling it in his right hand, which he holds palm up with the fingers extending upward to obstruct the audience's view. Gently shaking the left hand as if to force all the scattered pieces together at the bottom of the napkin bag, the magician allows the watch to slide down inside the napkin into his right hand as in Figure 25C. As soon as the watch is at the bottom of the napkin bag and hidden in his hand, the magician closes his fist on what the audiences supposes are the "pieces" and begins to knead them "back together."

At this point, the magician lowers his hands until they are just above the level of the table but so that they are back toward his body and not over the table at all. He then drops the corners of the napkin held in his left hand, and, with that hand, seizes the napkin just below the place where the watch is held. The left hand begins to twist the napkin to close it "so that none of the pieces will fall out." When the left hand releases its hold on the corners of the napkin, these corners will drop beneath the level of the table and the handkerchief containing its sugar will fall out into the magician's lap.

The magician, still hiding the form of the watch in the napkin with his hands, and still handling the napkin as if it were containing merely pieces of the watch, wraps the excess napkin around the watch, laying it in the center of the table where he commands it to restore itself into one piece. The spectator unwraps the bundle and finds his watch undisturbed, and the magician can, at his leisure, recover his handkerchief from his lap, brushing the sugar off onto the floor (if it is not the magician's floor!). The effect—because of the sound of crushing the lumps of sugar—is a rather startling one.

## 6. Flaming Proof

EFFECT: The tablecloth allows a burning cigarette to pass through it without harm.

PRESENTATION: Two spectators, sitting side by side, are asked to hold the edge of the tablecloth back toward their bodies so that a flat surface of cloth extends from the table to the spectators. Standing between them with a burning cigarette and a piece of paper of at least eight by ten inches in size (a menu is suggested), the magician says that the tablecloth is made of a very special material so as to be flame-proof.

To demonstrate this, the magician will attempt to burn it with the cigarette, to see if in fact the cloth will resist the flame. Trying to burn the menu will be thrown in as a further test of the general extent of fireproofing.

With the spectators holding the edge of the tablecloth almost horizontally, the magician takes the cigarette in his right hand and the paper in his left, holding it horizontally with his thumb on top and the fingers underneath. Carefully he examines the cloth to see just where to try his burning experiment. He flicks specks of imaginary dust off the cloth with his right little finger, and then, holding the cigarette upright with his right thumb and index finger, moves his right hand under the cloth. With his right hand in position, he covers the cloth with the piece of paper as in Figure 26A.

Momentarily changing his mind, however, he withdraws the paper until his left fingers are just over the edge of the tablecloth. Immediately the magician bends down and blows an imaginary speck of dust away from the area of the cloth over which he is working. As he is thus bent over, his right hand naturally moves out toward the edge of the cloth until

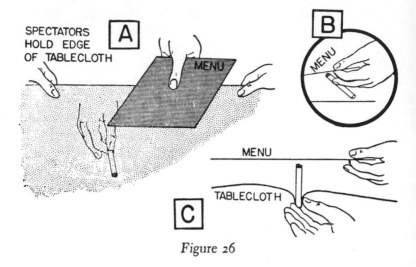

Figure 26

the left third and little fingers can pick up the cigarette from the right hand as in Figure 26B.

Immediately the magician straightens up and moves his now empty right hand back under the cloth. His left hand, holding the paper with the cigarette hidden under it, moves toward the center of the cloth until the cigarette is over the spot in the cloth where the penetration is to be made. The right hand underneath the cloth then grasps the cigarette through the cloth, and the left hand moves back to center the paper over the cigarette as in Figure 26C.

While the right hand holds the cigarette from below the cloth, the left hand allows the paper to rest on the cigarette until the latter burns its way through the paper. The left hand then releases the paper and grasps the cigarette which it pulls free of the burned hole. The right hand crumples the cloth together so that as one looks down through the burned hole, the tablecloth seems to have been damaged.

Remarking that the tablecloth does not seem to be as fireproof as he thought, the magician whisks away the covering piece of paper, and, at the same time, pulls the tablecloth downward a little and releases it suddenly, so that it springs up and apparently restores itself right before the spectators' eyes.

It will be noted that the positions of the spectators holding the cloth (the height of which is determined by the table) preclude their being conveniently able to bend down and see beneath the cloth, and hence the effect is quite mystifying. The only point needing particular care is the transfer of the cigarette from the right hand secretly to the left. This movement must be smooth and unhesitating for the effect to be deceptive.

There may be, of course, the possibility of sparks falling from the burning cigarette onto the tablecloth and actually burning it, although the possibility is slight. For that reason the magician may feel more at ease if he performs the effect using a small knife or large hatpin when confronted with a hostess' best imported Irish linen tablecloth. The working, of course, is the same.

### 7. Lumpy Legerdemain

EFFECT: Four lumps of sugar fly invisibly one at a time to congregate under a menu or napkin.

PRESENTATION: Before starting the trick, the magician secretly acquires a lump of sugar and places it in his lap where he can get at it easily when wanted. Then he tears a menu in half so that he has two pieces of cardboard about six by eight inches and lays one half on the table to either side, each protruding a trifle over the edge of the table. Finally, he arranges four lumps of sugar on the table in front of him at the four corners of an imaginary square about fifteen inches on a side as in Figure 27A. Lumps (3) and (4) should be just a few inches from the edge of the table.

While the magician is explaining that he is about to demonstrate an optical illusion, his left hand drops to his lap and picks up the extra lump of sugar hidden there, holding it between the tips of the second and third fingers. The left hand then comes up palm up and picks up the left piece of cardboard with the fingers underneath and the thumb on top. Since the cardboard was protruding over the edge of the table,

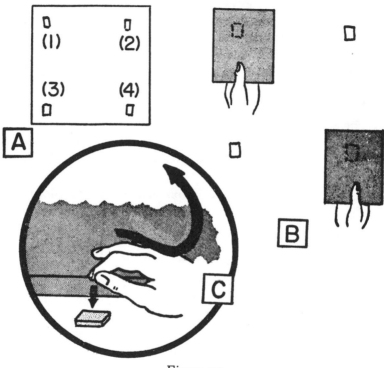

Figure 27

the left hand can grasp it easily and naturally without letting the lump of sugar between the fingers come into view. Simultaneously the right picks up the piece of cardboard at the right, holding it also with the fingers below and the thumb on top.

The performer points out that the lumps of sugar can each individually be covered by the pieces of cardboard. As he speaks he moves the cardboards so as to cover lumps (3) and (4), pointing out that, oddly enough, this process leaves lumps (1) and (2) uncovered. He then moves the cardboards so as to cover lumps (1) and (4) and then lumps (2) and (3), just to show all the possible combinations—and just to get the spectators used to seeing the cardboards moving around with no apparent reason (see Figure 27B).

Finally the performer covers lumps (1) and (2) and drops the cardboards on them, releasing at the same time the extra lump of sugar hidden under the left cardboard so that there are now two lumps under the cardboard at (1).

Now, says the performer, if we take one of the lumps and slap it down on top of a cardboard, it will go right through. So saying, he apparently picks up lump (4) in his right hand and slaps it down sharply on top of the cardboard at (1).

Actually what happens is that the performer slides lump (4) toward the edge of the table with his right fingers apparently so that his thumb can get under it. Instead of picking it up, however, he lets it fall off the table into his lap while he raises his right hand just as if he had picked the lump up and slaps his hand down on the cardboard. Figure 27C will indicate the mechanics of the move. It is not at all difficult. The reader need only spend a moment actually picking up the lump of sugar in this manner and then imitating his actions while letting the lump drop to his lap. There is no skill involved in the move—only a need for naturalness. The hand must move when apparently picking up the sugar exactly as it would in actually picking it up. Showing both hands unmistakably empty, the magician removes the cardboard at (1) revealing the two lumps of sugar beneath it. The left hand takes this cardboard and the right picks up the cardboard at (2) and shows it on both sides quite casually as the magician remarks that two lumps remain to be dealt with.

The three locations can now be covered by the two cardboards in several ways, says the magician. First he covers (3) with the left cardboard and (2) with the right, saying "Like this . . ." Then he covers (2) with the left cardboard and (1) with the right, saying ". . . or like this . . ."

While the left cardboard is covering the lump at (2) the left second and third fingers, hidden by the cardboard, pick up the lump at (2) and hold it under the cardboard. The magician then says ". . . or like this," again and moves the right hand and its cardboard from (1) over to (2). As soon as the right hand's cardboard covers the left hand's cardboard, the left hand moves its cardboard with the lump underneath over to (1) and both cardboards are dropped, the extra lump being released under the cardboard at (1).

Once again, the essence of this move is naturalness. The magician should not appear to wait until the right-hand cardboard is in position before moving the left-hand one. Rather the effect should be that both hands moved at once. Actually, however, the left hand lags behind just enough so that the two pieces of cardboard overlap in transit so that even if there were a lump of sugar still at (2) it would not be seen.

Now the right hand, using the same moves as it did before, apparently picks up the lump at (3) by sliding it toward the edge of the table and slaps down on the cardboard at (1). As the right hand slaps the cardboard, the left hand retrieves the dropped lump from the lap and places it between the tips of the second and third fingers. The right removes the cardboard from (1) and places it in the left hand, which emerges from under the table palm up just in time to take the cardboard with the fingers below and the thumb on top so as to hide the lump of sugar in the left fingers. The right hand goes back to (1) and points to the lumps there as the magician calls attention to the fact that three lumps have arrived.

Immediately the left hand drops its cardboard and the hidden lump of sugar down onto the three already at (1). The two hands then clap together as the magician says

"Watch!" before the spectators can wonder why he does not show the remaining lump they believe to be under the cardboard at (2).

The right hand then pretends to withdraw an imaginary lump of sugar right through the cardboard at (2) and slap it down through the cardboard at (1). Showing both his hands unmistakably empty, the magician carefully turns up both pieces of cardboard to show that all four lumps are now at (1).

NOTE: It should be emphasized that each of the three lumps arrived under the cardboard at (1) by using a different device. Thus the first lump was added before the trick began for the audience—that is, before the audience knew what was supposed to happen. The second lump arrived by stealing it from position (2) under cover of moving the cardboards. The final lump arrived at (1) by switching the cardboard from one hand to another while all attention was on the discovery of the three lumps at (1).

For this reason, should any of the spectators have noticed something unnatural about any one of these devices, there would still be the movement of two other lumps for them to figure out. Should a spectator notice, for example, that maybe something untoward happened when the magician passed one cardboard over the other in secretly switching a lump from (2) to (1), he would be inclined to discount that as a possible explanation since nothing of the sort happened when the other two lumps were transferred to (1). Should a spectator note that the magician might have added an extra lump from under the table in replacing the cardboard the last time, he would be completely thrown off the track by the fact that the magician had shown his hands unmistakably empty after the first lump arrived, and so on.

Thus the magician uses several different methods for doing exactly the same thing—that is, secretly introducing another lump of sugar under the cardboard at (1). One method allowed him to show that his hands were empty. Another allowed him to show that he was not switching the lumps around when covered by the pieces of cardboard. In this way the magician apparently disproves each of the possible solutions of the trick while still doing the very things he is disproving. In addition he has further confused the audience by actually using five lumps of sugar when only four ever appear in the trick.

This little effect, by the way, illustrates a principle that is almost fundamental in all types of tricks that involve the invisible transposition of an object from one place to another. For some reason or other the audience always expects the magician to try to introduce the object secretly at its destination just as he shows it has arrived. The thought that he could get the object to where it is going before it is supposed to have gone just does not seem to occur to the spectators. Thus the magician at each stage of the trick is one step ahead of the spectators. Each additional lump of sugar has actually arrived at (1) long before it is supposed to have left its former place. And that is why an effect as simple as this one can be successful.

As noted at the start, the magician might use a folded napkin instead of the pieces of cardboard, provided the napkin was stiff and bulky enough when folded so that it could be laid on top of the lumps without the spectators' being able to see how many lumps were under it.

# IV

## When Conversation Lags

"Wanna see a trick?" coming as a question from an eager young man with a deck of cards in his hand and a fiendish gleam in his eye usually elicits a more or less polite "No!" as answer. This situation we must somehow or other correct.

It is almost impossible to entertain people with magic if those people do not want to be entertained with magic. The stage magician does not have that problem. If his audience did not want to see a magician, there would be no one in the theater.

The amateur magician doing impromptu tricks with his friends, however, must have their interest *before* he begins or he may never succeed in capturing that interest.

Herewith, then, are a few hints as to a way to build up the impromptu audience's interest *before* the magician begins to do magic. Here are several suggestions to inveigle the audience into requesting that the magician perform, to give the magician an opening with which to start his tricks.

## CARD FLOURISHES

The magician is sitting at the bridge table. During a lull in the game he picks up a deck of cards and begins toying apparently absent-mindedly with it. Or the magician is sitting chatting with friends. He absently removes a deck of cards from his pocket and begins to toy with it. Almost immediately an interested question as to what he is doing will be directed his way.

The magician then (depending upon how much he likes to act) will either look surprised, as though he did not really realize he was toying with cards, or he will loftily explain that he is just getting in practice for his new hobby. If that does not bring forth a sincere, "Well, show us something, won't you?" the reader is heartily recommended to another hobby—or to other friends.

Most of the so-called card flourishes (the "toying" referred to above) involve a greater or less degree of manipulative skill. For that reason it is suggested that the reader learn some of the tricks in the other sections before devoting much of his time to learning these flourishes. A few of the simpler ones are given below just so that the reader may keep them in the back of his mind while he is acquiring more and more ability to handle cards.

### 1. Card Fan

Many words have been written about the various ways of performing card fans. Here is just one of the many explanations for this very effective flourish and, as will be seen later, very useful accomplishment.

Take the deck of cards in the right hand, holding it with the thumb at the bottom end of the deck and the second and third fingers at the top end exactly as in Figure 28A. The index finger rests lightly against the top corner of the deck.

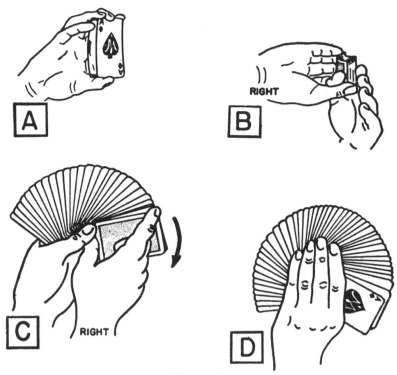

Figure 28

Hold the left hand relaxed and extended, palm facing the body, fingers parallel to the floor.

Holding the deck as described, place it against the inside of the fingers of the left hand so that about two-thirds of length of the cards protrudes above the left index finger and so that the left edge of the deck is against the palm side of the large knuckle of the left index finger. The deck is tilted a little to the left as in Figure 28B.

Now, using the second and third fingers of the right hand, press the top of the deck so that it bends backward slightly over the left hand. A good bit of pressure is necessary. When the whole deck is bent in an arc, sweep the cards outward to the right using the fingers of the right hand, and then downward and back in toward the body.

The second and third fingers of the right hand must keep their pressure bending the deck during the outward sweep, but as soon as the right hand starts its downward sweep, two important things happen almost simultaneously: The left thumb clamps down on the lower left corner of the top card, and the second and third fingers of the right hand let go all together, leaving the right index finger to do all the moving of the cards in their circle by pushing only on the upper left hand corner of the deck as in Figure 28C. The reverse side of the completed fan is shown in Figure 28D.

If the reader has dropped the cards all over the floor several times, it is suggested that he forget about fans now, and go on to something else. The fan is a pleasing flourish, but by no means essential. It should be noted, however, that a perfect fan, that is, one with all the cards evenly spaced, can only be executed with very good and very clean cards. So the reader should practice with a new deck. If both sides of each card are powdered with zinc stearate powder, they will be unbelievably easier to handle in fanning as well as for any other purpose.

### 2. Fancy Cuts

Two easy, meaningless, but very effective attention-getters are these fancy cuts. They should be done quite absent-mindedly while apparently toying with the deck of cards.

First hold the deck as in Figure 29A. Now, by squeezing with the left index and little fingers, pull some cards upward off the back of the deck holding them between the right index and little fingers, and replace them on the face of the deck. Do the same thing again, and as swiftly, and with as large a gesture as possible.

For the second cut, hold the deck again in the right hand, the fingers at one end, the thumb at the other as in Figure

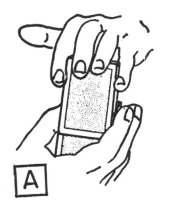

*Figure 29*

29B. Now, using only the left thumb, lift up a small packet of cards from the deck at the thumb end, and, by moving the left hand in the direction of the arrow, cause that packet to pivot against the right fingers and fall off the deck into the left palm. Drop the right hand cards on top of those in the left hand and repeat the flourish.

### 3. *Hindu Shuffle*

This device is described on page 165 as a method for controlling cards. It is, however, a perfectly legitimate way to shuffle cards (that is, it actually shuffles them) and its unusualness makes it a good flourish with which to attract attention.

## CARD TRICKS

Here are two card tricks that, as far as magic goes, may not be miracles, but as far as turning the conversation to magic or providing the magician with an opening, they are unsurpassed.

### 1. *Sloppy Shuffle*

This is done with no more warning than a pre-emptory "Here, let me show you something," when, during a card game, one of the players makes a particularly sloppy shuffle.

The magician takes the deck, and, without calling attention to it, nonchalantly gives it a good healthy bend across the middle by pressing the ends of the cards together so that

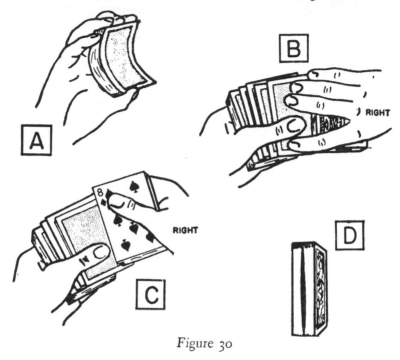

Figure 30

all the cards in the deck are curved as in Figure 30A. "I want to show you a really sloppy shuffle," the magician says, and, with the deck in dealing position in his left hand, he pushes several cards into his right hand as if he were dealing them. These cards, of course, are face down in his right hand.

Now the magician turns his right hand over (so its cards are turned end over end) and thumbs several more cards underneath those already in his right hand as in Figure 30B. Since his right hand is now turned over, these cards are now back-to-back with the first few cards in the right hand. "We not only mix them up, but we turn them upside down to boot," he says as he once more turns his right hand back to the normal dealing position and thumbs several more cards off the deck. These cards are now face down and he pushes them under the cards already in his right hand as in Figure 30C. Again the right hand is turned over and the cards are thumbed off and taken by the right hand under all the cards already there as in Figure 30B.

The magician continues until he is through the whole deck, turning his right hand over every few cards. The cards are always taken under the cards already in the right hand. All the while the magician is remarking about turning some of the cards face up and others face down. The sloppier the magician can be, the better.

When all the cards are in the right hand, the deck is evened up and the magician points out that the cards are all mixed in direction as well as in order. As he does so, he sneaks a look at the edges of the cards. Near the middle of the deck there will be a break resulting from the fact that all the cards were bent before starting as in Figure 30D. As the magician talks about the cards facing every which way in his deck, he splits the deck at this point, quite nonchalantly and without calling attention to it, and turns one half (either half) upside down.

"Now watch," he says, and runs his thumb quickly across the edges of the cards so that they make a snapping or tearing noise. "We snap the deck and all the cards once more arrange themselves in proper order!" and he spreads the cards on the table and they are once more facing the same way.

## 2. Easy To Fool

This effect as here presented, has proved itself invaluable as an opening for an impromptu display of magic, and, incidentally, it illustrates a very interesting magical principle.

If the conversation wanders around to a discussion of how unobservant most people are, or how illogical is our thinking, or any such discussion of human foibles, the magician offers to demonstrate how really gullible his listeners are. It is a good excuse for getting a deck of cards into action.

The cards are placed on the table and the magician tells his friend to cut a small number of cards from the deck—something less than half the deck—without letting anyone see exactly how many he took. Without seeing the spectator's packet of cards, says the magician, he can tell exactly how many cards the spectator took.

The magician then also cuts some cards from the remaining portion of the deck, *making sure to take more than the spectator took*. The magician points out that he did not take all the cards, since then it would be easy to deduce how many the spectator took.

Telling the spectator to turn his back and secretly count his cards, the magician does the same. *All the magician has to know to accomplish this demonstration is how many cards he himself cut off the deck*. Let us assume the magician finds that he has 22 cards. He turns to the spectator and says, "I have as many cards as you have, two more, and exactly enough to bring your total up to 20."

As will be seen presently, it makes no difference how many cards the spectator has to make this statement come true. The only critical figure is the number of cards the magician holds. If he had discovered upon counting his cards that he had 23, he would have said, "I have as many cards as you have, *three* more, and enough to bring your total up to 20." If the magician had had 18 cards, he would have said, "I have as many, etc., three more, and enough to bring your total up to 15"; if 20 cards, ". . . as many as you have, two more, and enough to bring your total up to 18."

In other words, *the magician is merely announcing his own total*, but in such a way that it appears that he knows how many cards the spectator has. As will be apparent upon a moment's reflection, saying "I have as many cards as you, two more, and enough to bring your total up to 20," is just another way of saying "I have two more than 20 cards," or 22 cards.

The deception lies in the fact that, in order to make any single one of the three statements: "I have as many cards as you do," "I have two more cards than you do," and "I have enough to bring your total up to 20," the magician would have to know how many cards the spectator held, but to make all three statements together, he does not need to know how many cards the spectator has!

The working of the trick should now be apparent. The magician counts his cards and finds he has 22 (or whatever he has). He turns to the spectator and says, "I have as many cards as you, two more, and enough to bring your total up to 20," (or whatever the appropriate figures are in each case). "Let's count our cards and see if I'm right," the magician continues, and both he and the spectator count their cards simultaneously one at a time on to the table. Let us assume the spectator has 12 cards.

When he has counted his 12 cards on to the table along with the magician, the magician stops and says—out of sheer bravado—"Twelve, I thought so! Now what did I say? I said that I had as many cards as you, which is the 12 I have just counted on to the table with yours, two more . . ." and the magician deals two of his cards aside, ". . . and enough to bring your total up to 20." Here the magician counts the rest of his cards on top of the spectator's pile, beginning where the spectator left off—in this case with 13. There will be just enough cards—in this case eight.

If the reader will try with cards in hand, the working will be apparent. The only condition is, as will be remembered from the beginning of the trick, that the magician must cut off *more cards than the spectator took*. The rest of the trick is just in the words the magician uses and the way they are interpreted.

Now, to get back to bringing the conversation around to magic: after the magician has completed the trick, he challenges the spectators to figure it out. Remember, the magician proposed to demonstrate human gullibility, and he did it with a puzzle. At no time has he mentioned magic or trickery; he is merely discussing human thought processes.

After the spectators have puzzled a while over the trick, the magician explains it to them as a joking exposition of their lack of perception, by pointing out that he did not know how many cards the spectator took. The surprise of that statement—coming after the spectators have been trying to figure out how he did know—will give the magician the floor without further competition.

The magician repeats the trick along with his explanation of it, just to demonstrate how gullible the spectators were to take his statements at face value. This time, however, the magician notes and remembers the top card of the portion he cuts off the deck.

When the cards are counted on to the table, this top card —the magician's key card—will, of course, be the first card counted on to the table. When the trick is over, the magician gathers all the counted-off cards and places them on top of his key card and returns the whole packet to the deck. The magician now knows the position in the deck at which his key card lies: thus, if the spectator took 15 cards and the magician took 23, when the deck was reassembled, the key card would be the thirty-eighth card from the top of the deck.

Now, while the magician is assembling the deck, he says that here is another way to do the effect and invites the spectator once more to cut a small packet of cards off the deck. The magician also takes some cards, making sure to take enough to include his key card. This time, while the spec-

tator is counting his cards, the magician looks for his key
card and notes its number from the top of his packet.

Thus he now knows exactly how many cards the spectator
took. If he finds his key card, for example, is eighteenth from
the top of his packet, the magician knows that the spectator
took 20 cards, since the key card was originally the thirty-
eighth from the top of the deck, and 18 from 38 is 20.

This time, then, the magician turns to the spectator and
smilingly says, "You removed exactly 20 cards from the
deck." After just having explained the trick to the spectators,
the magician fools them with what is apparently the same
trick: After having demonstrated the spectator's own lack of
perception, the magician heaps insult upon injury by fooling
them with the very trick they think they have just learned!

Naturally, the spectators will press for an explanation of
this second effect. The magician smugly points out that the
first example was merely a demonstration or puzzle, but that
the second was a trick. The magician will be glad to explain
puzzles, he says, but, since he is a magician, he cannot very
well be expected to give away his tricks. And there is the
magician's opening.

He has entertained the spectators with a discussion and
demonstration of how gullible people are. He has given them
a puzzle with which to fool their friends. Now he may go
ahead and do his magic. The spectators will be interested to
see if his other tricks are as easily explained as the one he
just demonstrated!

It might be well to note that the first part, at least, of this
effect may be demonstrated with any sort of counters such
as poker chips, matches, money, and the like so long as forty
or fifty of such counters can be assembled. Although without
the added finale possible with cards, the effect is still a good
impromptu device for turning the talk to magic or for at-
tracting enough attention to get the floor to do magic.

## IMPROMPTU OPENINGS WITHOUT CARDS

The following are several little effects that can be done without any apparent effort by the magician, to introduce his magic to the spectators. They are all performed with large mufflers, scarves (like the ones young ladies are currently wearing on their heads), neckties, clothesline, heavy cord, or anything of the sort. Actually, silk is the best material and, for best results, the silk should be about a yard long or more. A silk muffler or large scarf is wonderful; a necktie will suffice.

All the effects are done without an explanation, in a sort of offhand manner. Their purpose is not to deceive, but to get the audience interested in magic and its attention focused on the magician.

### 1. Flying Knot

Drape the scarf over the right hand as in Figure 31A. Notice that the part of the scarf hanging down over the back of the hand is longer than that over the palm and closer to the wrist, and, further, that the part of the scarf which hangs over the palm goes in behind the little finger.

(For greater clarity the drawings for this and the following effects show a tape being used. The moves are the same regardless of what object is used with which to tie the knot. One end of the tape has been colored black in the illustration to aid the reader in following the movements of the tape through the various drawings.)

The magician is going to toss the scarf in the air and cause it apparently to tie itself into a knot in mid-air. He moves his hand downward and then upward for the toss. As he moves his hand downward, the wrist bends so that the fingers point toward the floor as in Figure 31B. The third and little fingers pinch the scarf between them. The index and second fingers reach back and grab the scarf at Point X as in Figure 31C. The loop of the scarf slides off the back of the

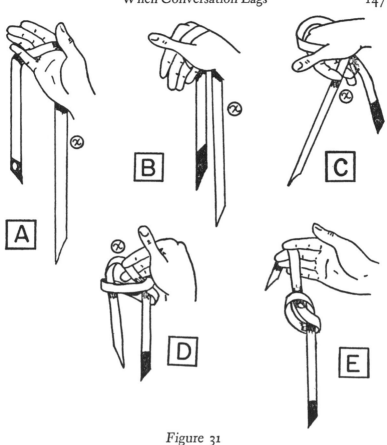

*Figure 31*

hand and a knot is formed as the first two fingers pull Point
X through the loop as in Figures 31D and 31E—all in one
down-and-up movement.

The reader should try it first without tossing the scarf into
the air in order to see what happens. Shaking the scarf a little
will tighten the knot to give the view of Figure 31E.

The reader should now toss the scarf in the air during the
tying. If the toss is made with a great downward and upward
sweep of the whole arm, the hand will have reached the point

shown in Figure 31D before the arm has finished its upward sweep. The knot is actually tied while the scarf is still in the hand, but the movement of the arm in tossing up the scarf hides this fact and makes it look as though the scarf tied itself into a knot in mid-air.

### 2. Vanishing Knot

Twist the scarf ropewise by holding its diagonally opposite corners to make it easier to handle. Grasp the twisted scarf about six or eight inches from one end between the index

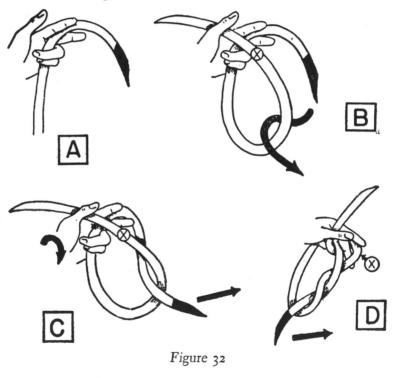

Figure 32

and second fingers of the left hand, letting the bulk of the scarf hang down against the palm of the left hand, closing the third and little fingers loosely on the scarf as in 32A.

Grasp the long end with the right hand and place it over the crotch of the left thumb as in Figure 32B, so that this end hangs over the back of the left hand, leaving a large loop. With the right hand, reach through the loop from the side toward the body and grasp the end of the scarf that is colored black in the drawing as it protrudes from between the left index and second left fingers. Pull this end through the loop and then to the right as indicated by the arrow in Figure 32B so that the loop gradually is tightened.

The second finger on the left hand, however, remains stiffly extended so that it hits Point X on the scarf. The left hand turns over in the direction of the curved arrow in Figure 32C so that the second finger points down as the loop is tightened by pulling the black end. The left second finger thus carries Point X through the large loop as it is tightened as in Figure 32D. Hence the second finger forms a loop around which the first loop tightens, making the knot a simple slipknot. Just before the Point X is drawn through the tightening loop the second finger is withdrawn.

The motions of tying and the bulkiness of the scarf (this knot is not at all effective with rope) makes it look like a real knot. Of course, the whole knot dissolves into nothing when the ends of the scarf are pulled—and, of course, the magician should blow on the knot for effect before making it dissolve.

### 3. Magic Hangman

The scarf is placed around the back of the neck as one would wear it, with the ends hanging down in front, the right end being somewhat longer, as in Figure 33A. With the left thumb and index finger, the right side of the scarf is picked up at Point Z in Figure 33A (about on a level with the top shirt button), and this point of the scarf is pulled toward the left, up, and around behind the neck as in Figure 33B. The part of the scarf below Point Z (that is, the part

Figure 33

from X to Z) at all times stays hanging in front; it is merely shifted from the right to the left side of the chest.

After the left hand has started to move as above, the right hand (going *below* the left forearm) grasps the end of the scarf colored black in the drawing (originally hanging down the left side of the chest) and carries it up past the left ear, around behind the neck, and down the right side to the front again. It will be seen that, in following the above directions, the black end of the scarf makes a loop around the loop formed by holding the white end at Point Z as in Figure 33C. These two interlaced loops must be behind the neck and hidden by it. The right hand must keep its end taut at all times.

Now, by grasping one end with each hand and pulling, the two loops will be pulled apart and the scarf will come off the front of the neck. When the movements can be made smoothly and the pulling done slowly and with much grimacing, it will appear that the scarf has been wrapped around the neck and then pulled right through the flesh.

### 4. Magic Bow

The scarf is held originally as shown in Figure 34A. The hands are brought together so that the left index and second

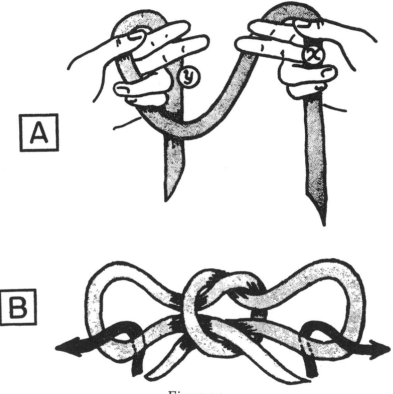

Figure 34

fingers can grasp the scarf at Point X on the palm of the right hand and the right index and second fingers can grasp it at Point Y at the back of the left hand. The hands are then separated, the first two fingers on each hand pulling their respective parts of the scarf out to form loops so that a bow-knot (see Figure 34B) is tied in just that one motion.

The magician asks his spectators if they ever experienced the annoyance of getting the ends of their shoe laces slipped through the loops in the bow so that a hard knot formed when they try to untie the laces. As he speaks, he very deliberately pulls the ends of the scarf through the loops and pulls the knot tight.

The magician explains that when such a misfortune happens to him, he simply blows on the knot and it falls apart. Suiting his actions to his words, he blows on the knot and it dissolves.

Figure 34B gives the explanation. The bowknot shown is the magician's view as soon as the knot is tied as in Figure 34A. The ends of the scarf are pulled through the loops as indicated by the arrows in Figure 34B. It is important to study the drawing and try to tie the knot, for if the ends are not pulled through the loops in exactly the manner shown, the trick will not work.

With the ends through the loops, the magician pulls the knot tight until it looks like a real tangle. Then, when he blows on the knot, he merely gives the ends one more tug and the knot dissolves. Putting the ends through the loops as shown changes the bowknot into a slipknot that can be dissolved merely by pulling the ends.

### 5. Blackout

A clever, attention-getting flourish that may be used every day is the following: Every time the magician strikes a match and uses it (with his right hand), he extinguishes the match by blowing up his left sleeve.

The flourish is very simply accomplished, but applies to paper matches only. When the magician tears a paper match from a book of matches and strikes it, he is careful to give it a sharp bend across the middle so that the upper half of the match is extending almost at right angles to the lower half.

When he is through with the match, the magician simply causes the match to rotate by moving his thumb and index finger slightly in opposite directions while pressing the match between them. By causing the bottom of the match to rotate quickly, the match head is very quickly rotated in a larger circle because of the bend in the match, and this quick passage through the air will extinguish the match. No movement of the fingers is perceptible since they have but little moving to do. Just as the magician flicks the match out, he blows up his left sleeve to give the impression that he blew the match out by some very circuitous route.

If accomplished without words of explanation in a completely nonchalant (even habitual) manner, this is a guaranteed attention-getter.

# V

## Handle with Gloves

Although the lack of necessity for difficult sleight of hand has continually been stressed in this volume, there are a few simple moves with which every magician must be familiar in order to handle cards and card magic properly. Such moves are collected for ready reference in this chapter.

If the written instructions and illustrations are closely followed, the reader should be able to familiarize himself with these maneuvers after a relatively few moments' study on each. The reader is recommended to a mirror for his own self-criticism, so that he may attain the most natural motions possible.

It should be emphasized that it takes an extremely talented manipulator to do even the simplest move indetectibly. That is, if the audience is watching for the move, it will detect it. A review of the effects published in this volume will show, however, that whenever these moves occur they are on the offbeat, so to speak. That is, they happen at a time when the audience is not expecting any skulduggery to occur or when the audience's attention is directed elsewhere. Thus the reader will find that he will be able to deceive his audience with the following moves long before perfection is attained in his execution of the moves themselves.

One all-inclusive, overriding dogma must always be kept foremost in the reader's mind: it is smoothness and naturalness that makes a secret move deceptive, not speed. A fast movement will only attract attention. There is always a natural tendency, however, to rush through with some secret move in order to get it over with in a hurry before anyone notices what has happened. Such an attitude may make the performer comfortable, but it hardly adds to the effectiveness of the trick.

It must be remembered that the spectators do not know what is coming next. If all eyes are focused fixedly on the performer when he is ready to palm a card or to get set to make a double lift, there is no reason why he cannot make some remark that will direct attention elsewhere. Nothing prevents the performer's taking his time. The spectators cannot possibly keep him under strict surveillance for an indefinite period. Sooner or later their attention must waver or succumb to the performer's misdirection, whether it be a gesture or a joke. And it really does not make too much difference, especially with the impromptu magician, whether he finishes his trick now or two minutes from now.

Familiarity and naturalness will come as the reader gains more experience in handling cards. Just a few minutes' work will suffice, however, for the reader to learn these few simple moves in a workable fashion.

## SIZE OF THE CARDS

A word should be inserted here about the size of playing cards. In this country most of the cards are made in two sizes, poker or "regular" size and bridge size. The only difference is that the poker size cards are a quarter of an inch wider than the bridge size. Before the game of bridge achieved its current popularity all cards were the wider size. When bridge took over as the leading card game, however, the necessity of holding thirteen cards in one hand led manufacturers to put the narrower cards on the market.

Although both sizes are currently available in fine-quality cards, it is more usual to find only the narrower bridge cards on hand in the home. Such a situation is fortunate for the magician since the narrower cards are a little easier to work with.

As far as the simple moves described below are concerned, it makes little difference which size the magician chooses, with the possible exception of palming. It is suggested, however, that if the reader intends to go on later to a study of sleight of hand, he should use the narrower bridge size cards, both for his own convenience and because that is the size that will be most frequently handed him with which to perform.

## RIFFLE SHUFFLE

There is nothing magical about a riffle shuffle. The reader probably already shuffles cards this way. It is rather more difficult, however, to riffle shuffle cards while standing than to shuffle them on a card table. The reader should familiarize himself with this method so that he can shuffle cards while standing before his audience without recourse to a table or to balancing himself rather indelicately on one leg while he shuffles the cards on his raised thigh.

Hold the deck face down in the left hand, the thumb at one end and the second, third, and fourth fingers at the other. The backs of the cards are toward the palm of the hand with the left index finger curled so that the fingernail

rests against the back of the top card. The deck is bowed outward by pressure from the left index finger.

The right hand is extended, palm upward, the fingers outstretched, beside the deck. At one end of the deck, the cards
are allowed to spring one by one off the left thumb on to
the tips of the extended right second and third fingers, while
still being gripped firmly by the left fingers at the other end
as in Figure 35A.

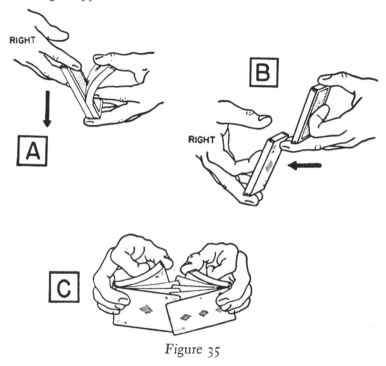

*Figure 35*

When about half the cards have thus sprung off the left
thumb, the right hand drops a trifle and the left third and
fourth fingers push their ends of the separated cards upward
and to the right so that they can be grasped with the right
thumb, the right index finger curling against the back of the
cards to aid in holding them in position as in Figure 35B.

With half the deck held in each hand with the thumbs at the top, the fingers at the bottom and the index finger curled behind to bow the cards outward, the cards are allowed to spring one at a time off each thumb and interlace with cards from the other packet as in Figure 35C. The tips of the second and third fingers of each hand are curled a bit underneath their respective ends to hold the cards as they fall and the index fingers of each hand clamp down on each packet as the shuffle is completed, Figure 35C.

At this point, the deck may merely be squared up, or the hands can move from the position of Figure 35C closer together, so that the interlaced cards are bowed upward in the middle, the left thumb regulating the height of the bowing. Bringing the hands together will cause the cards to spring together, thus squaring up the deck with somewhat of a flourish.

It is by no means necessary that the magician shuffle cards in this manner, but it is very useful if he does so. It is considerably more graceful to stand in front of the audience to shuffle the cards than to have to bend down to a table. Furthermore, since many persons seem to think that they cannot even shuffle cards, any ease and grace that the magician can accomplish with even such a simple thing as a shuffle will greatly accrue to his credit.

It will be seen how simple it is, also, to allow the original bottom card of the deck to fall first in the shuffle or the original top card (or top several cards) to fall last. Thus the magician is able to shuffle the deck apparently quite thoroughly and yet leave the top and bottom few cards undisturbed should the trick he is performing require it.

## OVERHAND SHUFFLE

A somewhat easier way to shuffle cards is the overhand shuffle, depicted in Figure 36A. The deck is held in the right

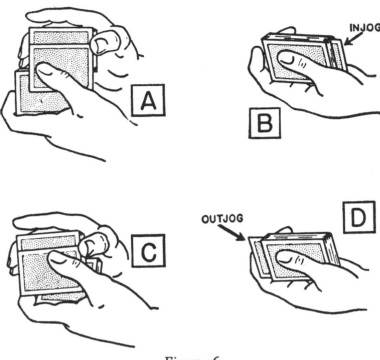

Figure 36

hand as shown and is repeatedly lowered into the left hand so that the left thumb can strip off several cards from the top of the deck, allowing the cards thus stripped off to fall back and rest against the upwardly extended left fingers. These moves are repeated until all the cards are in the left hand. For magical purposes this shuffle is as good as any other, although the riffle shuffle is considerably more spectacular.

TO CONTROL A SELECTED CARD. It will be noted here too, that with this shuffle the magician can control several of the cards. He may, for instance, strip the face card off the deck with pressure by his left fingers as the left thumb is stripping cards off the top of the deck on the first trip down into the left hand. Such a maneuver will mean that the original bottom card of the deck remains on the bottom after the shuffle.

Or he may simply take care that the last few cards stripped off the deck by the left thumb are taken one at a time so that the original bottom card of the deck is finally thrown on top at the completion of the shuffle. This is a very convenient way for placing a known card on top of the deck for the tricks where the magician must know and remember the top card. The magician merely glances at the face card of the deck, remembers it, and then shuffles the deck with the overhand shuffle, thus bringing the original bottom card—the remembered card—to the top of the shuffled deck.

Thus also can the original top card of the deck be transferred secretly to the bottom. The magician merely starts the shuffle by stripping only the top card from the pack. Since this card falls first into the left hand, it will be the bottom card of the shuffled pack at the finish of the shuffle.

Should the magician want to place the top card in the second-from-the-bottom position, he merely strips off the top card only with his left thumb and at the same time pulls the bottom card off with his left fingers. The rest of the cards are then shuffled on top of these two in the left hand.

If the magician, on the other hand, has several cards on top of the deck in a certain order, he may shuffle the deck and still keep them on top and in order. He merely has to make sure that the very first batch of cards stripped off the deck by the left thumb includes all his set-up cards. The second time the right hand goes down to the left for the left thumb to strip cards off, it moves out an inch or so away from the body as in Figure 36C, so that, when the rest of the cards are deposited little by little in the left hand, the original batch of set-up cards is left protruding an inch or so toward the magician. After completing the shuffle, the magician merely reaches down with his right hand and picks up all the protruding cards and throws them on top of the deck as if he were making one more move in the shuffle.

The above procedure is called a "jog." Should the magician want to mark his place in the deck for any reason, he could "jog" just one card by moving his right hand back toward the body while the left thumb takes off one card as in Figure 36A and then moving the right hand back to its normal position. Such a procedure will leave one card protruding or "injogged" from the end of the deck at the finish of the shuffle as in Figure 36B.

If the right hand is moved away from the body while one card is taken off (as in Figure 36C) an "outjog" will result as shown in Figure 36D.

## FALSE CUT

Since a truly convincing false shuffle of the whole deck (that is, where the order of none of the cards in the deck has changed although the deck appears to be shuffled) is rather difficult for any but experienced card manipulators, the magician frequently has recourse to a false cut to give the appearance of mixing the cards without actually doing so.

The simplest false cut is depicted in Figure 37. Consider the deck of cards as being divided into three packets as in Figure 37. (Note that the three packets are distinguished in the illustration by having their edges tinted—the top packet shaded, the middle one black, and the bottom one white. The arrows in the drawing indicate whether the hands are moving toward or away from each other.)

While the left hand holds the deck between the thumb and second fingers, palm downward, as in Figure 37, the right hand (also palm downward) using only the thumb and second finger, pulls the bottom third of the deck (white) away from the left hand. Still holding the white packet, the right hand goes back to the left and, using the thumb and

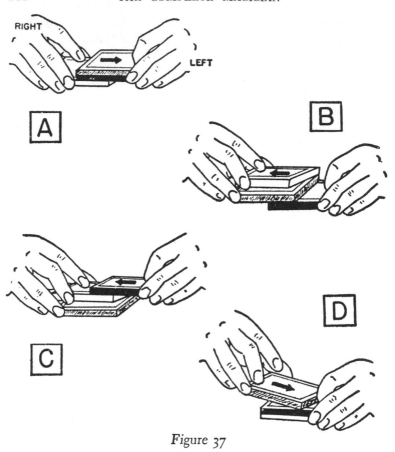

Figure 37

third finger, pulls the top third (shaded) away from the left hand as in Figure 37B, keeping the packets well separated.

Continuing without hesitation, the right hand again approaches the left hand and puts the white packet right back where it came from, immediately below the black packet. The left finger and thumb grip the white packet as it is forced between them as in Figure 37C. The remaining (shaded) packet is then thrown on top of the deck right back where it originally started as in Figure 37D.

Although the deck is in exactly the same condition after the cut as before, the effect of the above moves is that the deck has been cut in three parts and the parts mixed together.

If the performer is working at a table, the effect of the cut is somewhat enhanced if, after the right hand has acquired the top packet (shaded in Figure 37B), it throws the white packet onto the table (by releasing the right second finger while keeping the third finger still gripping its packet). The left-hand packet (black) is slapped on top and the remaining right-hand packet (shaded) slapped on top of all. The slapping and, indeed, whatever amount of nonchalance and sloppiness the performer can create seems to aid the effectiveness of the cut considerably.

It goes without saying that should the performer appear to be concentrating upon which packet to put where, the effect of the cut is nullified.

## THE GLIDE

This very simple and useful maneuver allows the magician to withdraw the next-to-the-bottom card of the deck while apparently removing the bottom one.

Usually the glide is done immediately after showing the audience the face of the bottom card of the deck, and the whole movement of the fingers is hidden by the large motion of turning the hand over. No speed is required, or even sanctioned. Smoothness and naturalness of movement are what make the glide successful.

Hold the cards as in Figure 38A, face up in the left hand, the entire weight of the deck being held by the thumb and index finger pressing against the edges of the cards only. The face card is thus shown to the audience. As the left hand turns at the wrist to turn the deck face down, the second, third, and little fingers of the left hand bend inward until they touch the face card of the deck. These three fingers

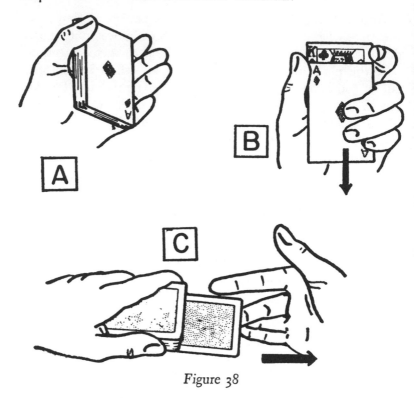

Figure 38

then slide the face card of the deck back toward the wrist with much the same motion as that of snapping the fingers. Figure 38B shows the position as viewed from beneath. The motion of the three fingers backward is completely hidden by the wrist turning and the left hand moving over toward the right hand. A little care must be taken to exert just enough pressure to slide only the face card back, and not two or three cards.

With the face card back an inch or so from the exposed end of the deck, the right hand—palm up and using only the tip of the right second finger and as much elegance and openness as possible—slides the next-to-the-bottom card out into view by pressing against the exposed part of the face of that card, as in Figure 38C. The card is allowed to drop onto the table or is taken with the right fingers, as the left fingers once more bring the original bottom card of the deck back into position. Since the audience must not now see the card on the bottom of the deck, the deck is usually laid aside at this point.

Of course, the glide move may also be made while holding the deck face up and withdrawing the next-to-the-top card, should the magician so desire or the trick so demand.

The only requirement for the move is that it look as much as possible as if the magician had really withdrawn the bottom card. A few moments of standing in front of a mirror withdrawing first the bottom card and then the next-to-the-bottom card will show the effect the magician must strive to attain.

## HINDU SHUFFLE

The Hindu shuffle is a rather unusual but quite legitimate way to shuffle cards and makes a convenient flourish for the magician to use habitually. In addition, as will be described below, it is one of the easiest and most effective ways for the magician to bring a selected card secretly to the top of the deck after the spectator has replaced it in the center of the pack.

The cards are held near one end by the right thumb and second finger as in Figure 39A. The left hand is moved palm upward under the deck with the thumb and fingers extending upward on either side of the deck. By squeezing the left thumb and second finger together a few cards are pulled off the top of the deck as in Figure 39A. These few cards are pulled away by moving the left hand to the left (following the arrow) and, when the cards are clear of the deck, the left fingers are relaxed so that the few cards just pulled off the deck are allowed to fall into the left palm.

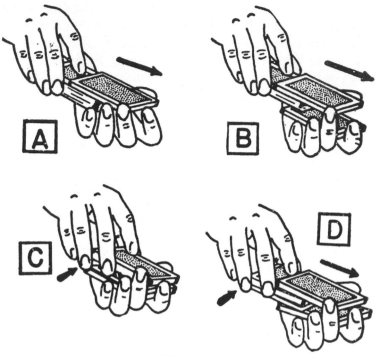

Figure 39

The left hand then goes back to the deck for another load as in Figure 39B. It pulls a few more cards off the top of the deck, carries them to the left until free of the deck and allows them also to drop to the left palm. This is repeated all through the deck—that is, until the whole deck is in the left hand.

TO CONTROL A SELECTED CARD. After the spectator has removed a card from the deck and while he is looking at it, the magician starts to do the Hindu shuffle as above. He tells the spectator to replace his card anywhere in the deck as the magician shuffles the cards.

As soon as the spectator starts to shove his card in the deck, the magician stops his shuffle and extends his left hand so the spectator can put his card on top of the left hand packet. The magician then apparently continues shuffling the cards, completely losing the selected card.

Actually what happens is this: The magician receives the selected card on top of the left hand packet and then continues the shuffle. When the left hand goes back to the deck to pull some more cards off the top, the cards already in the left palm naturally go underneath the cards in the right hand. In this position it is a simple matter to pick the selected card up between the right thumb and third finger and retain it under the cards in the right hand while the left hand moves away with more cards pulled off the top of the deck.

Figure 39C and D should make this clear. The weight of the deck in the right hand is borne by the right thumb and second finger. The right third finger is unoccupied. So, when the left hand carries its packet over to the right to pull more cards from the top of the deck, the right hand tilts slightly (as in Figure 39C) so the right thumb can engage the edge of the selected card as it lies on top of the left hand packet. The right third finger then reaches down and engages the other edge of the selected card as indicated by the arrow in Figure 39C. When the left hand then moves away, the selected card is retained between the right thumb and third finger under all the other cards in the right hand.

Since the cards originally in the right hand are held between the thumb and second finger and only the selected card between the thumb and third finger, there is a natural break above the selected card (as indicated by the small arrow in Figure 39D). Therefore the shuffle can be continued in the usual manner until the left hand pulls all the cards above the break out of the right hand. The selected card is then simply thrown on top of the deck in the left hand as the last move in the shuffle.

The description may seem involved, but if it is followed with cards in hand, the moves will be found to be quite simple. There is no need to look at the hands since the break above the selected card can be better felt than seen. Also, there need be no hesitation in picking up the selected card from the left hand packet since it is immaterial how many cards the right third finger picks up so long as it gets at least one.

Although smoothness is infinitely more important than speed with the Hindu shuffle, any briskness in execution that can be obtained is desirable. Not only do the cards seem to be getting a more thorough shuffle if they are moving rapidily, but the audience will be much more readily deceived if the magician executes the shuffle with ease and sureness than if he labors over each move in a manner to suggest that this is not the easiest way he knows to shuffle cards.

## PALMING

Of all the magician's secret moves that are known to the public, palming is far and away the most familiar. In fact the magician will soon find that his audience expects him to be able to palm (or hide in his palm) practically any object of practically any size. Unfortunately, palming is not quite so versatile. In card magic, however, it is a very useful tool. The following description of an easy way to palm a card from the top of the deck is given as only one of the many methods for palming cards with one or both hands, from the top, bottom, and middle of the deck.

Hold the deck, face parallel to the floor, in the left hand as if dealing the cards. The right hand covers the deck with the thumb at the end toward the body and the fingers together over the other end as if the right hand were squaring up the cards. The back of the right hand is toward the audience and completely masks the moves to follow. The first joint of the right little finger rests at the outer right-hand corner of the deck. The weight of the deck is now taken by the right hand between the tips of the thumb, index and second fingers with the hand arched above the deck.

The left thumb, resting on the back of the top card, pushes it to the right, pivoting the card at its outer right corner against the right little finger, as in Figure 40A. The card is

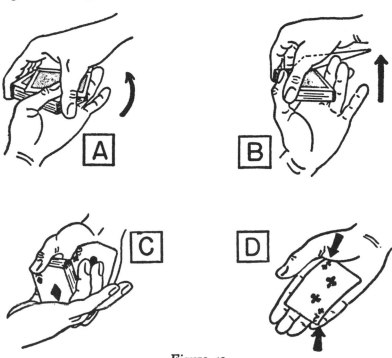

Figure 40

pivoted far enough to the right so that its right edge is aligned with the right edge of the right palm. The left fingers, then, extending upward along the right-hand side of the deck, push the top card up into the right palm as in Figure 40B and C. At no time does the right palm flatten out or come down against the deck. The right hand stays motionless throughout.

The left thumb and fingers once more grip the deck and

the right hand slides off the deck to the right, as if completing its mission of squaring up the cards, and drops to the side. The palmed card rests in the right palm as in Figure 40D, held in place only by the two diagonal corners between the base of the right thumb and the tip of the right little finger as indicated by the arrows. The hand is held completely relaxed and is neither bent unnaturally nor stiffly extended. The right thumb is relaxed and not stiffly extended. The card will stay there. No pressure need be exerted by the right hand. The fingers, of course, are kept close together, but they can be moved to some extent without affecting the palmed card.

In fact, it should be impossible to tell, even by comparing the two hands when held naturally, that there is a card palmed in the right hand. The magician, of course, never gives his audience a chance to study his hands thus. His main purpose in palming a card is usually to carry it secretly to or from his pocket and the card remains palmed but a few seconds.

In all tricks where palming is used, an effort is made to give the audience something to look at other than the hand with the card palmed. Care must be taken, therefore, not to call attention to the palming hand by holding it unnaturally.

In replacing a palmed card on the deck, the reverse of the above moves may be used or the deck may be placed on a table and picked up by placing the right hand (with the card palmed) flat on the deck and scooping it to the edge of the table where the right thumb can get under it, thus leaving the palmed card on the deck.

Care should be taken to move slowly and easily when palming a card. It is frequently convenient to stop after the card has been pushed into the palm (at the point depicted by Figure 40C) and make some gesture with the left hand. The deck is then tossed from the right fingers into the left hand, in a most natural manner.

It must always be remembered, however, when palming a card, that the palm is never placed down on the deck to receive the card. The right hand holds the deck quite naturally. All the work is done by the left hand. Also, it will be only after the move has become completely familiar that the magician will be able to avoid holding his right hand stiffly when a card is palmed therein. But it should be emphasized that the card is not held palmed by curling the fingers around it. It is held by pressure only at its two diagonal corners with the hand perfectly relaxed.

## DOUBLE LIFT

This very useful move performs somewhat the same service for the magician as the glide move described previously— that is, it allows the magician to show one card of the deck and then remove another but in such a way that the audience thinks the card that was shown was the one removed. In essence the move is that the magician turns the two top cards of the deck face up as if he were only turning one card and shows the face of the second card as if it were the top card.

The Double Lift has one advantage over the glide in that the cards are handled more naturally, the magician apparently turning over the top card in a natural manner. However, the reader will find the move somewhat more difficult than the glide to accomplish with complete naturalness. And it must always be remembered that naturalness is the keynote since the move must frequently be performed (as with the glide or any move whereby one card is switched for another) at a point in the trick when the spectators might possibly think something was amiss.

THE GET-READY. The main key to success with the double lift is the get-ready or preparation to make the move. Once the magician starts to turn the cards over, any hesitation or fumbling that occurs will attract unwanted attention to the possibility that something is wrong. Therefore the magician is careful to get all set to turn the cards over and then stop, gesture with his right hand, and make some incidental remark before actually doing the turnover.

The deck is held in the left hand just as it is held when dealing cards. The right hand, after having evened the deck up, rests lightly on the cards, the right thumb at the end

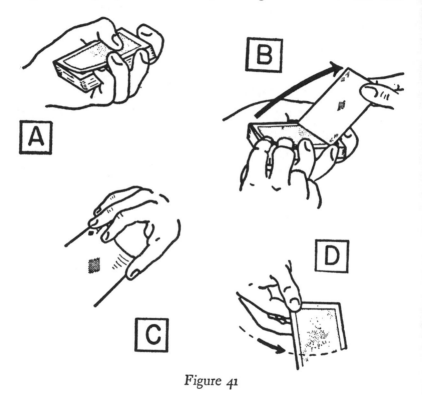

Figure 41

toward the body. As the performer patters about the trick in process or watches the spectators accomplish some necessary feat, the right thumb counts off the two top cards at the inner end of the deck and raises the inner right-hand corner of these two cards a trifle above the deck so that the left little finger can be inserted to keep the top two cards separated from the rest of the deck as in Figure 41A. The left thumb, by pressure on top of the deck, prevents any movement from being apparent at the end of the deck toward the audience. The right hand, having completed the get-ready, leaves the deck and gestures or drops to the side.

THE TURNOVER. When ready to accomplish the move, the right hand approaches the deck and grasps the inner right-hand corner of the two top cards with the thumb underneath and the index and second fingers on top. Pressing the two cards tightly together so they will not slip apart, the right hand turns them over end-for-end and places them both face up on top of the deck slightly protruding over the outer end of the deck. The composite diagram of Figure 41B shows the action of the right hand in the turnover.

The left thumb is withdrawn during the turnover to let the two cards past, but it clamps down on them immediately as they are laid face up on the deck so that any slight misalignment of the cards occurring during the move can be instantly corrected to give the impression that only one card was turned over.

It will be found that the grip recommended for use by the right thumb and first two fingers will allow the performer to pinch the cards in such a way that it is almost impossible for either card to twist away from the other and disclose an extra edge to the audience's view.

THE RETURN. Once the two cards have been turned face up and the original second card shown to the audience as if it were the top card, both cards must secretly be turned face down on the deck again. This can be accomplished by simply turning them back with the same movement as was used to turn them face up.

Many performers prefer, however, to indulge in a sort of flourish that seems to belie the fact that two cards could possibly be involved. The two cards are taken at their outer end

(end toward the audience) by the right hand as shown in Figure 41C. Pressure of the right thumb and second finger bows the card slightly outward.

The right hand then picks the cards off the deck and moves up so that its palm is toward the audience. The cards are then snapped—that is, they are further bowed and then allowed to slip off the end of the second finger so that they snap around to be held between the index finger and thumb as in Figure 41D.

When the hand is raised, the backs of the two cards are toward the spectators. When the cards are snapped, their faces are toward the spectators. The effect of the move is that the right hand merely picked the cards off the deck and snapped them around for the audience to take another look at the face.

The right hand does not, however, stop to display the cards. The chances are that some misalignment of the two cards will occur during the snapping and so the right hand— without ever stopping—replaces the two cards face down on top of the deck before anything can be noticed by the audience. This does not mean that the move is fast. The point is that the right hand never stops. The cards do not have to move rapidly, but they do have to keep moving. It is the motion, not the speed, that makes the flourish successful.

NOTE: Obviously, should the trick demand it, three or four cards could be turned up in the same fashion as if only one card were involved—that is, a triple or quadruple lift.

And once more it must be emphasized that ease and naturalness are the requirements for success. At first the reader will have the tendency to hold the deck in a viselike grip and accomplish the feat with studied and careful movements. Eventually, however, he will realize that a relaxed (or apparently relaxed) grip and a completely casual and nonchalant manner is not only necessary but easily accomplished.

Further it should be noted that almost every performer

has his own pet method for the double lift. The above method is given as but one of many effective ones. If the reader finds he can do the double lift more easily by some other method, he should by all means do so. The important thing is not just following these instructions; the important thing is to be able to turn over two cards in such a way that the audience will think only one card is being turned up. The method that the reader finds easiest for him is the best method he can ever use.

In considering the problem, however, the reader should realize that the double lift will be much more deceptive if the cards are handled just as if he were really turning over only the top card than if they have to be held in some special fashion and the turnover is made in some unusual manner.

## FAN FORCE

It is of obvious benefit to the performer if he can influence a spectator to "select" a card the identity of which the magician already knows—that is, "force" a card on the spectator. Methods for doing just this have been developed literally by the hundreds in the literature of magic. Several are mentioned elsewhere in this volume (at pages 198, and 278).

Many of the better-known methods of forcing, however, require prepared cards or some prearrangement of the deck so that they are of limited aid to the impromptu performer. Many more, in the author's humble opinion, are not worth the energy it took to think them up since they require such peculiar handling of the deck (if of the sleight-of-hand type) or such illogical flimflam (if of the take-a-number-divide-by-two-and-add-a-million type) that only the most stupid of spectators could possibly believe he is really getting a free choice of cards.

In this connection there should be emphasized a distinction that many magicians seem to miss: there is a difference between the effect on a spectator who knows he is being forced to take a certain card but does it anyway without comment just to be a good sport and on a spectator who is actually forced to take a certain card without the slightest idea that he did not have a perfectly free choice of all fifty-two. The performer may be content with either result, but it is important that he recognize the difference between them.

When the trick demands a 100 per cent sure-fire force for its success, the performer is entitled to go to any lengths to gain his objective. But as a general rule during an impromptu demonstration the reader is advised not to clutter his thinking with a lot of complicated methods of forcing unless he is really convinced that the effect he will attain by their use merits whatever limits the forcing may place on his free handling of the cards.

As was noted in the discussion of improvising impromptu tricks, however, it is useful for the magician to attempt to use the so-called classical fan force. This force is not by any means sure-fire, but its advantage lies in the fact that the cards are handled in exactly the same way as if the spectator were being given a perfectly free choice. Thus the magician loses nothing of the appearance of a perfectly free selection by trying the force and, if he succeeds in forcing the proper card, he is just that much to the good.

THE GET-READY. Before approaching the spectator to offer him a card, the magician notes the top card of the deck (or places the card he desires to force on top of the deck). It would then be well to give the deck an extra shuffle without disturbing the top card. As he approaches the spectator, the magician cuts the deck to bring the force card near the middle. He marks the location of the force card by inserting the tip of his left little finger at the right corner of the deck above the force card as the left hand holds the deck in dealing position.

THE FORCE. The magician is going to offer the spectator

the choice of a card as he spreads the cards between his hands, running them from left to right as in Figure 42 in the manner classical with magicians. In fact, the magician starts to run the cards as he moves toward the spectator, asking the spectator to take any card.

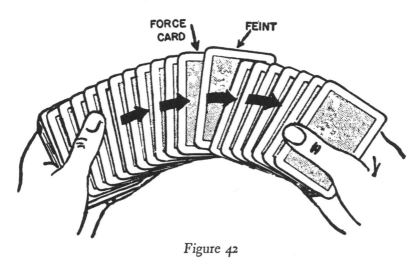

Figure 42

By the time the magician has got within the spectator's reach, some of the cards have already been run to the right hand. It is a fairly easy matter for the performer to keep the location of the force card marked with his left fingers as the cards are spread. He does so and keeps running the cards, offering them to the spectator.

As long as the cards are moving rapidly past, the spectator will not be inclined to dash in and grab one. He will, however, reach tentatively toward the spread. The magician merely attempts to regulate the speed with which he runs the cards from left to right so that, just as the spectator reaches for his card, the magician may thumb the force card by so it is the one the spectator will grab.

The device is purely a creature of timing and as such does

not readily admit of lucid explanation. It is not a question of running the cards until the spectator reaches for one and then stopping them. Nor is it a question of actually handing the spectator the proper card. Rather, the magician must contrive to run the cards at such a speed that, when the spectator reaches for a card, the force card just happens to be at the point to which he reaches.

It should be remembered that the spectator really does not care which card he takes—he simply reaches out and grabs one. The magician merely tries to arrange matters so the force card is the one the spectator grabs.

It is all too easy, however, to let the spectator get the idea that the magician is trying to give him a certain card. For this reason, many performers advocate running the cards as in Figure 42 so that the card next to the force card is allowed to protrude invitingly from the deck as a sort of feint, as if the performer were trying to force that card. The theory is that the spectator will sense the attempted force and deliberately refuse to take the protruding card. Having decided not to take the protruding card, however, he will probably take the next card since his eyes will follow the protruding card as it moves across the spread.

Further than the above, little can be added in the way of definite instructions on how to do the fan force. The rest is up to the reader's increasing familiarity with the idea and the development of his ability to time his actions so the force card reaches the proper place just in time to be taken by the spectator.

One useful bit of information can be added, however. If the spectator takes a card within two or three cards of the force card, the magician asks him to replace it in the deck. The spectator will naturally start to do so while the card is still face down. The magician draws his hands back and says, no, he means replace it face up. As the spectator turns his card face up, the magician separates the spread for its return so that the face-up card is placed in the deck immediately above the force card.

Telling the spectator that the card he took is to be merely an indicator, the magician closes up the deck and hands it to the spectator telling him to look through the cards and remember the card immediately below the face-up indicator, shuffle the cards, etc. In the author's opinion this is a rather weak device, but it is useful in a case where the performer feels it is really important to force a particular card at just that moment.

If the force card is not taken by the spectator, it may also be used as a known key card to help locate the card he actually did take. Thus, the spread can be opened at the force card for the return of his selected card or he may be invited to place his card anywhere in the spread, the magician counting to himself the number of cards between the known force card and the replaced selected card.

# PART THREE

# Prepared Magic

*The Masterpieces of the Magician's Program Where a Little
Preparation Means a Much Greater Effect*

Leaving for a moment the realm of impromptu magic, we now
go on to a consideration of some of the more advanced of magical
subjects which might be found in a planned magic program in a
show or on television.

By this statement, however, the author does not mean to imply
that he is about to consider how to saw a woman in half. Quite
the contrary. The effects collected in this part are merely more
advanced because they all require some preparation for their performance. The amateur magician will find these effects capable of
performance under all sorts of conditions, whether in his own living room or on a stage at a school or club or on television, where
impromptu card tricks would not be appropriate.

The only difference from the previous section lies in the fact
that—regardless of how impromptu they may appear to the audience—the tricks in this part do require some preparation of the

objects used. A little preparation allows for a much more startling result—and startling results are what we are after.

The effects in this section are still limited, however, to tricks of interest to the amateur magician, tricks that may be performed anywhere, tricks that do not require a trained assistant, tricks that do not need a lot of shiny, magical-looking apparatus, and tricks that eliminate the need for difficult sleight of hand.

Many of the tricks included in this section are new in either working or effect and have never before been published in book form. Others are the so-called standard items of the magician's repertoire. But all are audience-tested effects that, when presented in the proper routined relation to other tricks on the same program, will guarantee the performer a maximum of effect and entertainment value.

Following the plan of Part Two of this volume, prepared cards and tricks therewith are discussed first. Later sections describe advanced tricks with handkerchiefs, bills, books, and other objects which might be useful for any performance of a planned show on a stage or television program.

# VI

## Prepared Playing Cards

On all sides in magical circles one hears variations of the ancient argument of prepared cards versus "straight" decks. There are a great many wonderful performers who make it a point never to use prepared cards, relying on their sleight-of-hand ability to accomplish all necessary maneuvers with a completely unprepared deck. The main argument of such performers is that, as long as they use a straight deck, they can never be caught in the embarrassing position of having to refuse to do a trick because they are unprepared.

With this point, of course, there can be no argument. It is here suggested, however, that the performer is wise to use the easiest and surest method of accomplishing his effect. Unless the performer is an accomplished card manipulator, the easiest and surest method of accomplishing many very important and entertaining effects is by means of prepared cards.

No contention is here made that, with impromptu magic,

every effort should not be made to work with a straight deck. But with a planned magic program (whether it is a formal show in a club or on a television program, or a preconceived pocket routine to be used at a party or the like) much waste motion will be saved and many otherwise impossible effects will be made possible by "cheating" just a little on what the audience thinks is an unprepared deck of cards.

If, by using a prepared deck of cards, the performer can do a trick without even touching the deck or with giving the spectator complete freedom to act as he pleases, the final effect is just that much enhanced. If, by using a prepared deck of cards, the performer knows that he will force the spectator to select the proper card 10 times out of 10; if the prepared cards allow the performer to accomplish his ends with a minimum of flimflam and lost motion; if using prepared cards means that the performer will mystify and entertain his audience to a greater degree; if, because of the time limits of television, the performer must get the proper card selected *now*, this minute—then it seems he should certainly use prepared cards.

Of course, many performers are chary of prepared cards because they are afraid the audience will, in handling the cards, discover the unnatural qualities of the deck. It will be noted in the following effects that at no time is the audience given the opportunity to discover the nature of the prepared cards in use. In fact, if the presentation is followed carefully, the audience does not even have a chance to think that the cards might be prepared.

With impromptu, around-the-table magic, a prepared deck is limited to those circumstances where the performer is able secretly to exchange the prepared deck for an unprepared one. This is true because, with informally presented magic, the audience feels inclined to handle and to question the objects that the magician uses.

With a planned show, however, there is always the next

trick to occupy the audience's attention, just when the spectators get an idea they would like to see the deck or, which is more to the point, when they get the idea that the magician does not want them to see the deck. Also, with a planned show, the audience does not expect the magician to put all his apparatus on display for inspection after the show. Obviously, with a television demonstration, even the studio audience has no opportunity to demand (or to want to demand) a cross examination of the performer or his apparatus.

In using prepared cards, either for a formal show or a planned but apparently impromptu demonstration, there are several general suggestions that should be kept in mind:

a. Never say "This is an unprepared deck of cards." Simply handle the cards as if they were unprepared. If the faces of the cards can be shown to the audience, show them. If not, say nothing that might attract attention to the possibility that the cards are not unprepared.

b. Whenever possible, switch the prepared deck for an unprepared one. It should be remembered, however, that such a maneuver is not always necessary. Most of the time the trick is so constructed that the audience would gain little aid toward the solution even if it knew the deck were a prepared one. (Several methods of switching decks are considered below.)

c. The main advantage of prepared cards is that the audience thinks of a deck of cards first of all in terms of an ordinary deck and is actually incapable of imagining the many ways in which the cards can be faked or gimmicked.

d. Always remember that the audience wants to give the performer credit for sleight-of-hand ability and prepared cards mark the most readily available path to encouraging this desire.

## WHAT ARE PREPARED CARDS?

Let us now consider for a moment some of the many types of prepared cards. Only the most useful to the performer will be considered here, with tricks in which they can be used suggested in the next chapter.

### 1. Forcing Decks

Perhaps the most useful types of prepared cards for the magician are the so-called forcing decks. The simplest variety of such decks is the One-Way Forcing Deck. This is a deck made up of fifty-one identical cards with one indifferent card on the face. Thus, any spectator may be offered a completely free choice of any of the cards and, no matter which card he takes, it will always be the ace of spades (or whatever card the deck is set to force). Obviously this deck must be handled with the greatest of care to keep the spectator from discovering the fact that it is made up entirely of aces of spades. As will be seen in the following tricks, however, such a deck is extremely useful in tricks where the magician can switch an unprepared deck for the forcing deck or in tricks where the choice of a card is merely incidental to the effect and the magician wants a quick, simple, and absolutely sure-fire force.

Naturally, it is occasionally useful to have a forcing deck made up of two or three different forcing cards so that several cards can be forced on the audience by offering the choice from various sections of the deck. These are called two- and three-way forcing decks.

### 2. Rough-Smooth Deck

A very great improvement on the regular forcing deck is the so-called "Nu-Idea" or rough-smooth forcing deck. This deck is made up of twenty-six indifferent cards and twenty-six identical cards (the ace of spades, for instance). The cards are alternately placed in the deck, every other card being one of the force cards. Thus the top card of the deck would be an ace of spades, the second card an indifferent card, the third card an ace, and so on through the deck.

The *backs* of the *indifferent cards* and the *faces* of the *force cards* (the aces) are treated with a solution of resin, gum arabic, or some other tacky substance dissolved in ether or carbon tetrachloride. By wiping this solution over the proper surfaces of the cards and allowing the solvent to evaporate, the cards are made slightly sticky or rough. The *faces* of the *indifferent cards* and the *backs* of the *force cards* are then dusted with zinc stearate to make them slippery.

When the deck is assembled as indicated above, the force cards will stick ever so slightly to the backs of the indifferent cards. Thus the deck can be fanned with the faces toward

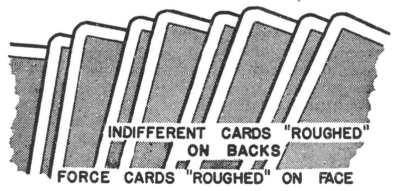

Figure 43A

the audience and only the faces of the indifferent cards will show, each force card remaining hidden and stuck to the back of the indifferent card just below it in the deck (as indicated in Figure 43A).

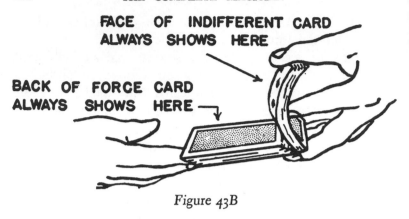

*Figure 43B*

For the same reason, when the deck is fanned with the backs of the cards toward the audience, only the backs of the force cards will be showing. Thus if the spectator is asked to point to a card while the deck is fanned face down in front of him, he cannot help but point to a force card, since only the backs of the force cards are visible.

The cards, however, can be readily separated by pressure of the fingers, so as not to appear to be sticking together. The end result, therefore, is a deck that can be shown to appear completely ordinary and yet from which the spectator can select only the ace of spades (or whatever card is the force card).

In the above description, mention is made of "fanning" the cards. When offering the spectator the choice of a card, it is generally more convenient to spread the cards between the hands or to spread them ribbonwise across the table rather than to attempt the fan flourish described on page 136. The reader will also find that this deck can be easily fanned with just one hand by holding the cards at the finger tips and then moving the thumb and fingers in opposite directions as when snapping the fingers. Since the fan is made up of twenty-six pairs of cards instead of fifty-two single cards, it is smaller and more easily handled than a fan made with an ordinary deck.

It is always recommended that the spectator be asked to "point" to a card rather than to "take" a card. The magician then removes the pointed-to card from the spread so there is no danger that the spectator might feel the fact that the two cards are sticking together slightly. Also the magician should never fail to emphasize that the spectator may point to any card, asking if he wants to change his mind after he has pointed to a card, and so on.

### 3. Svengali and Mene Tekel Decks

These two decks are well known to the magical fraternity and to the layman. Perhaps the reader has seen a street or carnival pitchman demonstrating them. The variety of tricks that can be performed with these decks is rather wide, but as a general conjuring tool their use is somewhat limited.

The decks are alike in that every other card is somewhat shorter than its neighbor. Thus as the decks are riffled or sprung from the thumb (as if flipping through a magazine or shuffling the cards using a riffle shuffle) the cards fall in pairs.

With the Svengali deck, the short cards are all alike so that it can be used for a forcing deck. The cards appear to be all different as the deck is riffled from top to bottom, since only the twenty-six indifferent (long) cards show, but when riffled face downward from bottom to top, the back of one of the force cards (short) is always exposed, no matter where the riffle is stopped (see Figure 43B).

The Mene Tekel Deck has the same long-short alternate arrangement with the exception that each short card is a duplicate of the long card immediately below it in the deck. Thus whatever card the spectator may select by cutting the deck, he leaves its duplicate undisturbed on the top or bottom of the deck.

#### 4. Marked Cards

Marked cards came into magic—as, indeed, did most of the tools of the card magician—straight from the gambling tables. At the gambling table, marked cards are a useful if slightly deadly weapon, but their efficacy for the magician is somewhat limited.

The magician, in order to use marked cards intelligently, must devise some system of marking that is readable ten or twenty feet away. Such decks are on the market, but their back designs are either so obvious or so well known that they lose their effectiveness. More subtle marking systems made with pen and ink to match the back design of the cards are usually so difficult to read at any distance that their use is practically limited to magicians who specialize in working exclusively at dining tables or under very close-up conditions.

#### 5. Short Card

The short card is perhaps the most useful of all magic utility items. Sooner or later, when the magician acquires the habit, so prevalent among magicians, of carrying a deck of cards with him in order always to be prepared to do tricks when called upon, it is suggested that he include a short card in his deck.

As the name implies, a short card is nothing more than one card with about one sixteenth of an inch trimmed off one end. The corners are rounded after trimming, of course, so that the card in all other respects looks normal as in Figure 44A. Indeed, only by the most minute comparison with another card can any difference be noted.

The sixteenth of an inch difference in length is just enough so that, with the short card near the middle of the deck, the magician is able to run his thumb across the ends of the cards riffling them, and stop unerringly at the short card. Thus if a selected card is returned to the deck on top of the

Figure 44

short card, and then buried with a cut, the magician can locate the selected card as he cuts the cards, preparatory to a
regular riffle shuffle.

It is obvious that such a method of locating a selected card
could well be used instead of the Hindu Shuffle for such
tricks as "Blackstone's Penetration" (page 71) and "That's
All" (page 76). Also, if the trick calls for noting the top
card of the deck as in "Look, No Hands!" (page 37) or
"Spellbound" (page 48), the magician merely riffles down
the deck until he comes to his short card and nonchalantly
cuts it to the top, thus placing a known card on top without
looking at the deck.

If several cards are to be kept in a certain order in the
deck, the magician, by placing the short card either directly
above or below the set-up series, can cut the deck several
times quite openly and freely and then, by cutting the last
time at the short card, return the set-up to the top or bottom
of the deck as he chooses.

As indicated by Figure 44B, C, and D, a short card can be
made in other shapes. The drawings, of course, are exaggerated to show the various methods of trimming. Some performers prefer the curved trim of Figure 44B, but it seems
to have little advantage over the straight trim indicated at A.
The corner and slanting trims shown at C and D are most
useful when the trick requires not one but two or three short

cards. Thus if one card were trimmed as in B, it would be located by riffling at the center of one end of the deck. A second card trimmed as in C would be located by a riffle at one corner and a third card trimmed as in D would be located by riffling near the other corner.

When using the short card, the performer should not try to feel for the little indentation in the end of the deck caused by the short card in order to know where to cut. Rather, he should riffle the ends of the cards and stop the riffle as soon as he feels the short card fall. Although the break in the riffling is indetectable to the audience, it is quite marked— even without practice—to the magician's thumb. Tapping one end of the deck on the table before riffling (at the other end of the deck) will cause the short card to settle in the deck so that its effect is easily felt.

The reader may find it convenient to trim somewhat more than the suggested one sixteenth of an inch off the short card at the beginning, until he acquires confidence in his ability to use this very useful conjuring tool.

The reader may soon see the advantage of carrying an extra card in his deck so as to be prepared to perform the many effects made possible by having a duplicate card. It is suggested that such extra card be a joker—that is, that the magician's deck have two identical jokers. Thus, the performer actually has a duplicate card although his deck is to all intents and purposes unprepared since none of the regular cards is duplicated. Furthermore, if one of the jokers is a short card, the performer is able to perform any trick using the short card idea as well as always able to locate one of his duplicate cards at any time without having to look through the deck.

### 6. Double-Faced and Double-Backed Cards

Both double-faced and double-backed cards are among the most effective of prepared cards, primarily because the audience will never conceive of a playing card with a face on both sides or a back on both sides. As the name implies, that is exactly what these cards are.

Without further discussion, the advantage of a single card with two faces should be obvious: it is the equivalent of a card that can be changed at will from the ace of spades to the deuce of hearts, or what have you. In addition to the double-faced card effects suggested below, the reader will soon be inventing his own effects for this intriguing item.

As with all the other prepared cards described in this section, double-faced and double-backed cards (as well as powder, "roughing fluid," marking ink and other such items) are available for sale at magic stores. It is, however, fairly simple to make the double cards.

Playing cards are made in three sections: there is a center layer of stiff cardboard to which are laminated two outside layers of glossy paper. By holding a card at one of its corners between the thumb and index finger and hitting the extreme corner of the card against the table to crush it, the three sections will be seen to separate a trifle at the crushed corner.

By placing the card face down on the table, it will now be possible to get a fingernail just above the face layer and, working very carefully, to peel the back and center layers upward off the face layer. If the peeling is done slowly and care is taken to keep the face layer held flatly and firmly against the table as the other two layers are peeled off, no tearing of any of the layers will result. The parts of two cards thus prepared (with the face layer removed from one and the back layer from the other) can then be reassembled and pasted together (rubber cement is suggested) to form one double-faced and one double-backed card to match the magician's own deck.

And, speaking of matching decks, it is most strongly urged that the magician make an effort to standardize the back pattern of the decks of cards he uses. Thus, if all the magician's prepared decks are of the same back pattern, which in turn matches the back pattern of the unprepared deck he uses, he will be able to interchange the various decks without the audience's knowledge.

In this connection it is suggested that a back pattern which has a white border is most useful. Then one card may be placed face upward in the face-down deck, as is desirable for many effects, without its white edges showing. All the prepared decks and prepared cards now sold on the magic market are made from the bridge size United States Playing Card Company's red- or blue-backed "Aviator" or "Fox Lake" pattern. This back pattern (in the bridge size cards) is not generally available in most retail stores, but can be found at all magic stores.

### 7. "Set-Up" Decks

There are many tricks requiring a special "set-up" or pre-arrangement of the order of the cards in the deck. Usually each of these tricks requires its own special arrangement. There are, however, several methods or systems of arranging the order of the cards that have a very wide application. One is given here.

This is the so-called "Si Stebbins Set-Up," originated by the very fine card magician who was known by that stage name. To accomplish this arrangement, lay all the cards out on a table face up, and arrange them in the following order, starting by placing the four of hearts face up upon the face-up ace of clubs, the seven of spades face up upon the face-up four, etc.:

AC, 4H, 7S, 10D, KC, 3H, 6S, 9D, QC, 2H, 5S, 8D, JC,
AH, 4S, 7D, 10C, KH, 3S, 6D, 9C, QH, 2S, 5D, 8C, JH,
AS, 4D, 7C, 10H, KS, 3D, 6C, 9H, QS, 2D, 5C, 8H, JS,
AD, 4C, 7H, 10S, KD, 3C, 6H, 9S, QD, 2C, 5H, 8S, JD.

Reference to the above list will show two things: (1) the suits always follow the order of the consonants in the word

CHaSeD—i.e.: clubs, hearts, spades, diamonds, and (2) the value of each card (counting the ace as one and the jack, queen, and king as eleven, twelve, and thirteen, respectively) is exactly three higher than the value of the card preceding it in the set-up.

Thus, with the deck completely assembled, the magician knows that the suits follow one another in a certain order and that the value of each card in the deck is three higher than the card immediately above it. Hence the magician can tell, by looking at any one card in the deck, the suit and value of the card next to it—or of several cards above or below it in the set-up. As will be seen presently, this is very helpful.

Also, the magician knows, for instance, that two aces are thirteen cards apart, or that every fourth card is a club, which, if dealt in a four-handed poker game, would give a straight flush to the person on the dealer's left, while all the others would have lower straight flushes and flushes only.

Naturally, a deck arranged as above cannot be shuffled, but it can be cut or false-cut as often as desired without disturbing the arrangement. Also, the cards can be fanned with their faces to the audience without any suggestion of being prearranged—especially if the fan is not very even so that the regular alternation of red and black cards is not apparent. Since the set-up is rather tedious to accomplish, the magician will probably want to use any trick requiring the set-up as the first trick of his demonstration.

After once remembering the CHaSeD and three-higher-than-above formulas, the magician will have no further need to follow the above table every time he sets up his deck. The start of the set-up is immaterial; that is, it does not have to begin with the ace of clubs as described herein, but can begin with any of the cards, so long as the order follows the CHaSeD and three-higher-than-above formula.

## 8. *Special Decks*

There are, of course, many special prepared decks—that is, decks which are especially prepared for but one trick. An example is the deck used in "Fifteen Miracle" (page 220), or "Precognition" (page 227). There is the "Haunted Pack" deck, made to move around as if it were alive, the "Brain Wave" deck, the "Peek Deck," and many others. There are decks arranged so that the magician can cut to any card called for, or so he can cause any card to reverse itself in the deck.

These decks all are useful and magically wonderful. Since most of them are made for only one effect, however, their description is omitted. Only such prepared decks as may be of a general utility to the magician have been described.

# VII

## Tricks Using Prepared Cards

With the following tricks, all using prepared cards, are incorporated any necessary suggestions as to the best way to take care of the prepared deck before and after the tricks are over. It should be noted, however, that each of these tricks should be performed not alone, but rather as part of a program or routine. The introducing and disposing of the prepared deck are considered in the light of another trick, both preceding and following the tricks here described.

In a formal magic program (that is, one in which the magician stands before his audience with his paraphernalia laid out on a table as distinguished from a demonstration of magic where the magician is working entirely from his pockets in an apparently extemporaneous manner) there is rarely any need for complicated deck-switching. If the magician begins his performance with several decks of cards (all with matching backs) lying along with other objects on his table, the audience will not note that he uses different decks for different tricks. If the magician removes all the decks from their boxes before he starts and if he does not do two prepared card tricks in a row (so that he must lay one deck down and immediately pick up another one), the audience will not worry over what deck he is using.

## SUCKER TRICK

EFFECT: In the course of a card trick, the audience sees that the magician has apparently missed the selected card, but all comes out right in the end. Especially is this trick effective against a smart-aleck spectator who attempts to confuse and distract from the magician's performance, but it is by no means so limited. Tricks wherein the magician apparently makes a mistake and then succeeds in fooling the spectators after all always rank high in effectiveness.

PREPARATION: This effect requires a duplicate card. For the purposes of this description, the duplicate card will be considered to be the joker, although it can be any one of the cards. It is convenient, though not necessary, if one of the two jokers is a short card (see page 190).

PRESENTATION: The magician, after having done several card tricks, announces that he will now attempt a very difficult experiment. He has secretly placed one of the duplicate jokers on the face of the deck (by riffling to it if it is a short card, and cutting it to the bottom, or by casually looking through the deck while shuffling it). He now proceeds to force the "selection" of the joker on some unsuspecting spectator.

The magician begins to execute the Hindu shuffle (page 165) rather swiftly. It will be noted that the Hindu shuffle leaves the bottom card of the deck completely undisturbed. As he shuffles, the magician tells the spectator to stop him at any moment. When the spectator tells him to stop, the magician holds up the packet of cards in his right hand so all can see the bottom card and says, "Remember that card!" He then slaps the right hand packet down on top of the cards in the left hand, hands the deck quickly to the spectator, and tells him to shuffle it well.

This is a very effective force. It appears that the cards are being well mixed and that the magician has been stopped at a random card in the midst of this mixing. If the magician is careful to handle the cards so that it is obvious that he is not sneaking a peek at any of the cards, and if he hands the deck immediately to be shuffled, the impression of a completely random selection will prevail.

The reason, says the magician, while the spectator is shuffling the cards, that this is such a difficult trick is simply that the card was selected in the midst of a shuffle and that the spectator and not the magician handled the cards immediately thereafter, thus precluding the possibility of controlling the card or of learning its identity by sleight of hand. Actually, says the magician, the trick is so difficult that he will not guarantee to discover the selected card upon the first try, but must take three chances.

The magician receives the well-shuffled deck back from the spectator and requests the audience to concentrate upon the selected card. The spectators are to visualize a picture of the card, etc., etc. The magician, meanwhile, studies the faces of the cards, muttering to himself about not getting a clear impression. He moves cards from place to place in the deck as if trying to decide which is the correct one.

Finally, he places one card—any card—on the face of the deck, squares the deck up and shows the face card to the audience, asking if it is the correct one. The answer, of course, is "No." Holding the deck upright with its face to the audience, he slides the face card upward a trifle as in Figure 45A, and then turns the deck face down, asking the spectator to place his finger on the back of the protruding end of the face card and press it against the table or floor as the magician

withdraws the rest of the deck as in Figure 45B, leaving the
face card face down on the table with the spectator's finger
upon it.

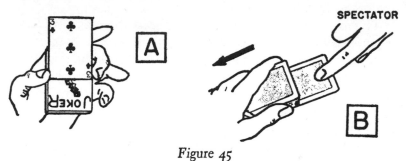

Figure 45

Well, that is one chance gone, says the magician, and scans
the cards again. He begins to question the spectator. "Was
it a red card?" "Was it a spade?" Since the card was a joker,
the answer is "No." Should the audience appear about to
volunteer the name of the card, the magician, of course, says
"Don't tell me!" and continues to scan the faces of the cards.

This time he places another indifferent card on the face
of the deck with one of the jokers behind it. Again he shows
his second choice, and, upon learning that it also is incorrect,
he once more asks the spectator to withdraw the bottom
card on to the table. This time, however, the magician executes the glide move described on page 163, as he turns the
deck face down after showing the face, so that the spectator
unknowingly withdraws the joker face down on to the table.

Being careful not to expose the faces of the cards, the magician points out that he has only one chance left. This time,
as he scans the faces of the cards, he places another indifferent card on the face of the deck and the other joker just
behind it. Once more he shows his choice. It is wrong.

The magician says he will just have to take one more
choice and draws the face card slightly upward as he did the
first time. This move, of course, exposes to the audience's

view the joker, which is next to the face card as in Figure 45A.

Letting everyone get a chance to realize that the "selected card" is still in the deck, the magician very openly has the spectator withdraw the face card of the deck as before. After that card is also resting face down on the table, the magician once more lets the audience get a glimpse of the fact that the selected card is still on the face of the deck, but he himself is careful not to notice.

The magician is embarrassed. He cannot understand why he missed three times in a row. He finally asks the audience what the card was. The spectators tell him it was the joker. Oh well, the magician exclaims, that was the trouble. The joker is always confusing matters and trying to ruin tricks. But all is not lost yet.

The magician puts the deck into his coat pocket and turns his attention to the three cards on the table in front of the

Figure 46

spectator. (See Figure 46.) He asks the spectator to point to two of the cards (the other joker is the middle one, remember, although the spectators believe it is still in the deck). If the spectator points to the two indifferent cards, the magician picks them up, reaches into his coat pocket and removes the deck (except for the extra joker which he leaves behind in his pocket), adds the two cards to the deck and lays it aside.

If, on the other hand, the spectator points to the joker and one of the indifferent cards, the magician picks up the third card and adds it to the deck, requesting that the spectator "pick one of those two cards." If the spectator now picks the indifferent card, the magician picks it up and adds it to the deck. If, on the other hand, he points to the joker, the magician says "You want that one," and removes the indifferent card.

In other words, the magician by this means induces the spectator to "select" the joker from among the three cards. When the joker has been "selected" (remembering all the while that the audience does not know that it is the joker on the table), the magician explains that, though the joker causes trouble, it can be kept under control. In fact, he says, although he missed discovering that the joker was the selected card, he will try to change the lone card on the table into the joker. He mutters the magic words, asks the spectator to turn the card over, and it is found to be the joker.

Obviously this effect could be done without two jokers, but it would lose thereby the added punch of the audience seeing the duplicate joker in the deck and not on the table until the last moment. The duplicate joker, of course, is left in the pocket, and the deck will now bear as much scrutiny as possible.

## POCKET PICKINGS

EFFECT: A card selected by the spectator leaves the deck and ends up in the magician's pocket or his wallet.

PREPARATION: For the first effect only a short card is required. For the alternate effect, a duplicate card is needed and it should be a short card (see page 190).

PRESENTATION: I. The magician shuffles the cards, using both riffle and overhand shuffles to bring the short card to the bottom of the deck (see page 191). He then offers a spectator the choice of any card. While the spectator is looking at his card, the magician squares up the deck and pulls the bottom half of the deck out of his left hand as in Figure 47·

Figure 47

He then offers the left-hand portion (the top half of the deck) to the spectator, telling him to place his card "right on there," pointing to the top card. As soon as the spectator puts his card on the packet, the right-hand packet is slapped down on top. Thus, the magician points out, the selected card is buried in the deck. The short card, of course, is directly above the selected card.

In order to make the trick very difficult, says the magician, he will ask not just one, but two spectators to shuffle the deck. So saying, he riffles across the ends of the cards until he feels the short card fall. At that point, he splits the deck, offering the top half to the spectator who selected the card, asking him to shuffle. The selected card is now the second card of the half of the deck that the magician holds.

Taking the top card of his packet (the short card), the magician shows it to the spectator, asking, "That's not your card, is it?" The spectator says it is not and the magician, smiling, says that is good and casually replaces the card on the bottom of his packet. Thus, the selected card is now on top of the magician's packet.

Turning to another spectator to his left, the magician asks him to shuffle the other half of the deck and starts to hand it to the spectator. Suddenly the magician's attention apparently is attracted to the first spectator. The magician stops and asks him why he has not started to shuffle (or why he has, as the case may be). Both spectators must shuffle at the same time and in the same manner, the magician explains. As he speaks, and while all eyes are on the spectator, the magician palms the top card (the selected card) in his right hand and then hands the packet to the second spectator with his left hand (see "Palming," page 168).

Immediately, but not hurriedly, the magician reaches into his right trousers pocket. He leaves the palmed card in his pocket and his hand comes out holding whatever coins or other objects were in the pocket. These he lays on the table. Apparently the magician has merely emptied his pocket in preparation for some effect.

When the spectators have finished shuffling, the magician places the two halves of the deck together and says he will make the selected card rise out of the pack. He asks the spectator to call his card by name. Nothing happens and the magician looks distressed. He asks the spectator to call on his card again. Still nothing happens, but the magician realizes what is wrong.

The selected card is a little shy, he explains. This time, instead of rising from the deck when called upon it has invisibly flown out of the deck to hide in the magician's pocket. Showing his hand unmistakably empty, the magician reaches into his pocket, and, smiling, pulls the selected card into view.

II. There is an alternate method for accomplishing essentially the same effect:

The magician has a duplicate of his short card previously placed in his wallet (or his lady friend's purse, or elsewhere). Using the force described on page 198 (or any other force the performer desires), the magician forces the short card on one of the spectators. He hands the deck to the spectator, asking him to shuffle the cards. While the spectator is shuffling, the performer casually places his wallet on the table or floor. When the shuffling is finished, the magician asks the spectator to look through the cards to see if his selected card is still in the deck. The spectator does so, and, of course, finds his card still there.

Well, says the magician smiling, in that case the cards had better be shuffled some more! He takes the deck and shuffles it himself, bringing the short card secretly to the top. To accomplish this the magician need only find the short card as he riffles through the deck to cut it into two packets for a riffle shuffle. He simply breaks the deck at the short card and gives it a regular riffle shuffle, allowing the short card to fall last. If the card is too close to the top or bottom to make this possible, the magician does a regular riffle shuffle and then gets the short card with a second shuffle.

With the short card on top of the deck, the magician says "Watch!" and runs his thumb across the edges of the cards to make them snap while making a tossing motion at his wallet. The selected card has just flown secretly into the wallet, the magician says, and, after asking the spectator to name his card, requests him to open the wallet and remove the selected card.

While the spectator opens the wallet, the magician quietly palms the short card from the top of the deck and casually drops his hand into a trousers pocket, leaving the palmed card there. He then lays the deck down on the table for all to examine.

## DOUBLE TROUBLE

EFFECT: Two apparently freely selected cards invisibly change places and then one of them vanishes right before the spectators' eyes. This clever routine, which was shown to the author by Dr. F. V. Taylor, combines two very startling magical effects: the transposition of two objects and the mid-air vanishing of a card. Credit for devising the vanish goes to Mr. Allan Lambie.

PREPARATION: All that is needed is a double-faced card (see page 192) with, for example, jack of clubs on one side

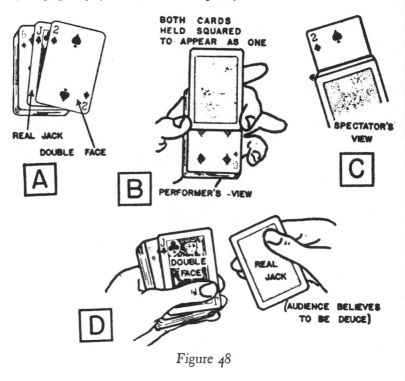

Figure 48

and the two of spades on the other. The real two of spades is removed from the deck and placed in the magician's wallet or hidden somewhere about the room. The real jack of clubs and the double-faced card (with the deuce side showing) are placed on the face of the deck as in Figure 48A.

PRESENTATION: The magician starts to do the Hindu shuffle (see page 165) and requests the audience to stop him at any point it chooses. As soon as the audience says Stop, the magician says, "We'll cut the deck right where you called 'Stop,' " and saying so, places the packet of cards in his right hand underneath the packet in his left hand, thus putting the two prepared cards right back on the bottom of the deck where they started. The effect of this is, of course, that the magician did stop in mid-shuffle and cut the deck at a random point.

Turning the deck face up, the magician throws out the two bottom cards (the double-faced card with the two showing and the real jack of clubs) face up on the table and asks the audience to remember those two cards. Picking up first the jack and then the double-faced card, he returns them to the face of the deck with the two showing as the face card —that is, just as they were at the start of the trick as in Figure 48A.

Turning so that the spectators cannot see the face of the deck, the magician slides both the cards out beyond the end of the deck so that the back of the jack can be seen, being careful to keep the cards lined up so that it looks as though only one card were protruding. "Since I am a magician," says the performer, "I must make magical moves. I am now giving the deuce a magical turnover!" The magician turns both cards over as if they were one so that the two side of the double-faced card protrudes from the edge of the deck where all can see as in Figure 48C.

The effect of this on the audience is that only the deuce was protruding from the deck and only the deuce was turned over. Figure 48C indicates all that the spectators see. If they could see what the magician sees (Figure 48B) they would know that both cards had been turned over. For this reason, then, the deck is held so the audience cannot see the face card.

Now that the deuce has had the magical turnover, says the performer, he is a very magical fellow. With this, the magician evens up the cards with the deck, and turns it so the audience can once more see the face of the deck. He deals the face-down card face down onto the table or floor. The audience thinks that card is the two of spades whereas it is actually the jack of clubs. This belief is strengthened when the audience sees that the jack is apparently still on the deck after the face-down card has been dealt off. Of course, the jack that is showing on the face of the deck is the jack side of the double-faced card. The real jack was dealt face down onto the table.

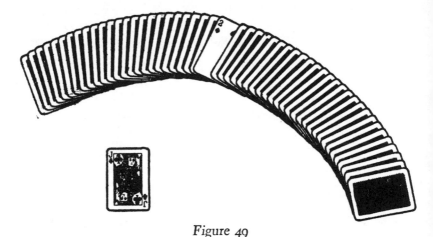

Figure 49

Since the deuce is a very magical fellow, continues the performer, let us see if we can make him perform. With that, the magician openly cuts the deck, burying the visible jack with the cut and saying that, having buried the jack in the deck, he will make the deuce come from over there (pointing to the face-down card) and trade places with the jack in the deck. As an addition—just to make it harder—the magician continues (before anyone has a chance to ask to see the deuce "over there") he will make the deuce turn face up while all the rest of the cards remain face down!

The magician claps his hands or mutters the magic words and says that the change has taken place. He reaches over and flips up the face-down single card, and, sure enough, it is the jack of clubs and not the deuce. The magician then spreads the deck across the table or floor face down until the two side of the double-faced card comes into view, appearing to be the two of spades turned face up in the face-down deck. (See Figure 49.)

Gathering up the deck, but leaving the double-faced card and the real jack of clubs on the table, the magician says that is only the beginning of the jack's power to jump invisibly from place to place.

The jack of spades is placed once more casually on the face of the deck. The double-faced card is picked up and placed in the right hand (being careful not to expose the jack side) lying flat in the palm with the two side showing as in Figure 50B. The deck is held in the left hand, face outward, with the fingers along one side and the thumb at the other, the backs of the fingers toward the floor, the backs of the cards toward and parallel to the body as in Figure 50A.

Some magicians, the performer says, when they want to vanish a card, pass their hands over the deck. Suiting actions to his words, the magician passes his right hand across the face of the deck, with its back toward the audience, leaving the double-faced card on the face of the deck as indicated by the composite diagram Figure 50A. Since the last thing the audience saw before the magician's hand went across the face of the deck was the jack showing on the face, and since what the audience sees after the double-faced card has been deposited on the face of the deck is the jack side of the double-faced card, no change will appear to have taken place. The magician is careful to hold his hand as if it still contained the card, its back toward the audience.

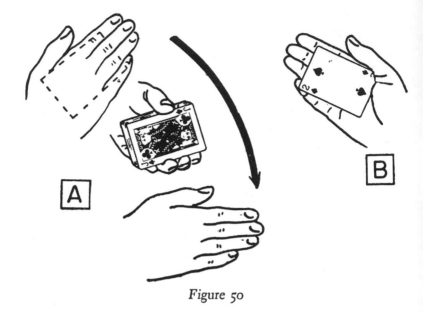

Figure 50

Some magicians, the performer continues, pass the deck over their hands. Once again, suiting action to words, the magician rubs the deck across the back of his right hand.

But he, the performer says, merely crumples the card into little pieces, and he closes his right hand with a crumpling motion and then shows that the deuce has vanished and that his hand is empty.

Where has the deuce gone? He certainly has magical jumping qualities! The magician then reveals the whereabouts of the real deuce that he had hidden before beginning this effect. While one of the spectators retrieves the deuce, the magician quietly palms the double-faced card from the face of the deck (see page 168) and casually puts it in his pocket. The deck is now completely ordinary.

## DIVINING DAGGER

EFFECT: The magician demonstrates a very phenomenal divining dagger with which a spectator is able to touch one card and then locate blindly with the dagger the identical card in another deck. This effect, once acclaimed by a newspaper critic at one of the author's performances as the most perfect card trick he had ever seen, was first performed for the author by Mr. Richard Dubois. Because of its simplicity, both in effect and working, and because everything is apparently done by the spectators, this trick makes a very profound impression on an audience.

PREPARATION: The objects needed here are a piece of paper (newspaper will do) large enough to wrap up a deck of cards, a dagger or paper knife (the more peculiar and exotic the design, the better) and two rough-smooth forcing decks (see page 186), both forcing the same card (let us say it is the ten of clubs, for example).

PRESENTATION: Producing the dagger, the magician tells of how he once acquired this very special knife from an ancient Chinese conjuror, or whatever patter story he may choose. He presents the dagger to the audience, expounding its phenomenal divining properties. Anything that touches the dagger the dagger will then follow, just like a bloodhound on the scent.

To demonstrate the dagger's peculiar properties, the magician picks up a rough-smooth deck of cards from the table. (If another deck has been used previously, it was casually replaced on the table near the first forcing deck when the dagger was picked up).

He fans the deck briefly with the faces toward the audience, using the deck as a pointer in asking a young lady to come assist him. Still holding the deck fanned so that all can see there is apparently nothing prepared about it, the magician gives the piece of paper to the young lady and, closing the fan, asks her to wrap the deck in the paper and hold it. The magician helps to be sure that the deck is not dropped. It may be considered safer if the magician merely places the paper in the young lady's hands and wraps the deck himself before giving it to her to hold.

Taking the dagger, the magician hands it to another spectator, requesting that he too help with the demonstration. Then the magician picks up the other prepared deck of cards and fans it with the faces toward the audience so that all can see that the deck is apparently unprepared, although no mention is made of that fact.

Holding the deck in front of the assisting spectator, the magician asks him to run the dagger over the faces of the cards. This allowing the spectator to study the faces of the cards will eliminate even the strongest suspicion that anything is wrong with the deck.

Suddenly, spreading the deck face down between his hands, or ribbonwise across a table, as if changing his mind, the magician requests the spectator to point to the back of any card with the dagger. After repeated admonitions by the magician to make sure he has a completely free choice and is completely satisfied with his choice, the spectator is allowed to select one of the cards with the dagger. This, of course, is one of the force cards, the ten of clubs. The magician removes it from the deck, and, holding it aloft for all to see, he disposes of the deck of cards in his jacket pocket.

This ten of clubs is the bait, the magician explains, the scent. He rubs the card across the blade of the dagger several times "just to make sure the dagger has the scent." Now, says the magician, we will see if the dagger can still divine.

The assisting spectator is instructed to go over to the young lady spectator, who has been holding the other forcing deck wrapped in newspaper, and to insert the dagger any place he wants to in the wrapped deck, by pushing it through the paper wrapping and into the side of the deck as in Figure

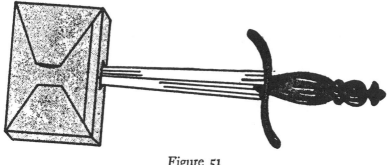

Figure 51

51. The man does so, and the magician again admonishes him to make sure he is inserting the dagger exactly where he wants to.

With the dagger still protruding from the wrapped deck, the man is asked to tear away the wrappings and expose the stabbed deck. (It is apparent that when the dagger was inserted in the wrapped deck, it went either above or below one of the twenty-six tens of clubs in that deck, since every second card is a ten of clubs.) The magician, then, after showing quite plainly that he has nothing concealed in his hands, lifts off the portion of the deck above the dagger.

A quick look will tell whether the face card of this portion is the ten of clubs. If it is, the magician holds it aloft for all to see, exclaiming that the divining dagger, once it had the scent of the ten of clubs, found that very card blindly in this wrapped deck! If, on the other hand, the face card of the portion above the dagger is not the ten of clubs, the magician knows that the card below the dagger is. In that case he pockets the top portion, asks the man to remove the dagger, and very openly takes the card below the dagger, the ten of clubs, and shows it explaining that the dagger blindly found its mark in the wrapped deck.

The magician then relieves his assistants of the rest of the cards, the dagger, etc., and thanks them for their help. As the magician returns to his table, he quite openly removes the cards from his pocket (the first deck and half of the second) and, adding the dagger, the rest of the second deck, and the scraps of wrapping paper, he puts the whole confused mass aside. Thus he provides a perfectly logical excuse for using a new deck for his next feat rather than attempting to straighten out the confusion of two decks of cards mixed together with scraps of paper, etc., right in the midst of his demonstration.

Needless to say, either or both decks could be Svengali decks (page 189) instead of the rough-smooth variety, but the working is a little easier and the effect considerably stronger as described. As another alternative the second deck could be a plain forcing deck (all tens of clubs) but the rough-smooth deck allows the faces to be shown.

Because of the necessary two prepared decks, it is most convenient to perform this trick during a planned demonstration where the magician has at his disposal a table, etc., rather than as part of a seemingly impromptu routine of tricks that the performer "just happened to have in his pocket." It is also one card effect particularly adapted to a television performance because the identity of the "selected" card is never a secret.

NOTE: Many tricks of the take-a-card-and-I'll-find-it variety are entirely unsuited for audiences of more than just a few spectators. However, tricks like "Divining Dagger," although they are card tricks, are effective before even the largest audiences because they do not depend on the fact that only one spectator knows the identity of a selected card, etc. Here everyone knows what card is involved and the whole audience can follow all that goes on. The audience does not have to wait until the climax to see if the spectator who selected the card acknowledges that the performer has been successful, and the effect is equally successful whether the audience is all present in an auditorium or watching at home before a television screen.

It is well, however, for the magician to choose as the card he will force one that is easily recognized at a distance. Thus, a black ace, two, four, five, or ten can be recognized at a glance, even when the spectator is not close enough to read the index number on the card. All the face cards, on the other hand, look pretty much alike from a distance and it is difficult to distinguish among a six, seven, eight, and nine without noting the index number. A three from a distance closely resembles a two.

The black cards, of course, are to be preferred over the red, but the ace of spades should be avoided since its uniqueness seems to suggest, for some reason or other, that it was forced on the spectator. If, however, the trick calls for forcing several cards, contrast is important so the performer should choose some such combinations as a black ace or deuce, a black ten, and, for variety, a red face card.

## FOUR TOLD

EFFECT: The magician is able to predict the names of four cards selected by four different spectators before they even have selected their cards. This effect, using the so-called "one-ahead" principle, long a standard tool of the spirit medium and mind reader, illustrates one of the proper ways to utilize a set-up deck.

It will be noticed that the setup is not used to tell the magician the identity of the selected card so that he may merely announce it to the audience. The setup tells the magician which card was selected only after the audience thinks he already knows it.

PREPARATION: A two-way forcing deck, that is, a deck made up of twenty-six tens of hearts and twenty-six queens of spades, for instance, with one indifferent card on the bottom,

is needed for this effect. This deck is resting in the magician's
left jacket pocket next to an envelope or stiff piece of paper.
Also needed is an unprepared deck arranged in the Si Stebbins set-up (see page 194) with the ten of hearts and the
queen of spades (or whatever cards are in the force deck)
removed. This deck is standing on end in the little change
pocket inside the magician's right-hand jacket pocket. A
pencil and a small pad of paper are also necessary.

PRESENTATION: After completing a card trick, the magician
drops the deck he has been using into his right-hand jacket
pocket and picks up the pad of paper and pencil. Asking
two couples (let us say Mr. and Mrs. A and Mr. and Mrs. B,
although any four persons divided into pairs may be used)
to assist him, he says that he will attempt a demonstration
of his fortune-telling ability.

After long practice, says the magician, he finds that he has
acquired a little of the ability of an oracle; he can sometimes
foretell the future. Of course, says the magician, he has not
as yet acquired the ability to foretell exactly what the stock
market will do next week, or who will win the fifth race at
Jamaica this afternoon, but he can predict the future to a
certain limited extent.

With that, he takes the pad and pencil, and, turning to
Mr. and Mrs. A, he says he will write them a prediction.
What the magician actually writes on the paper while studying Mr. and Mrs. A is: "Mrs. B will select the ten of hearts.
Mr. B. will select the queen of spades" (or whatever are the
cards of the forcing deck). He tears this paper off the pad
and folds it in half so no one can see what he wrote. The
folded prediction is placed on the floor or table in some con-
spicuous position.

Advancing toward Mr. and Mrs. A, the magician removes
the set-up deck from his right jacket pocket. (Since he deposited the deck used in the last trick in this same pocket,
the audience will think he is using the same deck. The set-up

deck was in the little change pocket, so it has been kept separate and will not be confused with the deck previously used.)

Fanning the set-up deck, or spreading it between his hands, and glancing at the faces as if to assure himself that all the cards were there, the magician says he wants Mr. and Mrs. A each to select a card. He turns the deck so the audience can see the faces of the cards. This can be done with impunity if the fan is not too even since the only apparent evidence of any set-up is the alternating red and black cards, which is not obvious in an uneven fan.

Unfortunately, says the magician, he is only able to predict the future under certain limited conditions. So, for the purposes of his demonstration, he will use playing cards, since they are such common objects familiar to everyone, etc.

As he talks, he spreads the cards face downward between his hands, requesting Mrs. A to remove one card. As she removes her selected card, the magician separates the cards at the point from which she takes a card, placing those in his right underneath those in his left hand, and squaring up the deck. This maneuver brings the card that was directly above the selected card to the bottom of the deck.

Gesturing with the deck, the magician asks Mrs. A to show her card to Mr. A. *That gesture enables the magician to glance at the face card of the deck.* Immediately he knows what card Mrs. A took, because of the set-up. That is, the magician glances at the face card of the deck (suppose it to be the deuce of spades), adds three to its value (getting five) and follows through the CHaSeD formula (to diamonds), thus calculating that the identity of the selected card was the five of diamonds.

When the magician has figured out what card Mrs. A took, (and he can take as much time to do so as he needs by telling Mrs. A to put her card in her purse, etc.) he offers the cards to Mr. A for his selection. He cuts the cards after Mr. A's choice also, squares up the deck, and places it in his left jacket pocket, being careful that the envelope or stiff paper in the pocket separates this deck from the forcing deck already there. As he puts the deck in his pocket, he glances at the new bottom card, thereby being able to calculate what card Mr. A took. Let us suppose it was the ace of diamonds.

The magician now turns his attention to Mr. and Mrs. B. He picks up the pad and pencil and studies the second couple, apparently trying to decide on their prediction. What he actually writes is: "*Mr. A will select the two of diamonds. Mrs. A will select the five of diamonds.*" That is, while apparently writing the prediction for the second couple, the magician actually writes down the cards selected by the first couple. This prediction he also folds and places with the previously written one.

The magician now approaches Mr. and Mrs. B, removing the force deck from his left jacket pocket (which he is able to do easily because it is kept separated from the other deck in that pocket by the envelope or piece of stiff paper). The magician offers Mrs. B the selection of a card, by spreading the deck between his hands exactly as before except that he spreads only the top half of the deck so that she is forced to pick one of the tens of hearts.

The magician then offers the cards to Mr. B, spreading only the bottom half so that he must pick one of the queens of spades.

Immediately the magician places the force deck back in his left hand coat pocket and turns his attention to the predictions. He hands them to a member of the audience to read. The spectator reads the predictions, and, of course, they all prove to be correct. As the selected cards are called out, the magician removes the set-up deck from his left pocket and takes the cards back from the spectators to replace in the deck. A shuffle of the set-up deck, then, will destroy all evidence of the set-up, and the spectators can inspect the deck (they think only one was used) as much as they choose.

NOTE: I. It should be remembered that, at the start of the trick, the ten of hearts and the queen of spades were removed from the set-up deck. Naturally, after Mrs. A selected the five of diamonds, it too was no longer in the deck. Therefore, after Mr. A's selection, if the bottom card indicates that Mr. A took one of these three cards, it merely means that his card would have been directly under the card indicated if that card had been in the deck.

Thus, after Mr. A picks his card, if the bottom card is the nine of hearts, this would indicate that Mr. A had drawn the queen of spades. That is impossible since the queen was not in the deck, therefore, the magician knows that Mr. A picked the card next to the queen in the setup. He calculates from the queen of spades and knows that Mr. A actually selected the two of diamonds.

II. It should be needless to point out that there is no limit to the number of persons or the number of predictions that the magician can use with this same system. So long as he is able to force the last card (so he can write the last prediction first) he can continue the idea as much as he wants, having cards selected from the set up deck and writing the name of the selected card while apparently writing the next prediction.

The presentation as here suggested, however, will probably be found most effective since it allows the magician to predict four different cards while having to write only two predictions. No matter how it is accomplished, the writing does slow the trick down. Then, too, repeated use of the set-up deck might give the audience a clue of the working of the trick since the magician must glimpse the bottom card after each selection.

Many performers use three spectators and write three predictions, one for each. Such a working allows them to use a rough-smooth forcing deck for the single final force (see page

186). They can, therefore, show the faces of the force deck before the final card is selected. Since there are only twenty-six force cards in such a deck, however, the rough-smooth principle is not so practical for a two-way deck.

III. It is further suggested that, if the set-up deck contains a short card which starts out on top of the deck, the magician may accomplish the trick (using two spectators) with only one deck of cards. This necessitates forcing the short card on the last spectator by one of the various methods described elsewhere for forcing a single card (see pages 95, 198, 278, and 279). Since most of the sure-fire forces for a single card require the magician to handle the deck differently for the last spectator from the others, such a working does not have the apparent fairness of the effect given. It is frequently useful, however, as an impromptu method for accomplishing approximately the same effect.

IV. Attention should also be called to the way in which the decks were switched one for the other. As a general rule, if the magician has one deck in his pocket (either with a stiff piece of paper to keep the deck separate or in the change pocket of his right jacket pocket) he can always switch another for that deck if he can arrange a logical excuse for putting the deck into his pocket. Perhaps the most logical excuse is the one used here: to free both the magician's hands for writing a prediction.

## FIFTEEN MIRACLE

EFFECT: Each of two spectators counts fifteen cards off the deck and each seals his fifteen cards into an envelope. Notwithstanding the sealed envelopes, three selected cards pass invisibly from the packet held by one spectator to the envelope held by another. The magician apparently never touches the cards.

This very startling effect is a product of the magical genius of the contemporary card magician, M. F. Zens. As will be seen, this effect is practically, although not completely, limited to use in a planned formal demonstration rather than in an apparently extemporaneous routine. No one who has seen Mr. John Mulholland perform his own version of Mr. Zen's miracle, however, will ever deny that the effect is well worth the little preparation required. It is also another card effect particularly adapted to a large "live" audience or a television demonstration although it takes somewhat longer to perform properly than is usual in most television routines.

PREPARATION: First of all, a special deck is needed for this effect. It is very simply made from three decks of cards, all with matching backs. Fifteen miscellaneously selected cards are taken from one of the decks and the identical fifteen cards from each of the other two decks. All three sets of fifteen are arranged in the same order and put together one set on top of the other to form a deck containing forty-five cards in three identical series of fifteen.

Secondly, a stack of six or eight regular letter envelopes is needed. In one of the envelopes are sealed twelve cards that are all different from any used in the special deck (but with matching backs). Using a colored pencil (preferably one of the variety that is red at one end and blue at the other) a short red line is drawn across the edge of the sealed flap.

Finally, the rest of the envelopes are placed flap-side down in a stack. The envelope with the cards sealed inside is placed flap-side upward on top of the stack. Two more empty envelopes are added flap-side down on top of the sealed envelope. Underneath the top envelope are placed three indifferent cards face down. Figure 52 shows an exploded diagram of the arrangement.

With the stack of envelopes on the table (or in a pocket fastened with a rubber band so as to be sure the above arrangement is not disturbed) along with the special deck and the red and blue pencil, all is set to perform.

PRESENTATION: Without announcing the climax he hopes to achieve, the magician invites two spectators to assist him. A man and a woman make an excellent combination for the effect. The magician stands the lady to his left and the man to his right.

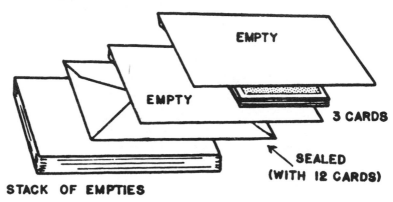

Figure 52

Picking up the special deck of cards, the magician fans them or spreads them so that the lady and the audience can see all the faces for just a moment. He does not comment on the fact that the deck appears unprepared (as it will, since no signs of the repeated series of fifteen will be evident upon a casual glance at the faces of the cards). If the magician feels he must say something about the cards, he can content himself with some variant of the witticism "A deck of cards: all the faces different (showing the faces), but exactly alike on the back" (showing the backs and smiling).

He requests the lady to give the cards a "couple of cuts," making sure she completes each cut. It will be apparent that the special deck can be cut any number of times without disrupting the order in which the cards are arranged. There will always be a series of fifteen cards followed by a duplicate series of fifteen, etc. All that the cutting does is start the series with a different card after each cut. The lady is then to count fifteen cards face down onto the table.

While she is counting (and the magician is counting with her to make sure she does not make a mistake), the magician has picked up the stack of envelopes. He holds the top envelope with the three cards hidden beneath it slightly separated from the rest of the stack, with the right fingers beneath the envelope, holding the cards up against it, and the thumb on

## 3 CARDS UNDER ENVELOPE

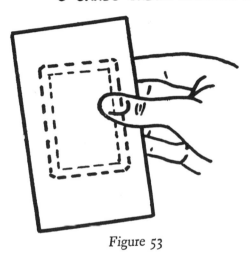

Figure 53

top as in Figure 53. When the lady has finished counting, she is asked to lay the deck aside.

As she does so, *the magician nonchalantly drops the top envelope and the cards under it directly on top of the pile of fifteen cards the lady has just counted.* The magician asks her to take the envelope and examine it carefully. This she does. It looks quite innocent. But the magician has thus secretly added three cards to the fifteen the lady counted on to the table.

When the lady has satisfied herself as to the unprepared-

THE COMPLETE MAGICIAN

ness of the envelope, the magician asks her to place her packet of fifteen cards in the envelope and to seal it. This she does, but unwittingly seals eighteen instead of only fifteen cards in the envelope.

Picking up the red and blue pencil, the magician reaches over and, using the blue end, makes a short mark across the edge of the sealed flap, pointing out that such a mark across the seal will be a way of knowing if the envelope is opened. The magician then asks the lady to initial the front of the envelope and not let it out of her possession. During this business, the magician does not take the envelope or touch it except to make the mark over the sealed flap.

Turning his attention now to the man on his right, the magician asks him to take the rest of the deck which the lady has discarded and to count fifteen cards onto the table just as the lady did. Obviously these fifteen cards will be exact duplicates of the fifteen now in the lady's envelope. His fifteen cards the man is to show to the first row of the audience, asking three persons therein each to remember one card. It is well to have the "remembered" cards called out so that all present can help remember the three cards selected.

Still holding the stack of envelopes, the magician moves away from the table toward the man and hands him the top envelope to examine, and in which to place and seal his cards. The prepared envelope is now flap-side up on the top of the stack that the magician is holding and he must be careful not to let the audience be aware of that fact.

Taking the man's sealed envelope from him, the magician places it *flap-side up* on top of the stack he holds in his left hand. As both men are now away from the table, the magician places the envelope on the stack apparently so that the stack will act as a support for writing on the envelope. The performer remarks that he will place a mark over the sealed flap so that any tampering will be obvious, "just as we did with the lady's."

The magician draws a line with the red end of the pencil exactly like the line on the prepared envelope, and, seizing the *two top envelopes* of the stack, he turns them both over as one and proffers the stack to the man for his initials on the front of the envelope, "just as the lady did."

This turnover is quite simply accomplished. As he makes the mark across the seal, the magician inserts the fingers of his left hand under the prepared envelope, separating it from

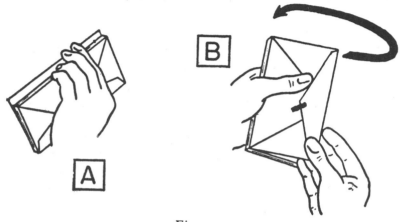

Figure 54

the rest of the stack as in Figure 54A (viewed from below the left hand). The magician turns to his left (with his back to the man assistant) apparently so that the audience can see where he is putting the mark on the envelope. He then grasps both the top envelopes as one by the right edge with his right hand and pulls both envelopes out to the right and flips them over as he turns back once more to the right, to face the man assistant as in Figure 54B.

The body turn will cover the double turnover, but neither should be at all hurried. This turning over of the two top envelopes as one, of course, brings the prepared envelope containing twelve cards to the top, and *it is the front of this pre-*

*pared envelope* that the man initials as his own. The magician tells the assisting spectator to hold his envelope and not
let it out of his possession.

Disposing of the rest of the stack of envelopes, the magician now recapitulates what has happened. The lady counted
fifteen cards and put them in an envelope which she sealed,
initialed, and is holding. The man did likewise, except that
three of his cards were noted by members of the audience.
The magician has at no time touched the deck of cards since
the trick began, etc.

The magician will now make the three cards selected by
the members of the audience (naming the three cards) pass
invisibly from the man's envelope into the lady's. So saying,
the magician goes through the pantomime of plucking three
invisible cards from the man's envelope and flipping them at
the lady's.

It is done, says the magician, and he asks the man to open
his envelope and count his cards. There are only twelve! The
very three cards that were selected by the members of the
audience are gone! The lady is asked to open her envelope
and the fifteen originally counted have been increased to
eighteen cards, and among those eighteen cards arc the three
selected by the audience!

It should be obvious that the only weak point of the trick
is switching the envelope actually sealed by the man for the
one containing twelve cards previously sealed by the magician. The whole business about marking the envelopes and
placing initials thereon is directed solely at giving the magician a logical excuse to turn the envelope over and make the
switch.

The marking business may seem tedious and unnecessary
during the performance, but it adds materially to the success
of the deception, and is completely forgotten by the spectators in the amazement created by the invisible flight of not
just any three but three selected cards from one sealed enve-

lope to another without the magician's apparently ever having touched the cards.

## PRECOGNITION

EFFECT: The magician demonstrates that he was able to know even before he arrived for his performance exactly what card a spectator would choose when allowed to scan the faces of the whole deck in making his choice.

This effect is especially useful as a trick with which to commence a demonstration of card magic before a small audience. It takes but a moment to perform and yet it seems so thoroughly unbelievable that it cannot fail, as the saying goes, to stand the spectators on their ears. Therefore, it is a welcome punch as an opening effect just at the moment when the performer's magic is most on trial.

PREPARATION: A special deck of cards is needed. It is a rough-smooth deck made up of twenty-six cards with blue backs and twenty-six cards with red backs chosen so that the faces of all the fifty-two cards give a complete deck. The backs of all the cards should have a white border. Obviously any two colors would suffice but for purposes of this description, red and blue will be used. It will further be assumed that the reader's ordinary cards have blue backs identical with the twenty-six blue cards.

The *backs* of the *red-backed cards* and the *faces* of the *blue-backed cards* are coated with roughing fluid (see page 187). The *faces* of the *red-backed cards* and the *backs* of the *blue-backed cards* are powdered with zinc stearate powder. The cards are then assembled into a deck with red and blue cards alternating so that the *top* card has a *blue back*, the *second* a *red back*, and so forth. The faces of the cards (both colors) should be in random order in the assembled deck.

The rough-smooth treatment will cause the cards to stick together in pairs, a blue-backed card adhering slightly to the back of every red-backed card. When a deck prepared as above is fanned, only blue backs will show and it will appear to be an ordinary blue-backed deck. Yet, if any of the cards whose faces show in the fan is removed, it will have a red back.

The prepared deck is in its box. An unprepared deck with matching blue backs is in the performer's left jacket pocket along with an envelope or stiff piece of paper.

PRESENTATION: The magician explains that, just to get his performance under way, he would like to demonstrate his ability to see into the future. He removes the prepared deck from its box and fans it in his left hand with the faces toward the audience. In fanning the deck, he separates one of the pairs of cards (any one) so that there is one red back visible among all the blue-backed cards.

Before arriving for this performance, says the magician, he considered the problem of just what card this particular audience was likely to favor most and he decided on one particular card. He has indicated his choice by placing one red-backed card in this blue-backed deck. As he says this, he turns the fan around and shows the one visible red back in the blue fan.

Closing the fan, the magician says he now wants to see if he was right. He cuts the deck "just so the audience will lose track of where the red card was" and fans the cards once more, faces to the audience. This time he makes sure that none of the red backs is visible among the blue cards.

Advancing to the nearest spectator, the magician extends the fan toward the spectator so that he can see the faces. He asks the spectator to study the faces of the cards carefully and then quickly to point to any card there. By thus asking the spectator to point to a card, the magician obviates the possibility that the spectator might call out one of the twenty-six cards not showing in the fan. By insisting that the spectator do so quickly, the performer refuses to allow the spectator to study the faces long enough to come to the conclusion that all the cards are not showing. If, by watching the spectator's eyes, it becomes apparent that he is looking for a particular card in the fan, the magician says "Quickly, point to one of the cards—any one!" in a firm voice.

When the spectator points out one of the cards whose face is showing in the fan, the performer reaches over the top of the fan with his right hand and pulls that card up so it pro-

CARDS STICK TOGETHER IN PAIRS SO THAT ONLY BLUE BACKS SHOW IN FAN

SELECTED CARD WITH RED BACK

Figure 55

trudes above the fan as in Figure 55. He announces what card was chosen but does not yet show its back.

Stepping back out of reach of the spectators (so they will not be tempted to reach for the cards to inspect them) the magician smiles contentedly and announces as dramatically as possible that he apparently succeeded in predicting the very card the spectator chose—even before he had ever seen the spectator. As he says this, he slowly turns the fan around so that the audience can see that the protruding card has a red back—the only one in the blue-backed fan!

Pausing just a moment for the effect of this disclosure to impress itself on the audience, the magician removes the red-backed card from the fan, shows its face once more, and hands it to the spectator who picked it with the request that he hold the card a moment. Before anyone can demand to see the rest of the deck, the magician closes the fan and drops the deck into his left jacket pocket so that the piece of paper there keeps it separated from the unprepared deck already in the pocket.

He then removes his handkerchief and very carefully wipes his hands as if to prepare his fingers for the forthcoming performance. The effect of this procedure in the minds of the spectators—especially any few who might distrust the innocent appearance of the deck—is that the magician will continue with the same deck of cards and, indeed, the same red-backed card that he asked the spectator to hold for him.

Thus the prepared deck is got out of circulation in the simplest manner possible and before anyone is the wiser. Having finished wiping his hands, the magician reaches into his left jacket pocket and removes the unprepared deck of cards with which he performs his next trick. He is careful to choose as his second trick one during which the spectators handle and have an opportunity to see that the deck is unprepared.

Since the performer handed the red-backed card to his assisting spectator with the request that he hold it a moment, it appears as if both the card and the spectator have something more to do with the performance. Therefore, the meticulous performer who desires to come as close as possible to perfection will make use of both the assisting spectator and the single red-backed card in his second effect in order to complete the logical sequence of misdirection covering the switching of the prepared deck for the unprepared one.

Thus the magician might dispense with the hand-wiping and place the prepared deck in his pocket apparently to free his hands for writing on the face of the red-backed card some note required by his second effect. Or the red-backed card might be used in a torn-and-restored card effect, or handed to the spectator with the request that he keep it as a memento of the performance. Finally, the simplest device would be to have the spectator use the red-backed card as a pointer with which to select from the unprepared deck a card for the performer's second trick. Since symmetry is very effective as an aid to misdirection in magic, the performer might place the prepared deck in his pocket apparently to free his hands so that he could tear the single red-backed card in half. Handing each half to a spectator, he would request each to use his bit of card as a pointer with which to select a card from the unprepared deck for the performer's second miracle.

NOTE: It is not to be suggested that this effect is useful only as an opening trick. It deserves a place in any part of the performer's routine, especially among tricks that allegedly demonstrate the performer's mentalistic or psychic powers. The reader is also recommended to the closely analogous effect sold at all magic stores under the name of the "Brain Wave Deck."

It should also be noted that if "Precognition" is used during a formal program—especially where the performer is on a stage or platform—there may be little necessity for devising a way to switch the prepared for an unprepared deck. The magician would simply lay the deck aside after showing the red-backed card and bow for applause or go on to his next effect. "Aesthetic distance," that indescribable psychological advantage that any person on a stage has over the lone dissenter in the audience, would take care of any doubts anyone might have as to the genuineness of the cards used.

As will be apparent, this effect can have a tremendous impact as a very short but highly astonishing trick for a routine limited in length as most performances are on television. The differently colored backs, while sufficiently contrasting for color television, may, however, lose some effect with the black-and-white medium, and should be especially selected for such use with this limitation in mind. Wildly contrasting colors, such as purple and yellow, for example, would be more effective on black-and-white television.

# VIII

## Tricks with Silks and Handkerchiefs

Magical effects using silks and handkerchiefs are among the most successful of the amateur magician's repertoire. The use of gaily colored silk squares adds materially to the spectacle and grandeur of the magician's performance. The amateur magician cannot hope to have at his command the colorful, brightly painted scenery, drapes, and costumes of the professional stage magician. Tricks using a large variety of bright silks, however, do help fill the gap. They add the brilliance and color so helpful in attaining the effect the magician wants.

Furthermore, as items to be magically produced from empty hats, pockets, boxes, etc., silks are eminently effective. A yard-square piece of fine Japanese silk can be compressed to less than the size of a golf ball, and thus easily introduced secretly into an empty hat or some such object. Yet several such silks fully expanded give the impression of an enormous quantity of material.

The proper type of silk for use as an item to be produced

magically from an empty hat or box is very fine oriental silk. It is available at all magic stores and at some other stores that sell yard and piece goods, although the true imported silk is not easily found in the regular retail market. Though rather expensive, the imported silk is infinitely superior to its domestic counterpart, since an addition of rayon fibers to the silk detracts from its springiness. Domestic silk with a high rayon content cannot be wadded into such small compass, and, when released, does not expand so fully as does pure oriental silk.

Usually, a suitable variety of silk can be found bleached white. It can be readily dyed with whatever bright colors are desired. Since the magician is interested in brilliant, forceful colors, the more or less pastel-colored kerchiefs widely sold as objects of feminine apparel do not entirely fill the need.

For use with silk tricks other than magical productions from empty containers, any sort of handkerchief will do. Silk is usually found more practical, however, because of its appearance and its slick surface. For most purposes, lighter silk will be easier to handle.

The most practical size for most silk tricks is from fifteen to eighteen inches square. Bright contrasting colors give the best effect regardless of what sort of material is used. Also, when the trick calls for tying two silks together, square knots should be used (see Figure 21B, page 100). Not only will they hold most securely, but they can be "upset" by pulling backward on either of the short ends so that the silks can be drawn apart without picking at the knot with the fingernails to untie it and thus damaging the silk. If silks are kept rolled up in a smooth bundle rather than folded flat, they will be easier to handle because of the lack of creases, and they will last longer.

## TARBELL SILK

EFFECT: From time to time throughout his program, the magician nonchalantly removes a green silk handkerchief from his pocket and wipes his brow. Before returning it to his pocket, the magician, casually and without calling any attention to it, pulls the handkerchief through his fingers and it is seen to change instantly from green to red.

Dr. Harlan Tarbell, who has given many startling effects as well as many informative books to the magical fraternity, is responsible for this ingenious device.

PREPARATION: The device can be purchased ready-made from any magic store, but the following description is included for completeness. Two silk handkerchiefs of bright contrasting colors (usually red and green since those are complementary colors) are used. Lay the two silks one upon the other as in Figure 56A, and sew them together along edges *ab* and *bc*. The silk bag thus formed is turned inside out (so that the edges of the seam are on the inside of the bag) and the two seams just made are brought together and sewed to each other as in Figure 56B. The green half now is turned completely inside out so that the final product is a green cone of silk with the red silk sewed inside it as a lining, as in Figure 56C.

The very tip of the cone (*b* in Figure 56C) is now cut off and a small plastic embroidery ring (about the size of a quarter and available at any notion counter or the dime store) is sewed securely between the silks to form a stiff opening at the top of the cone. It may also be necessary to "tack" the two silks together with a few stitches about midway of the long side of the triangle.

When the device is completed according to the above instructions, the corner of the red silk (X in Figure 56C) is thrust upward through the ring, thus turning the red lining

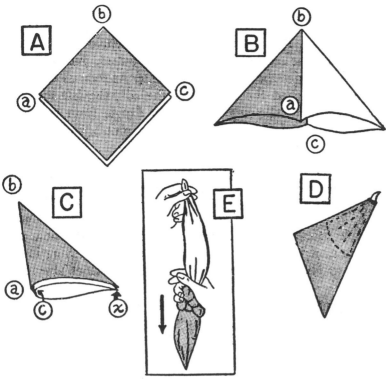

Figure 56

of the cone partly inside out. With the device as shown in Figure 56D, the trick is ready to perform.

The silk is removed from the pocket with the left hand holding the ring and hiding the tip of red silk that protrudes therefrom. When it is desired for the silk to change color, the silk is allowed to hang down from the left thumb and first two fingers. The right hand strokes the silk several times starting at the top. On the last stroke, the right thumb and index finger grasp the ring at the top of the silk while the left thumb and index finger maintain a firm hold on the tip of the red silk. The left hand carries the ring downward, pulling it along the silk as in Figure 56E.

This move, it will be seen, turns the whole device inside out so that the red lining becomes the outside and the green outside becomes the lining of the cone. As soon as the right hand has reached the bottom of the silk, the *left* hand releases its hold, allowing the silk to dangle from the right hand as that hand hides the ring and protruding corner of green silk.

The silk is now returned to the pocket, being careful not to expose the ring and green tip. Later in the program, the silk is again removed, the brow wiped, and the color changed back to green. Each time this happens, the magician makes no reference to the silk. Indeed, he handles the whole procedure as if it were the most natural and usual thing in the world to change the color of one's handkerchief after each use.

The first time the audience will be taken by surprise. The second time it will chuckle. By the end of the program, the continued changes of the silk will cause considerable comment by the spectators.

## TWO TO ONE

EFFECT: The magician places two silks in a regular glass tumbler and either one selected by the spectators vanishes right before their eyes. The effect is primarily an opening trick since the magician must leave the room before performing it. The effect is so startling, however, it is considered well worthwhile, and is almost a "close-up" effect by nature so that it can be performed right in the eye, so to speak, of a television camera. Mr. Roy Benson first introduced the author to this effect.

PREPARATION: A piece of stout cord is necessary for this effect. It should be long enough to reach from the magician's left wrist, up his left sleeve, across his back, down his right sleeve, and to his right fingers. The length should be adjusted so that the magician may hold one end in his right hand and have just a little freedom of movement in his arms as he stands with his elbows at his sides and his hands extended before him. One end of the cord is fastened to the left wrist and a small loop (about one inch in diameter) is tied

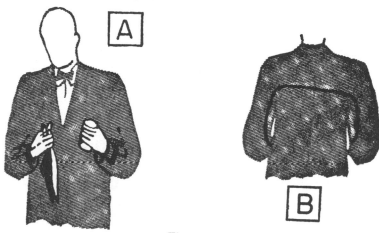

Figure 57

at the other end. The arrangement is indicated in Figure 57.

With the cord in position, the magician takes two small silks of contrasting colors and sticks them both through the loop at the right end of the cord. The silks are held by their corners with the right thumb and second finger and allowed to dangle downward. The right index finger keeps the tops of the two silks separated and the third finger goes between the silks to hold the loop of cord so it will not slide down the silks (as in Figure 58A). The left hand then takes a regular drinking glass and the magician is ready to make his entrance and begin his performance as in Figure 57A.

PRESENTATION: The magician comes before his audience and points out that he has a red and a green silk (or what-

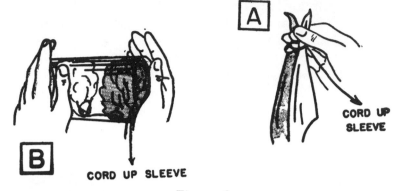

Figure 58

ever colors they are) in his hand. He asks the audience to select one. Let us suppose the red one is chosen. The magician grasps the green silk with the index and second fingers of his left hand (the hand holding the tumbler) and pulls it away from the right fingers. He then pulls the red silk upward through his right fingers, thus sliding the cord loop to the center of the silk, and stuffs the red silk into the glass tumbler, cord and all. With the right fingers (which are now free) the magician takes the green silk and stuffs it into the tumbler on top of the red silk "just for a cork."

He now places the palm of his right hand over the mouth of the tumbler and the palm of his left hand over the bottom of the tumbler, holding the tumbler horizontal, as in Figure 58B. "Watch!" exclaims the magician, and he jerks his hands forward and upward. The red silk vanishes in a flash from the glass up his right sleeve, leaving the green one still there in the tumbler held between the palms of the hands.

A little experimenting will show just how long to have the cord to insure the greatest freedom of movement and still make sure the red silk is pulled completely out of sight up the right sleeve. The speed and flash with which this effect is accomplished makes it a very startling opening effect. The visible disappearance of the red silk right before their eyes has a great effect on the spectators and immediately assures them that a competent magician is about to entertain them. After the silk has been pulled up the sleeve, the cord will no longer prove to be of any bother to the magician during the rest of his demonstration.

## TWENTIETH CENTURY

EFFECT: Two colored silks are tied together and given to a spectator to hold. A third silk is made to vanish magically and then reappear firmly tied between the two silks held all the while by the spectator.

PREPARATION: Four silks are needed for this effect, two of which must be identical in appearance. Let us say that a red, a blue, and two white silks are used.

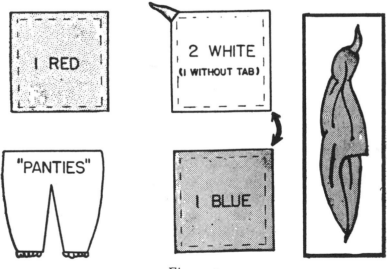

Figure 59

To one corner of one of the white silks is sewed a piece of blue material of the same color as the blue silk. This little tab is about two inches long. The white silk is then tied, at the corner diagonally opposite to the little tab, to one corner of the blue silk. Figure 59 shows the required silks. The white silk is then gathered into a small ball and hidden in the folds of the blue silk just beneath the knot. The little blue tab is left protruding, and the blue silk is slightly twisted around the white silk to hold it in place as shown in the inset of Figure 59.

The blue silk thus prepared, the other white silk, and the red silk are on the table ready for the trick. Another piece of white silk, cut as shown in Figure 59 to resemble a pair of ladies' panties (with, perhaps, a bit of lace sewed to each "leg") is resting in the right trousers pocket so that one corner of it can be readily pulled into view.

PRESENTATION: The magician picks up the red and blue silk, holding the blue in his left hand with the fingers hiding the bulge where the white silk is hidden and with the blue tab protruding upward. Remarking that the two silks came to him as part of an old Chinese treasure—or any other sort of nonsense that the performer chooses—the magician quite openly ties the little blue tab to one corner of the red silk, being careful to use up all the tab and yet not allow the audience to see any of the white silk, as in Figure 60. To the audience it appears as though the magician has merely tied the red and blue silks together at the corners.

Now that the silks are tied together, says the magician, he will give them to a spectator to hold for a moment. Quickly he bunches the two silks up and hands them to a nearby spectator, requesting that he hold them up high so that all can see (and, incidentally, so that the spectator will not be able to meddle with them!).

The magician picks up the white silk and blandly announces that he is going to cause the white silk to vanish. Using both hands, he starts to wad the white silk, telling the audience, if he chooses, to keep one eye on the spectator holding the red and blue silks, one eye on the white silk, and the other eye on himself. If, as, and when the audience laughs at that witticism, the magician pretends to close his left fist on the white silk and holds his hand up high, gazing at it fixedly. His right hand, tightly closed, makes a dive for his right trousers pocket.

*Figure 60*

The audience, naturally, is not fooled by what appears to be a clumsy attempt to divert attention from the right hand's trip to the pocket. The magician has apparently blundered completely, for, as his right hand is withdrawn from the pocket, a corner of the white silk is seen to appear.

What actually happens is this: The magician is wadding the silk with both hands. When it is entirely inside his hands, he takes the silk in his *right* hand, and, closing his *left* fist as if it held the silk, he raises his left and stares at it. The right hand, containing the silk, goes into the right trousers pocket and *stuffs the white silk up into the very top far corner of that pocket* where it will be held by the pressure of the waistband of the trousers. As the right hand emerges from the pocket, it draws into view a corner of the white "panties" that are in the pocket.

The magician says he will vanish the white silk by simply crushing it, and he makes a crumpling motion with his closed left fingers, finally showing the left hand empty. He turns to the audience as if he expected some applause for the feat of vanishing the white silk. The audience, of course, will be more inclined to laugh at what appears to be a very clumsy demonstration. The spectators will call the magician's attention to the corner of white silk protruding from his trousers pocket. The magician is very careful not to notice it or to understand what the audience means.

Finally, however, he looks down and sees the corner of white silk. Oh that, exclaims the magician, pulling the "panties" out of his pocket and displaying them smilingly, he just carries those along for laughs. While the audience is chuckling at having been so patently taken in by the magician, he

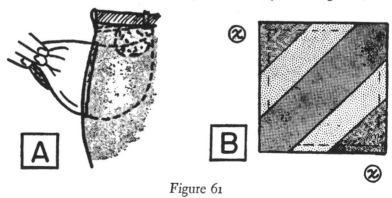

Figure 61

reaches down, and, showing his right hand empty, pulls his trousers pocket inside out, thus proving that it is unmistakably empty. This maneuver can be done with impunity since the white silk remains stuffed into the far top corner of the pocket even when the pocket is pulled inside out, as shown in Figure 61A.

If the audience really wants to know what happened to the white silk, the magician says, look here. The magician then grasps one corner of the silks that the spectator has been holding all this time and jerks them out of his hand with a flip. The white silk will come into view, tied between the very two silks that the magician tied together at the beginning of the trick!

NOTE: As an alternative method, many performers use a variegated silk instead of the white one. This variegated silk is dyed several different colors as in Figure 61B, with two corners (the ones marked X in the drawing) dyed to match the blue silk, thus doing away with the necessity of the tab. Such an arrangement may be superior to that first suggested, but it does require a specially dyed silk.

It should also be noted that, if a variegated silk is used instead of the white one, the "panties" should match one of the colors of the silk. In this case, the magician, while wadding the silk in his hand, will be careful to allow the part matching the "panties" to be the last to disappear and to call attention to its color to build up the sucker effect.

The required silks for either method and "panties" to match are available at any magic store.

## SILK PRODUCTIONS

The seemingly endless magical production of dozens of brightly colored silk handkerchiefs is the one-man magician's equivalent of the musical show "production number." Silks are compact, easy to handle, and yet expand into a colorful, apparently enormous display of matter. The picture of a magician standing in the midst of numberless yards of silk which he has magically caused to materialize from nothing is an applause-provoking one that many performers overlook.

There are, however, two grave faults of which many a performer has been guilty. First of all, there comes a point where enough silks have been produced. After the surprise of the first batch of silks, any further production, no matter now magical, ceases to be startling and begins to be simply redundant if not downright boring. Secondly, the idea behind a silk production is to give the effect of an enormous quantity of silk, not an enormous number of silks. The performer who takes pains to display each silk singly soon finds himself losing his audience; whereas the performer who tosses silks to right and left with apparent abandon in a veritable shower of color has the proper approach.

It should be remembered further that there is very little point in utilizing any of the many false-bottomed boxes and other contraptions on the market for a silk production. Considering the comparative ease with which silks can be produced from the bare hands and the immeasurably increased effect of the bare-hand production, the performer is wise who accomplishes his silk productions without the aid of visible mechanical apparatus.

The final general admonition regarding silk productions is the most important: Just as with a musical composition, a play, or the entire magic program itself, a silk production routine must be made up of a number of short, startling climaxes ending with a clean-cut flash finale. Translated into material terms, this means that each step of the silk production must be more startling than the last, with the finale being the most surprising of all, hence if any given step in the routine cannot be topped by the next step, the next step should not be done.

Thus, in attempting to work out a suitable production, the possibilities might be considered somewhat as follows, always thinking in terms of short, well-defined progressions from one climax to the next:

Step 1. From the empty bare hands, a single silk is produced.

Step 2. With minimum of flimflam this first silk is changed into (or has added to it) first one, then two, then three or more silks one at a time.

Step 3. These four or five single silks suddenly (with one motion) double or treble in quantity so that a double handful of silk appears.

Step 4. Without warning that double handful of silk suddenly expands into the main body of the production which overflows the performer's hands onto the floor in seemingly endless quantity—a great gushing fountain of brilliant color—perhaps with the size of the individual silks getting greater and greater.

Step 5. (Obviously the only "topper" to Step 4 is a sudden and obvious change in appearance of the silks.) The gushing stops as quickly as it began and the stream of small silks changes into a long, narrow varicolored streamer which the performer unreels, sending it flying yard after yard into the air like a wildly writhing serpent.

Step 6. Finale. All has been movement thus far. For a climax, a sudden stop coupled with surprise and flash is needed. The remaining silks and streamer are tossed high in the air and the performer is seen to be holding spread between his outstretched hands a gaily colored silk four or five feet square over which he takes his bow.

Within this general outline, then, the silk production act must be devised in order to achieve the desired effect. Both the late George Stillwell (whose entire vaudeville act consisted of nothing but a bare-handed production of silks) and the contemporary magicians Keith Clark and Franklin M.

Chapman (whose "Fountain of Silks" has been applauded for some years) unwittingly or otherwise adhered to the above formula. It is only when the magician attempts to substitute overbearing quantity or a slow, silk-by-silk display for the required ever-increasing series of climaxes that he will fail to entertain audiences of both men and women with a silk production routine.

The two routines given below try to bear out the above ultimate outline within certain practical limits. The author has borrowed freely from the methods and principles devised and published by Stillwell, Clark, Chapman as well as Jean Hugard, Samuel Berland, and the many other performers and inventors who have, by their ingenuity, added to the magic of silk.

## FAST AND TRULY BAREHANDED

PREPARATION: Several dozen eighteen-inch square silks of various brilliant colors are needed. Instead, a smaller number of two- or three-foot square silks cut diagonally in half and hemmed all around may be used. (The sheerer the silk the better it will serve here unless it is so sheer that the brilliance of the color is affected.)

Also needed is a large (four- or five-foot square) silk or a large flag and a Stillwell Handkerchief Ball. This latter item is merely a hollow ball (about the size of a golf ball) with a hole in it as shown by Figure 63A. By scouting around the toy counters of a dime store, the reader should be able to find a hollow plastic ball in which he can make a hole about the size of a quarter. The ball is painted with flesh-colored paint. It may be found convenient to paint the ball first with glue and then sprinkle with very fine sand (to give a rough finish which can be more easily handled) before painting with flesh paint. Any magic dealer can supply the necessary handkerchief ball.

Two small bulldog clips are needed (of the type illustrated

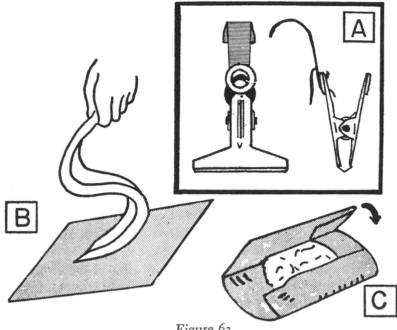

Figure 62

in Figure 62A) with jaws about one inch or less long, with a double-lipped hook arrangement as shown in the drawing. Bulldog clips will be found more convenient than pins or thread for holding loads because of the ease with which they can be released. Two buttons are sewed to the top two corners of the large silk or flag.

TO PREPARE FOR PERFORMANCE: The large silk or flag is folded in half from side to side and in half again and finally in thirds. The resulting long, narrow bundle is accordion-folded, starting with the bottom (the side away from the buttons) until a bundle about six by eight inches is obtained. One of the bulldog clips is fastened to the top (button side) of this bundle and the bundle is hung inside the front of the trousers on the right side with the lower of the two hooks on the clip hooked over the waistband.

If full dress is worn, the bundle is placed clip-downward under the right side of the vest. If a tuxedo (double breasted) is worn, the bundle is hung on a safety pin fastened inside the V front of the coat. The trousers load will, however, probably be the reader's most frequently used one. Full (pleated front) trousers held up with suspenders (so that the belt is not too tight) will hide the loads successfully and conveniently until needed.

Another of the eighteen-inch silks is spread out flat on the table and the rest of the silks to be used are folded into it in the following manner: Each silk is taken by one corner separately and folded into a tight bundle as if the silk were allowed to form a letter "S" and then was squashed flat (see Figure 62B). A heavy book will keep each silk flat as the next is being folded.

When all the silks are folded flat, the sides of the eighteen-inch silk are folded over the bundle (as in Figure 62C) and finally secured at one end with the other bulldog clip. This bundle (pressed flat) is hung on the left side of the trousers exactly as the large silk bundle. Figure 63B shows the two silks loads in position.

Three contrasting eighteen-inch silks are then stuffed into the hollow handkerchief ball. The silks are put in the ball one at a time. After the first silk is almost entirely inside the ball, its protruding corner is twisted together with the corner of the second silk so that when one silk is pulled from the ball, it will pull the corner of the next silk out of the hole just enough to be readily grasped by the fingers. One corner of the last silk is left protruding from the ball as in Figure 63A. The loaded ball goes on the table or in the right-hand pocket.

PRESENTATION: Turning his back on the audience as he replaces some item used in the previous trick on his table, the magician places the loaded handkerchief ball in the crook of his right elbow, covering it with a fold of his right sleeve.

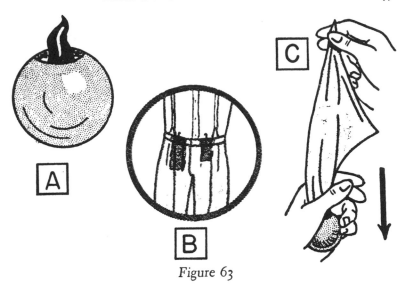

*Figure 63*

The ball will remain hidden there if the right arm is carried bent (but not stiffly) at the elbow.

Turning to the audience, the magician announces "Something from nothing!" He turns with his right side toward the audience and shows his left hand unmistakably empty back and front, at the same time pulling up his left sleeve slightly by grasping it at his left elbow with his right hand. He turns then to the right and shows his right hand similarly empty, similarly hitching up his right sleeve. In the process of pulling up the right sleeve, however, the left hand steals the loaded handkerchief ball from its hiding place in the right elbow crotch.

Throughout the time that it is being used, the handkerchief ball is held "palmed" in the hand—that is, resting easily in the hollow of the palm and held there by slight pressure of the base of the thumb. The lightness and rough surface of the ball make this easy. The hand remains relaxed. The hole in the ball is in such a position that the silks may be pulled from the ball through the crotch of the thumb as in Figure 63C. As soon as the ball is taken by the left hand, the hand drops listlessly to the left side, holding the ball easily and without apparent stiffness or strain.

But first, says the magician, we need some "nothing," and he reaches into the air with the right hand and picks an imaginary silk therefrom, holding it by one corner with the right thumb and forefinger. "Here we have some 'nothing,'" says the magician, indicating the imaginary silk he holds, "Now watch!"

If the performer desires, he may use this reaching-for-nothing movement as sufficient cover for his left hand to steal the loaded handkerchief ball from a paper clip hanging just beneath the left side of his jacket instead of getting the ball from his elbow.

Standing with his left side toward the audience, the magician strokes the imaginary silk dangling from his right fingers several times with his left hand. On the third stroke, the left hand is raised close enough to the right so that the right thumb and index finger can grasp the protruding corner of the first silk in the handkerchief ball. The left hand is then brought sharply downward as the right fingers (without moving) pull the first silk from the ball as in Figure 63C. The effect is that the imaginary silk has been made visible by stroking with the left hand.

Without moving his body (the left hand is again at his side) the magician pauses to look at the audience and shifts the single silk in his right hand so that it is dangling from between the tips of the right index and second fingers, the palm of the right hand toward the audience and perpendicular to the floor. The left hand, held thumb up and back toward the audience, reaches over and takes the silk from the right hand between the tips of the left index and second fingers.

In the process of this change, the two hands rub across each other palm to palm and the handkerchief ball is trans-

ferred from the palm of the left hand to the palm of the
right hand. As the change is effected, the magician swings
around so that his right side is toward the audience. At the
end of the change, the silk is dangling from the left fingers
and the ball is palmed in the right hand so that the position

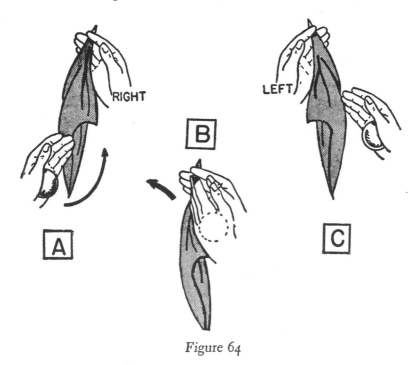

Figure 64

in all respects is exactly the reverse of the situation before
the change. The change is diagramed in Figure 64.

Because of the change, the audience has seen a silk materialize in one empty hand and be transferred to another
empty hand. Now the second silk is produced from the ball
by stroking with the right hand the silk held in the left, just
as the first silk was produced. The third silk is similarly produced with or without changing the palmed ball back to the

left hand (depending on the performer's ability to execute the change smoothly enough to merit a repetition of it).

The three silks are now taken with the right hand and draped over the left forearm, which is extended horizontally across the front of the body about waist high as in Figure

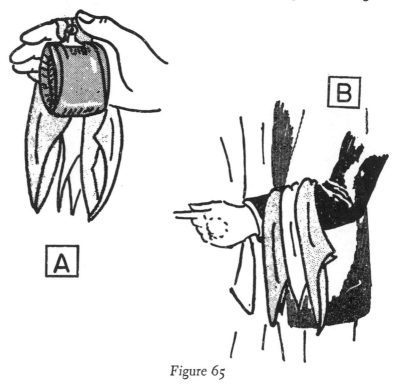

Figure 65

65B. The empty handkerchief ball is left in (or taken by, as the case may be) the left hand.

The performer glances at the silks and then at the audience, pointing out that there are three silks, all from nothing. Immediately the right hand, moving up from beneath the extended forearm and *between it and the performer's body* (palm toward his body), grasps the inside ends of the three silks and picks them off the arm so that the three silks are lying through the crotch of the right thumb.

As the right hand came up between the performer's fore-arm and body, to pick up the three silks, it also picked up the bundle of silks inside the left side of the trousers by catching the hook on the bulldog clip over the top of the right index finger and pulling the bundle free to be hidden by the three silks hanging over the back of the right hand as in Figure 65A. If the coat is kept open and the abdomen drawn in, there need be no trouble and no hesitation in stealing the load with the same motion that picks up the three silks.

The two hands are brought together, the bulldog clip is released, and the silks are allowed to well up, much to the performer's apparent surprise. Both hands are waved slowly up and down as the silks are worked into view to flow over onto the floor or the table.

As the hands are being moved up and down, they are brought over to the right side of the trousers and in close to the body. Under cover of the remaining silks in the hands, the bundle containing the large silk or flag is stolen from the trousers (or vest or coat front, as the case may be) and held ready for production.

When only a few silks are left in the hands, the bulldog clip on the large silk is released. The two buttons on the large silk are grasped one with each hand and the remaining small silks are tossed into the air as the hands separate to display the large silk.

It will be found that the empty ball and the two clips can readily be retained in the hands during the development of the silks, and then simply put aside with the large silk after the production is finished.

## OLD HAT

There is one exception to the remarks made above regarding bare-hand versus apparatus silk productions. Productions from a hat are so inextricably connected with magic and magicians that a hat does not seem to come in the same category as the shiny box that is shown empty and then fills with silks, especially when used in some such context as the following.

This routine is especially effective as an opening either to the magic program or to some special part of it.

PREPARATION: A silk opera hat (the type of top hat that folds flat) and an eight-inch square of black silk are needed. In addition will be needed a bundle of eighteen-inch silks made up like that described in the foregoing routine (though it may contain fewer silks and should be smaller—that is, more tightly compressed), a twenty-four-inch red silk and two long (twenty-foot) silk streamers twelve inches wide (or diagonally cut halves of eighteen-inch silks tied together in a long string may be used).

Figure 66

The streamers (or the two strings of tied silks) are accordion-folded. It will be found that a streamer of the type described (and sold by magic dealers) can be compressed into a bundle about the size of two packages of cigarettes. If desired, the bundles may be kept folded tight by means of two small bulldog clips.

When a silk "topper" or opera hat is folded flat, it will be found that the sides of the hat fold inward. If these inwardly folding sides are pulled upward, space will be found for a great quantity of silk as indicated by Figure 66. The two folded streamers in addition to a deck of cards (or some other small object that will be used in the trick that is scheduled to follow the silk production) are placed into the folded hat and covered with the square of black silk. Although the hat is now somewhat thicker than it should be, it is still apparently merely an opera hat folded flat. Pressing the sides of the hat back down on the load with a heavy book should result in a perfectly innocent-appearing folded top hat.

The twenty-four-inch red silk is folded in half diagonally and the resulting triangle accordion-folded in one-inch pleats. The long, thin strip resulting is then rolled tightly and fastened with a straight pin. The resulting roll (one inch thick and about an inch in diameter) is pinned (with the same pin) to the magician's lapel, where it will resemble a rosebud. If desired, one corner of the red silk may be dyed green and allowed to show as a leafy background for the "bud."

The bundle of eighteen-inch silks is once more hung inside the right side of the trousers but this time a catgut loop large enough for the thumb to slip through is fastened to the bulldog clip.

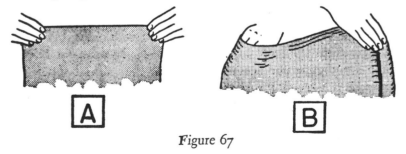

*Figure 67*

PRESENTATION: This routine is to be performed immediately preceding whatever trick uses the deck of cards or other small item that was included in the hat load.

The magician reaches up and removes the "rosebud" from his lapel button hole. Grasping it by the exposed corner, he shakes it out into a twenty-four-inch silk. Holding the silk by the two top corners, he displays it to the audience, holding it with his hands about waist high as in Figure 67A.

Moving his right hand (and arm) over to his left and his left hand and arm to the right (the left arm nearer the body), he shows the other side of the red silk as in Figure 67B. As the left hand goes to the right side of the trousers, the left thumb slips into the catgut loop of the load of eighteen-inch silks hidden there.

After getting the loop, the left hand moves straight upward, pulling the bundle of silks free of the trousers, the right hand moves up and over to the right, and the magician steps back (away from his hands) swinging the bundle of silks hanging over his left thumb outward. As the bundle of silks hits the red silk, the latter is folded over the bundle, giving the impression that the magician has caught something in the air, using the red silk as a net or seine.

Gathering the bundle enclosed by the red silk into his hands, the magician releases the bulldog clip and allows the silks to well into view, apparently both surprised and rather annoyed.

Taking all the silks (which are dribbling onto the floor) in his left hand, the magician reaches over with his right and picks up the folded opera hat. He displays the hat briefly so the audience can see what it is; he then flips it open by tapping it against his raised thigh. Into the hat he dumps the silks remaining in his hands. He has made sure that most of the silks have developed and fallen to the floor as he looked around for something to do with all these silks that he apparently did not want. He places the hat back on the table and starts to turn away in disgust to continue his efforts elsewhere, when his attention is attracted by something inside the hat.

Puzzled, the magician reaches into the hat with both hands. In each hand he grasps an end of one of the streamers and starts to pull them out. As the length increases, so does the magician's wonderment. With large gestures and a rather hectic haste, the magician continues to pull the streamers out of the hat, tossing them to the right and left. Perhaps he pauses to tell the spectators that he will be with them in just a moment.

He continues pulling the streamers out of the hat in a fast and frantic display, completely oblivious of what is happening, concentrating his attention apparently only upon reaching the bottom of the hat. Great sweeping gestures and a hectic manner that keeps the streamers flying can create the impression at this point that there is simply no end to the amount of silk streamers involved. Pulling the streamers out of the hat will also send the few smaller silks which were dumped into the hat flying up with very good effect.

When the end of the streamers is reached, the magician, very much relieved, reaches into the hat and removes the deck of cards (or whatever item was included in the hat load) and turns to the audience with a sigh, saying, "I knew this was here someplace!" and then goes on with his next trick. The effect of this "throwaway" type of presentation for the silk production (that is, with the magician treating the production as an unwanted interruption concocted by an impish fate) is immensely effective, especially with an audience that has had to sit through a silk-by-silk display by a performer who is laboring under the misapprehension that a lot of pretty silk is a substitute for showmanship.

## ALL OUT—OF NOWHERE

The reader will notice that neither of the two foregoing routines conforms entirely to the formula suggested at the beginning of this section. Such a formula is, of necessity, a general guide to be approached if not equaled. The reader may, however, devise a silk production routine comprising all the elements embodied in the outline referred to, by combining, perhaps, part of the two foregoing routines.

Emphasis should also be laid on the possibility of utilizing a silk production routine as a follow-up for any of the silk tricks in this chapter. Also a production of other items (such as feather flowers, spring flowers, etc., with which the reader will become familiar upon his closer association with magic) —especially the traditional fish bowl full of water and even fish—might well follow the first of the foregoing silk production routines. In such a case the final large silk would be used as a foulard or cover under which to produce the additional items.

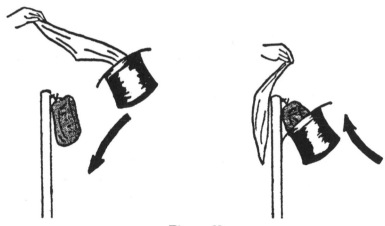

Figure 68

Attention should be directed also to the possibility of hanging one or more of the bundles of silk on the back of a chair or table (or an assistant if one is used) to be picked up when needed, either in the hands covered by silks already contained therein or with a top hat while other silks are being removed therefrom as in Figure 68. Since the average reader will probably not want to invest in a quantity of silks in excess of the amount required in the first routine given above, such possibilities are only to be suggested to the reader's contemplation as he matures in his study and ability in the magical art.

NOTE: Instead of a bare-hand production or the "rosebud" device for acquiring the first silk, any of the many gadgets on the magical market designed for leading into a silk production may be used. Thus the performer's cane or his wand may be changed magically into a single silk with which to start a silk production as in the Walsh "Vanishing Cane" or the Petrie Lewis "Vanishing Wand." A box of wooden matches (with the silk stuffed inside the cover where the drawer goes) may be made to yield a silk as the performer closes the drawer after lighting a cigarette. Even a single lighted match itself can be flipped into a silk as with Berland's "Silks at the Finger Tips."

Infinite, too, are the liaison tricks that may precede a silk production. Thus, if the performer is doing a trick using balls, the last ball used may be a hollow one containing a silk as described. This last ball is then "changed" into a silk and the production proceeds. Candles, glasses, pencils, flowers, and all manner of other items may be similarly used to yield the starting silk.

Also, the possibility should not be overlooked of using whatever silks the performer may be holding at the completion of any of the silk tricks in this chapter as a cover behind which to steal his first load.

## MASTER SILK ROUTINE

There is almost an infinitude of magical effects made possible by the use of faked or prepared silks (faked, that is, to a greater extent than the silks in "Twentieth Century"). Such effects are frequently either overlooked or performed in such a way that their worth is somewhat diminished. The difficulty is that a silk prepared for a certain trick can usually be used only for that particular trick. Thus the magician is forced to do only that one effect or to pick up a different silk for each trick, a procedure that seems to impeach the innocence of the silks to a high degree.

The following routine is devised to eliminate such difficulty. Although each of the component parts will stand alone in its own right as an effective silk trick, when routined as described, the combined effect is much enhanced. All the parts of the routine use faked silks of one sort or another and yet apparently the same silks are used throughout. The entire routine comprises representatives of the most popular types of silk effects: "Sympathetic," "Twentieth Century," "Blendo," and "Mis-made Flag," each presented in its most baffling manner. For this reason the routine should be done as an entity and no other silk tricks should be included in the same program. Thus the magician will have five minutes of silk magic in his show beyond which he need never go. Since none of these effects requires the assistance of a spectator, this routine is readily performed on television.

As with most faked silk tricks, the preparation seems complicated and tedious. It should be remembered, however, that the silks need be prepared but once no matter how often the routine is performed.

No attempt will be made to trace the performer who first suggested the various effects contained herein, all of which have now assumed classical proportions in the art of magic. The self-tying device utilized was published some years ago by Mr. Keith Clark. The method for working the well-known "Mis-made Flag" finale is the author's own invention.

PREPARATION: THE FLAG SILK: The description of this item is necessarily rather involved and the reader may have little reason to study it in detail until he is actually starting to make his own flag. The reader may, however, find the following device helpful in trying to visualize quickly the construction and principle of the Flag Silk.

The reader should think of a pillowcase that is turned halfway inside out—that is, the end seam is pulled up inside the case until it is even with the edges of the open end. If the reader now were to reach into the open end of the pillow case, grasp the corners of the end seam, and shake the case violently, it would turn itself the rest of the way inside out, apparently doubling in size and bringing a completely new surface of cloth to view.

This simple idea is the action that underlies the Flag Silk. Two changes occur in the trick: By shaking the prepared silk from one side, two plain-colored silks apparently change into a "mis-made" flag—that is, an American flag that has red and white stripes but no blue field. Then, by shaking from the other side, the "mis-made" flag apparently changes into a regular flag twice the size of the "mis-made" one. Both of these changes occur in the one self-contained device simply by reaching inside, grasping the proper corner and shaking the device inside out.

CONSTRUCTION OF THE FLAG SILK: Two silk American flags are needed of a size approximately twenty-four by thirty-six inches. The weight of the silk used should be slightly heavier than is usual for magical silk so that it will be more nearly opaque. Also are needed two "mis-made" flags—that is, American flags from which the blue field has been cut out and replaced with a square of white silk. The size of the "mis-made" flags should be about eighteen by twenty-four inches. A red and a white silk the same size as the "mis-made" flags complete the requirements.

It will be noticed that the "mis-made" flags are a trifle shorter than the usual proportions for an American flag, but this is necessary and will pass unnoticed by the audience. All the above flags and silks now have a one-inch border of gold ribbon sewed all the way around them.

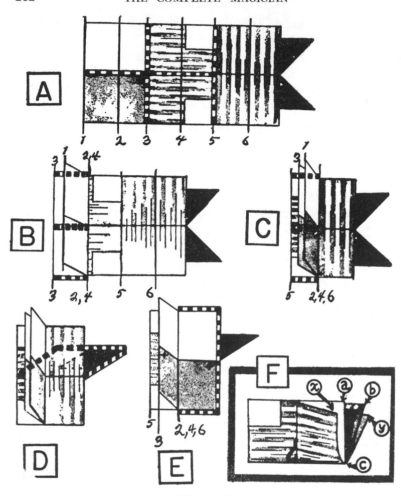

Figure 69

Now consider Figure 69. It will be noted that the gold borders around each silk have been omitted in an effort to make the drawings less confusing. The device of the heavy dotted line is used in all the drawings to indicate a seam that must be sewed.

The gold-bordered red and white silks and the two gold-bordered "mis-made" flags are laid out as in Figure 69A and sewed together along the edges indicated by the heavy dotted lines. The resulting piece is then sewed as indicated to half of each of the two large flags, leaving half of each large flag unattached and extended out behind the other silks as in the drawing.

The red and white silks are then folded over to the right along the imaginary line (3) in Figure 69A so that line (2) coincides with the line (4) down the middle of the "mis-made" flags. The edges are sewed together along half the length of the silks as indicated by the dotted lines in Figure 69B. Once more the left end of the assembly is folded along line (4) so that line (2) is carried to the right to coincide with line (6). The edges are sewed as shown by the dotted lines of Figure 69C—that is, the edges between lines (4) and (5) are sewed to the edges between lines (5) and (6).

Now the two free halves of the large flags that have been extending out behind the assembled silks are brought together and sewed along all three edges as in Figure 69D. The red and white silk flap (between lines (1) and (2) in Figure 69D) is folded down and its edges are sewed to the edges of the large flags as in Figure 69E.

Finally, the remaining flap (red and white on one side and part of the "mis-made" flags on the other) is folded down, but not sewed, so the plain red and white silks are hidden, and the whole contraption is folded in half along the horizontal center seam in Figure 69E to give the almost finished result shown in Figure 69F.

The edges ac and bc in Figure 69F are sewed together. The corners (not the edges) x and y are brought together and sewed firmly just at the very corner. One half of a snap fastener is sewed to each of the corners of the red silk indicated by the two little crosses in Figure 69E. A small tape loop about two inches in diameter is sewed near the center of the bottom seam of the "mis-made" flag as in Figure 69F.

TO PREPARE THE FLAG SILK FOR PERFORMANCE: Considering the device as it appears in Figure 69F, the right-hand halves of the "mis-made" flags are folded back on themselves, thus making a rectangular gold-bordered silk packet, red on one side and white on the other. Care must be taken to get all parts of the folded packet to lie flat without wrinkles.

The gold borders should hide any of the inside red and white striped edges so that when the silk contraption is held by the corner between the two open sides and allowed to dangle from the fingers, it will appear as if the magician is merely holding a red and white silk together. The purpose of the gold borders is to adjust the sizes of the various silks one to the other. The gold borders may be trimmed to various widths so that there will be no inside edges protruding where they are not wanted.

Now, as the performer holds the Flag Silk by one corner, it should resemble a red and a white silk. If both hands grasp the edge protruding from within the opening at the short side of the red and white silk and give the entire silk assembly a violent shake or downward snap, the red and white silk will appear to change into a "mis-made" flag. If the consistency of the cloth requires, several pieces of lead shot may be sewed into the gold border so that their weight will facilitate this change. Actually, of course, the red and white silks are merely folded down on themselves bringing the "mis-made" flag into view.

After the "mis-made" flag is exposed, the two halves of the snap fastener are face to face and the magician snaps them shut as he displays the "mis-made" flag. The same shaking move is now repeated by grasping the end of the large flag which protrudes from the opening along the top of the "mis-made" flags. This final shake will turn the whole device inside out displaying a large American flag just as though the "mis-made" flag had expanded and changed into the large complete flag.

THE SYMPATHETIC SILK: Two gold-bordered silks about twenty inches square are needed here. One silk is prepared as

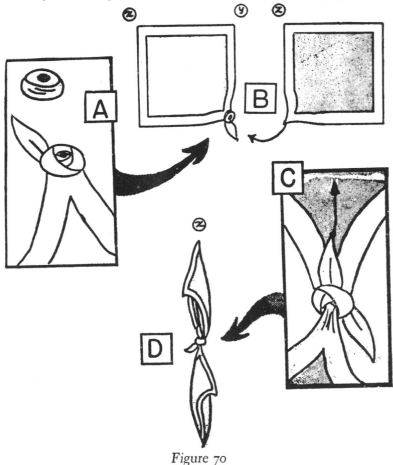

Figure 70

follows: Using some heavy lead wire (such as wire solder without an acid core), a small doughnut-shaped object is made about the size of a large knot that might be tied with the two silks. This doughnut weight is sewed into the corner of the red silk with the silk going around it so as to look like a knot in the corner of the red silk as in Figure 70A.

A piece of black thread is tied to the corner of the weighted red silk that is diagonally opposite to the weighted corner. The other end of the thread is led downward through the hole in the weight and fastened to one corner of the gold border of the other red silk. The length is adjusted so that when the weighted silk is held by the threaded corner (X in Figure 70B) and allowed to dangle from the fingers, the weight will slide down the thread and over the tip of the other red silk to give the impression that the red and white silks are tied together as in Figure 70C and D.

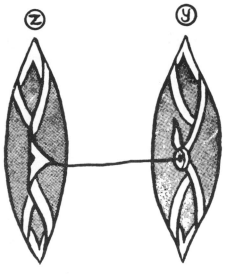

Figure 71

TO PREPARE FOR PERFORMANCE: Both red silks are picked up by the corners marked Y and Z in Figure 70B. When held by these two corners, the weighted corner of one and the threaded corner of the other will naturally fall behind or inside the folds of the two silks. It will be seen that the two silks can then be separated just enough (the thread running between them) to show that they are not tied together in any way as in Figure 71.

THE AUTOMATIC TWENTIETH CENTURY: Although the effect of this part of the routine is similar to the "Twentieth Century" trick described earlier in the chapter, the working is considerably different. Two gold-bordered blue silks and one gold-bordered white silk are used in this effect.

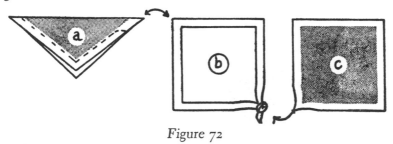

Figure 72

One of the gold-bordered blue silks is folded diagonally in half and sewed together along the dotted line of (a) in Figure 72 to form a pocket in which the white silk can be hidden. The pocket corner of the blue is then tied to one corner of the white.

Another of the doughnut-shaped weights is sewed into the diagonally opposite corner of the white silk as described above for the "Sympathetic Silks" (see Figure 70A). A piece of black thread is tied to the very tip of one corner of the second blue silk and is then led up through the hole in the weight and fastened to the white silk where it is tied to the blue. Figure 72 indicates the arrangement. If the blue silk to which the white is really tied (the one with the pocket) is picked up, the weight will slide down the thread, pulling the white silk from its pocket in the blue, and will slide over the tip of the other blue silk so that the three silks will appear to be tied together just as with the "Sympathetic" effect above.

TO PREPARE FOR PERFORMANCE: The white silk is tucked

into the pocket in the blue and the edge of the blue folded around it. The two blue silks are held by the pocket and threaded corners, the hand holding the pocket silk, hiding the white silk by holding the pocket closed. The thread is long enough so that the two blue silks can be held to appear completely separate.

MISCELLANEOUS ITEMS: A single gold-bordered red silk and a gold-bordered white silk complete the silk requirements. Also a handkerchief "pull" is needed. This last item is merely a metal cup or a cloth bag (with its mouth stiffened with wire) fastened to the end of a piece of strong black elastic

ELASTIC TO BELT

*Figure 73*

cord (see Figure 73). The cord is threaded through the belt loop on the performer's left hip and carried around behind his body, where it is pinned to the right side of the trousers. The length of the elastic is so adjusted that when the cup is held in the left hand in front of the body and then released, it will suddenly fly back out of sight beneath the left side of the coat. One corner of the white silk is fastened inside the cup of the "pull" and the silk and cup (with the elastic in position) are placed in the left trousers pocket.

Two chairs with solid backs (or with a cloth thrown over the backs to make them opaque) are standing one on either side of the magician, their seats pointing to the rear. On the seat of the chair at the magician's right is placed the Flag Silk ready to perform. The pair of red and blue silks is over the back of the left-hand chair.

PRESENTATION: The magician picks up all four of the prepared silks, holding them by the proper corners with his left hand, being careful not to get the dangling threads tangled with each other. He counts the silks for the audience, taking the first red one in his right hand and separating it as far as he can from the other red one. Then the right hand takes the second red one, saying "Two red." The right hand then takes the next silk (blue) and separates the two blues as far as the thread will allow, saying, ". . . and two blue."

The performer asks the audience to "pick a color—red or blue." If the spectators pick blue, the magician says: "Blue for the audience, so I'll use red." If the spectators pick red, he says: "All right, we'll use red." In any case, he hangs the blue pair of silks over the back of the left chair and, showing the red ones once more separated, hangs them over the back of the right-hand chair, with most of the silks, and especially the weighted and threaded corners, hanging to the rear. He takes care to arrange the silks so that he will be able to grasp the proper corner of the weighted one to show the two tied together.

Removing the single red silk from his pocket, he executes the "Vanishing Knot" described on page 102. The performer pretends to take the knot he has just tied in the single red silk and throw it at the two red silks on the chair. Then he lifts the two silks off the chair by picking up only the proper corner of the weighted silk as in Figure 70C and shows that the knot has apparently flown to the two red silks because they appear to be now tied together. He drops the two "tied" red silks together with the single red one onto the seat of the right-hand chair beside the Flag Silk already there.

Throwing knots into the air is one thing, the performer says, but now let's try to throw a whole silk. The performer crosses to show the two blue silks still separated at the left chair. He replaces them, weighted and threaded ends to the rear, making sure to arrange them so that the white silk slides from its hiding place in the blue silk while hidden by the chair back.

Removing the white silk and "pull" from his pocket, the pull hidden by his hand, he stuffs the white silk inside the cup of the "pull" while apparently wadding it between his hands. The hands are held together and in front of the body. As soon as the silk is inside the "pull," it is released to fly back underneath the coat, but the hands still keep wadding as if the silk were still there. Finally, the magician makes a tossing motion toward the blue silks on the chair, and shows that the white silk has vanished. Crossing to the chair, he picks up the blue silk with the corner opposite from the pocket and shows that the white silk is apparently knotted between the two blue. As he raises the blue silk the weight slides down the thread to form the "knot" behind the chair back.

That is not all the wondrous things these silks will do, the magician explains. He walks back toward the right chair and as he goes he unties the blue silk with the pocket from the white. Holding this single blue silk in his left hand, he lowers the blue and white pair to the seat of the chair and drops them, picking up the Flag Silk. Apparently the magician has merely reached down with a blue and white silk in his hand and picked up instead one of the red silks used previously so that he is now apparently holding a red, a white, and a blue silk. The blue silk and the Flag Silk are all held in the left hand in a bunch to aid the illusion of holding only three silks.

Walking forward, the magician says he will rub the red, white, and blue silks together. As he begins to bunch up the silks in his hands, he allows the blue silk to fall to the floor, but is careful not to notice it. Should someone in the audience attempt to point out that the blue silk has dropped, the magician stops him with "Watch," said in a voice that indicates that he does not want to be interrupted.

The magician shakes the Flag Silk, causing the "mis-made" flag to appear. He does not notice that the flag is incomplete, but looks about for applause. (He uses this opportunity to close the snap fastener on the flag.) At last he realizes that the blue is missing. Spotting the blue silk on the floor where he "inadvertently dropped" it, the magician picks it up and tries again.

Under cover of "rubbing the silks together" the magician slips the blue silk (doubled) through the tape loop and executes the second change to the large flag for his colorful finale complete with surprise at the increase in size of the flag and the sucker effect of the dropped blue silk.

NOTE: Neither the foregoing routine nor the tricks suggested earlier in this chapter pretend to be exhaustive or definitive examples of the magic of silk. Rather the material here was selected merely to suggest to the reader the scope and limits of silk tricks and to present some of the various effects and techniques for the reader's contemplation.

When even competent performers are seen to bore an audience with silk magic, it will be realized just how much the ultimate effect depends on the intuitive artistry of the performer's presentation rather than any mystery or beauty inherent in silk tricks themselves. It was felt necessary, however, to include some materials on silk magic since the reader will desire familiarity with all aspects of magic before he can consider himself proficient in the art.

But the reader should not be discouraged. After all, the audience really cares very little if the performer pulls silk handkerchiefs or flowers or anything else out of an empty hat. It is not the object produced but rather the éclat and showmanship of the producer. If the performer could not entertain the audience by producing dirty rags from a hat or causing two pieces of very prosaic string to tie themselves together, he will not be much more successful with brightly colored silks. But, if the performer has that necessary understanding of what makes entertainment, if he can get laughs or mystery from the most unexotic object, then he will find in silk magic a fountain of inspiration and effect.

# IX

## Mental and Spirit Effects

The perennial appeal of the so-called mind reading or spiritualistic variety of performance stems from the same inherent characteristic of human nature that has made soothsaying a good profession since the world began. The interest here completely transcends the limits of conjuring and approaches a truly personal desire on the part of every member of the audience to be able to read minds.

A great mass of heterogeneous effects and devices have been rather indiscriminately categorized under the terms "mental magic" and "mind reading." For the purposes of this discussion, two distinct classifications should be made, on the basis of effect rather than method. Those effects in which the performer himself attempts to "read" the spectator's mind or look into the past or the future are considered as "mental" effects. Those effects in which the "spirits" do the work of figuring out the answer and, in particular, of reproducing or displaying it (that is, effects involving words or objects that have been mysteriously "materialized" by the spirits) are considered as "spirit" tricks.

It should hardly be necessary to point out that every time the performer discovers the identity or whereabouts of a playing card which the audience has selected, it is merely a matter of whim whether he credits his success to sleight of hand or magic or mind reading. Whenever an object mysteriously vanishes from one place or appears in another, it is immaterial whether sleight of hand or magic or the capricious spirits are blamed for the transposition.

Hence the reader must eventually reach the obvious result that, whether a sleight-of-hand performance is being discussed or a spirit medium's occult seance, only the patter and presentation are different; the methods are more or less the same. It is, then, up to the performer whether he desires to present whatever tricks he may know as a conjuror or as a mind reader or spirit medium.

The strong appeal of the mental or spirit presentation, however, indicates that this chapter should be included both to describe those tricks that lend themselves readily to such coloring and also to suggest how other "straight" tricks may be presented in a mental or spirit light.

For the general purpose of acquainting the reader with certain of the mentalistic cliches and terms, as hooks on which to hang his own presentation, it might be well to review momentarily a few of the many scientific and quasi-scientific ideas, arguments, and *non sequiturs*. For further patter material, the reader is referred to the devoutly sincere spiritualistic works of Sir Arthur Conan Doyle and his followers, as well as the works (and publicity releases) of some of the modern mind readers such as Dunninger. The debunking exposés of fake mediums by such men as Houdini and Dunninger are also fruitful sources of ideas for presentation, effects, and methods. The work of Dr. Rhine at Duke University on "extrasensory perception" should not be overlooked as patter material.

Generally speaking, a "mental performer" has two choices. He can present his effects as tricks which *duplicate* the methods of fake spirit mediums or mind readers or he can present them as *actual examples* of spirits at work or of mind reading. Should he choose the latter road, he has always one beautiful "out" to explain the sometimes illogical objects and motions he uses (an "out" used by spirit mediums since time began). That is, the spirits are willing to work only under certain specialized conditions. Or, if the performer is reading minds and misses, the spectator obviously is not "psychic" or cannot concentrate sufficiently.

For the purely practical purpose of organizing effects in his program, the magician might consider the division used in the routine described at the end of this chapter: reading the future is precognition, the present is either telepathy or mind reading, and the past is clairvoyance. Being able to "feel" the same ideas as the spectator in the present may be extrasensory perception (a sixth sense that only some persons have) or it may be mind reading, or the spirits may be "feeling" what the spectator is thinking and leading the performer around.

On the other hand, the performer may be nothing but a go-between and the spirits may do all the work, displaying the results thereof by some mysterious manifestation that forms the climax of the effect. Still a further refinement is for the performer to provide a "medium" (usually his wife!) who is able to read his mind as he moves among his audience.

Whatever presentation the "mental" magician prefers to apply to his tricks, his methods will be virtually the same as his brother, the "magic" magician. It should be remembered, however, that the "magic" magician cannot hope to present, in the midst of his magic, a "mental" routine except in a tongue-in-cheek manner. A performer like Dunninger can convince an audience that he is really reading minds, because that is his major premise. He appears as a mind reader and not as a magician.

The performer who is a conjuror and an admitted fake or charlatan cannot hope to convince his audience that he can read minds or evoke the spirits to do his bidding. Hence the conjuror must present a mental routine completely with tongue in cheek, admittedly as a trick, without relying on the "mentalist's" greatest weapon: that the audience would like to believe that someone can read minds.

## SPIRIT SLATES

First of all the spirit tricks will be considered, within the definition given above.

EFFECT: The spirits write the required information on a previously blank slate. This is the traditional method of getting the spirits to communicate with their earthly brothers (namely, the audience).

REQUIRED: One or two slates are needed of the kind associated with the little red schoolhouse. Also a black cardboard flap which will fit inside the frame of either slate, completely covering the black area of the slate, must be procured. The exploded diagram of Figure 74 shows the slates.

PRESENTATION: ONE WAY: The desired information (whether it be the name of a card, a word, or a number, or what have you as described later) is written on one of the slates. The flap is put in place over the writing.

The magician shows both of the slates perfectly blank on both sides. Naturally, since the flap is hiding the writing on one slate, they both appear completely blank. The two slates are put together with the flap in between, the slate with the writing on top, and laid aside or given to a spectator to hold. The part of the trick wherein the question (the answer to which appears on one of the slates) is asked, the card selected, or the number chosen is then accomplished.

The magician takes the slates and opens them. Gravity alone has pulled the flap from its position covering the writing on the bottom of the top slate and has deposited it un-

Figure 74

noticed against the face of the bottom slate as is suggested by Figure 74. The spirits have apparently written the required information on the previously blank slate in a ghostly hand while the spectator held the slate.

ANOTHER WAY: Only one slate is used. The required information is written on one side of the slate and the flap put in place to cover the writing. The slate is then wrapped in a piece of black cloth just as though the performer always carried it so wrapped to preserve it.

The slate is unwrapped, flap side up and shown to be blank on both sides. It is then laid (flap side down) on the black cloth. Apparently realizing that the audience cannot get a clear view of the slate, the magician immediately picks it up again and stands it against a table leg (writing to the rear), where all can see it at all times. The flap, of course, was left lying unnoticed on the black cloth which is then folded up and discarded with the flap.

A THIRD WAY: Both of the above are combined. Two slates, one of which has writing on it covered with a flap, are wrapped in a black cloth. The written-on slate is first shown and wiped with a handkerchief. It is laid aside flap side down on the black cloth as the other slate is cleaned. The two slates are then put together (minus the flap) with the writing hidden between them and given to a spectator to hold.

A FOURTH WAY: The back of the flap is covered with newspaper and the slate or slates are wrapped in newspaper. The working is exactly as with the black cloth.

There are also several hundred more ways of getting rid of the flap, of using a flap that locks on the opposite slate, and of doing the effect without any flap at all. It is here submitted that, however ingenious these methods may be (and some are very ingenious), they hold little advantage over the methods above outlined, except for an audience of magicians who would not be fooled by the usual devices.

The problem is to get a message written on a slate and then hide it sufficiently for the slate to appear blank until the existence of the message is revealed. As always, the easiest and most straightforward method should be used. What is more straightforward than showing the slates blank on both sides, putting them together, and then showing that the spirits have written a message?

The above discussion will, of course, bring to mind the "Spirit Calling Card" on page 91 wherein a blank calling card was used instead of a slate. As a pocket trick, the calling card effect seems to be stronger because of the usualness of the objects used. Although the usual size of the slates used in spirit effects is around eight by ten inches, there is a set of "Pocket Slates" for sale on the magic market about two by three inches with which many startling effects can be obtained.

## THE MESSAGE

The above discussion, naturally, brings up the question of what to write on the slates. Obviously whatever the spirit message is, it must be "forced" in part or in the whole on the audience. The following discussion will reveal several methods of accomplishing this feat.

## PLAYING CARD FORCES

The theory behind the entire effect, of course, is that the spectator picks a card and the spirits not only divine what card is selected but also write its name on the previously blank slate. The slates are shown to be blank before the card is "selected." Any of the card forces described elsewhere in this volume may be used. Especially recommended in this connection are the forces using prepared cards, simply because they are more straightforward.

In addition, the following are several card forces that lend themselves readily to spirit tricks:

A. The magician's patter slips over from spiritualism into the realm of astrology and numerology as he asks the spectator for any number between ten and twenty. This, says the magician, is the number that is inextricably linked with the spectator's personality. Assuming the spectator's number is fifteen, the magician counts fifteen cards from the top of the deck. Now, he says, as he puts the remainder of the deck aside, he must deal with this number exactly as do the numerologists.

He picks up the counted-off packet of fifteen cards and says, "The number fifteen is made up of a five . . ." and he counts five cards off the fifteen cards he holds, ". . . and a one . . ." and he lays the sixth card aside. The spectator is now asked to take that sixth card as the one indicated by his own numerological pattern. That card is the card the magician wants to force.

The force card is placed tenth from the top of the deck. If the above procedure is followed with any number between ten and twenty, the force card (originally tenth from the top) will always come up.

B. Nine identical cards are grouped in the deck between tenth and twentieth from the top and the spectator asked for a number from ten to twenty. Obviously he will get one of the force cards. Even with the nine stranger cards in place, the deck can be fanned casually for the audience's inspection if the nine cards are not spread too well in the fan.

C. All the cards of one suit (say hearts) are placed in the deck so that every second card of the top twenty-six is a heart. The spectator is asked to name a number. (If his number is over twenty-six, the magician asks for a lower one "to save time in counting.") If he names an even number, he is asked to look at the card that lies at that number. If his number is odd, he is asked to count that number of cards off the deck and look at the next card. In any case, he ends up with a heart.

For this effect the message is written on the slate in the following manner:

```
┌─────────────────┐
│ YOUR CARD       │
│ WAS THE         │
│ OF HEARTS       │
└─────────────────┘
```

The message is covered with the flap and the slate shown to be blank in the usual manner.

It will be seen that the value of the card is omitted from the message. As the magician turns to the table to deposit the deck after the spectator has selected his card, he presses his right thumb down on the sticky side of a short piece of flesh-colored adhesive tape to which has been fastened a tiny piece of chalk or a lump of cornstarch. He picks up the slate (without the flap), holding it message-side to himself with one hand at either end as he asks the spectator to show the audience the card he selected.

Figure 75

As soon as the magician hears which of the hearts was selected, he writes the proper figure in the blank space in the message following the word "THE," using the piece of chalk taped to the end of his thumb as in Figure 75. Since only one figure (or "J," "A," "K," or "Q") need be written, it is quite easily accomplished by moving the right thumb. The piece of tape is discarded at the earliest opportunity.

This method serves to allow the magician to use an absolutely clean-cut selection of the card with an apparently unprepared deck of cards, since the deck may be scrutinized quite closely before it is apparent that there is a heart especially placed as every other card.

## OTHER CARD FORCES

Before the above effects are discarded (as many performers may want to do) on the rather logical grounds that they utilize playing cards and hence are subject to the spectator's suspicion and distrust, the reader should consider the following suggestions:

Any of the tricks in this section that are described for use with playing cards can also be accomplished with a packet of any number of cards bearing any of the following items:

| | | |
|---|---|---|
| numbers | letters | famous people |
| girls' names | boys' names | cities or countries |
| brands of autos | cigarettes | brands of liquor |
| postage stamps | colors | movie stars |

Picture post cards, facsimiles of the auto license plates of all the states, pictures of bathing girls, etc., all leap to mind as substitutes for playing cards for mental effects.

It should be noted that a packet of cards containing any of the above can be made up according to the principles outlined for prepared playing cards in Chapter VI (for example, "Svengali" deck, "Rough-Smooth" deck, etc.). Any of the forces with unprepared playing cards can also be used with such a special deck of picture or word cards. The effect obtained in mental tricks, it is believed, is considerably stronger than a similar effect using regular playing cards, simply because "magician" combined with "playing cards" brings trickery and sleight of hand immediately to the spectator's mind.

## CLIPBOARD FORCES

The effects described in this section can with equal ease be applied to a pad or tablet of paper. Experience has shown, however, that the use of a clipboard enhances both the convenience and the effect. The clipboard, if used, should be handled throughout as though it were merely a convenience for the magician and not an integral part of the trick. Not only should it be used as a writing desk but also as a tray with which to handle the various items needed. It will thus assume no more importance than a pencil in the minds of the spectators. The size is up to the magician and is determined only by the size of the paper he wishes to use.

### 1. *Clipboard Svengali*

In the proper context, this is a very effective force. To achieve that proper context, two circumstances are necessary: first, the performer must use clipboards throughout his "spirit" routine merely as adjuncts to his efforts and, second, the force must be presented in a manner that suggests that it is merely incidental to the really important goings-on.

TO PREPARE: twenty or thirty pieces of paper to fit the clipboard are needed. An eighth of an inch is trimmed off one end of half of the sheets of paper and the force word or number, etc., is written on these pages. Various other random words or numbers are written on the other pages. All the sheets are then put into the clipboard so that every other sheet is a short one. The entire clipboard will then resemble a "Svengali" deck as described on page 189 and the working is the same as for that deck. As the magician riffles through the pages (which he has first shown to contain different words) the spectator stops him. Because of the short pages, the spectator will always stop on a force word or number.

## 2. *Clipboard Addition*

The essence of this effect has long been a concomitant of spirit or mental magic. Many performers utilize the same idea as here suggested with pads of paper, blank cards, and the like. Mr. Al Baker has applied the idea to a slate with a locking flap.

EFFECT: Each of several spectators writes a four-digit number on a piece of paper. The column of numbers is totaled by another spectator. The spirits are seen to have been faster at the addition, however, because they have already written the total of the freely selected figures on a previously blank slate.

Although the method can be presented as though the magician were predicting the total that the spectators would eventually get or as though he were reading the spectator's mind, the strongest presentation seems to be as here described. The necessary "switching" of the selected numbers can be accomplished with greater ease (or at least with greater confidence) if the performer's control over the clipboards is not impeded by the fact that he is not supposed to see the figures. With the spirit presentation, the spirits do the work so it is immaterial whether the performer sees the figures as they are written or not.

PREPARATION: The paper used should be heavy enough so that writing will not show through it. It is suggested that a large clipboard be used and that the writing be done with a black crayon so that all present may see the figures clearly (or apparently are able to).

Several sheets of paper are placed under the clip of the clipboard. The bottom of the top sheet is folded upward until it touches the clip at the top as in Figure 76A. The sheet is creased so that it will lie flat. With the top sheet (X) thus folded, another sheet of paper (Y in Figure 76A) is pasted to the folded part of the top sheet and also to the exposed part of the second sheet. When the paste has dried, the top

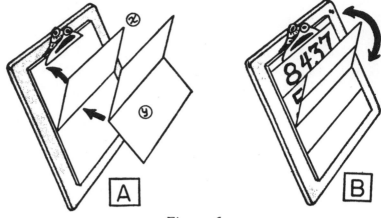

Figure 76

sheet is folded back downward until it lies flat, thus folding the top half of the pasted-on sheet downward onto itself. The fraction of an inch of the pasted-on sheet that protrudes from the bottom is carefully trimmed off.

The clipboard will now resemble Figure 76B. There is a flap of paper that can be folded upward or downward, thus completely changing the top sheet of the pad.

The flap is folded down and four horizontal lines are drawn on the exposed sheet, one of which coincides exactly with the crease of the flap and hides it. If crayon is used, one stroke will give a line wide enough to hide the crease. The top line is drawn so that it coincides exactly with the top edge of the flap when the flap is up.

Four varied four-digit numbers are then written (in different handwritings and different sizes) in the four spaces thus formed. The four numbers are then added up and it is their total that is written on a slate and covered with the flap of the slate to be later "materialized."

The clipboard flap is then folded to the up position so that the numbers are completely hidden. Four horizontal lines are now drawn across the exposed sheet. Once again one line coincides with the crease of the flap and the top line coincides with and hides the top edge of the flap. The paper on the clipboard is slid toward the top just enough so that the least bit of the top edge of the flap can be caught under the clip of the clipboard, thus locking the flap into the up position. The complete clipboard is shown in Figure 76B.

As many other sheets of paper as the performer intends to use in connection with the clipboard before getting to the addition trick may now be placed on top of the prepared sheet, if desired.

PRESENTATION: With flap locked in the up position, the clipboard is held in front of a spectator and the magician hands him a piece of crayon, requesting that he write any four-digit number in the top space. This is repeated with three other spectators.

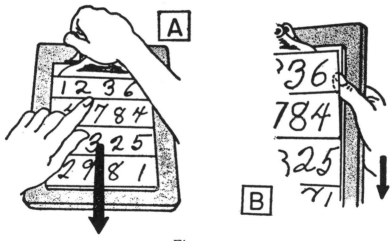

Figure 77

When all four numbers have been written, the magician stands in front of the audience holding the clipboard horizontally with his right hand at the top pushing the bottom of the board against his stomach. He runs his left finger down the list of numbers as if counting them, remarking to the audience that four numbers have been written. During this motion, the heel of the right hand presses the clip so that the left hand can slide the sheet downward enough to free the top edge of the flap from the clip as in Figure 77A.

The magician then raises the clipboard so that he holds it vertically with the paper toward and almost touching his body, one hand on each side with the fingers in front and the thumbs to the rear. Looking around the audience, he says that he now needs someone who can add. As he peers about over the clipboard seeking such an educated soul, he slides his right thumb downward along the side of the clipboard, carrying the flap with it into the down position (as in Figure 77B) so that the numbers written by the spectators are hidden and those written by the magician are exposed. He then gestures with the clipboard in his right hand as part of the same movement.

Handing another clipboard, a card, or pad of paper to the spectator who volunteers to do the addition, the magician holds the numbers in front of him so that he can add them and write the total on the other card or pad. The magician's thumb keeps the flap in the down position. The adding spectator is, of course, chosen so that he is sitting where none of the spectators who volunteered numbers can see the numbers he is adding. Naturally his total is the one previously written by the magician on the slate.

The clipboard is now discarded as the message on the slate is shown, the performer explaining that the spirits are faster with their addition than was the spectator.

## MENTAL EFFECTS

Following the classification mentioned at the beginning of this chapter, tricks in which the performer attempts to read the spectator's mind without the aid of the spirits will be considered here.

Obviously, any of the methods of forcing the spectator to select any given item suggested above may, of course, be presented as mind reading instead of as a spirit effect. The spectator is requested to concentrate on his selection while the magician gets an "impression" of his thoughts bit by bit. Many of the card effects (presented either with playing cards or with some other variety of cards as discussed above) may also be used.

The main limiting factor is the necessity of making it completely self-evident that the magician cannot gain his information except by mind reading.

In addition to forces and card tricks, there are many methods for the performer to discover the spectator's thoughts. A description of a representative selection follows.

## BILLETS

The use of "billets" or small pieces of paper on which the spectator writes his "question" or the word or item of which he is thinking has long been a standard item of both spirit mediums and mental performers. The spectator is induced to write his thoughts on a slip of paper with the excuse that it will be easier for him to concentrate, that writing the thought will insure everyone's knowing if the performer is correct in his mind reading, that each spectator should write a thought and the performer will read the minds of a selected few, etc.

Once the information is written by the spectator, the performer must somehow or other gain possession of the slip of paper.

### 1. Billet Switches

The most obvious (though not necessarily the easiest) way of gaining possession of the written information is for the performer to take the folded billet and, by means of sleight of hand, secretly exchange it for a blank piece of paper, which he burns in order to read the spectator's mind by looking into the ashes.

Moves and devices to accomplish such a secret exchange have been worked out in great profusion, some of which are both ingenious and effective, but all of which take the masterly showmanship that comes only from years of experience. It is indeed a daring performer who will attempt the usual mind-reading routine after the manner of a Dunninger or an accomplished spirit medium.

There is, however, one effective impromptu method to gain possession of the spectator's written information. The spectator is given a small piece of paper (two by three inches) with a penciled oval encircling the center portion. The spectator is asked to write a word or number (something short) inside the "magic circle" and then to fold the paper in quarters, writing inside.

The magician takes the quarter-folded slip and holds it in his right hand with the open edges to the left, the folded edges to the right. He tears the folded slip (without unfolding it) once down the center, putting the left-hand pieces in front. He tears it again in the other direction down the center, once more placing the left-hand pieces in front. The right hand is now holding a packet of torn pieces about one-half inch square.

All these pieces are apparently dropped into an ash tray and burned while the performer "reads" the spectator's thoughts by staring into the flames. Actually, however, the performer retains with his thumb the piece nearest his body when dropping the torn bits into the ash tray. This piece, it will be found, is the entire center of the original slip folded in quarters. While looking into the flames, the magician opens this piece secretly under the table or while making notes on the pad of paper and simply reads what the spectator has written. Figure 78 should make this clear. The piece marked X is the folded center portion.

## 2. One Ahead

One application of the "one ahead" system has already been discussed in "Four Told" on page 215. As far as the mind-reading performer goes, however, this is perhaps one of the easiest devices available.

In essence, the performer collects a series of folded slips of paper on which the spectators have written their thoughts. The contents of one of these slips the performer must know,

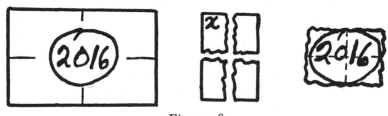

Figure 78

either by having a confederate or by some other of the methods discussed in this section. Tossing all the slips in a hat, the performer requests each person to concentrate on whatever he wrote.

The performer reaches into the hat and removes any folded slip, which he holds to his forehead. He says that he gets the impression of whatever it was that is written on the known slip, and asks if one of the spectators was thinking of that. In announcing his "impression," the performer is, of course, careful not to use the same words as are written on the slip. For instance, if "Cary Grant" were written on the known slip, the performer would first get the impression of a man, then a performer of some sort, then an actor, then a name like Grand or Gant and finally Grant. "Was it Cary Grant?"

Opening the slip he is holding, the performer "confirms" his announcement. Actually he merely reads whatever is written on that slip and is thus able to get an "impression" of the next slip. After announcing his second impression, he looks at the second slip to "confirm" it and gains the information needed for the third "impression." The known slip, of course, is the last removed from the hat, the performer pretending that it bore the message actually written on the next-to-last slip.

### 3. Impressions

One very direct way of gaining knowledge of what a spectator has written on a slip of paper that the spectator continues to keep in his own possession is by the use of carbon paper impressions. A piece of soft carbon paper introduced under the second sheet of a pad of paper on which the spectator writes will pick up an impression of his writing which the performer can read at leisure while apparently making notes upon the pad in the process of reading the spectator's thoughts.

A number of devices are on the market with which to pick up such carbon impressions of the spectator's writing. Notable among them is a small prepared clipboard, which is handed to the spectator with but one sheet of paper on it. Nonetheless the clipboard will later deliver to the magician's hand an impression of whatever the spectator wrote. Similar ideas have been used in the covers of books and card boxes, handed to the spectator to support the paper on which he is writing.

The use of such devices must be managed with some care. The spectator should always be provided with a very hard pencil so he has to bear down firmly. And it should be remembered that it is easy to arouse in the spectator the suspicion that some such device is being used.

## LIMITED CHOICE

This is perhaps the most intriguing of the many devices used in mental tricks. The basis of the idea is to limit the spectator's choice to a relatively few items while still making it appear that his choice is almost unlimited.

Actually, of course, when a spectator is asked to think of any card in the deck or any of the popular makes of automobiles, any of the headlines on one page of a newspaper, etc., his choice is really limited to a relatively few possibilities as compared with asking him to concentrate on any name or any word or any number. At the same time this limitation is not immediately obvious, as is asking for a number between one and ten, simply because the limitation on his thinking is implied rather than expressed.

The device becomes more obviously useful, however, when the spectator's choice is even more limited. Thus, in the third of the "Playing Card Forces" above, the spectator's choice was limited without his knowledge to one of the thirteen hearts instead of to any of the cards in the deck. In "Book Test" below, the spectator can choose only one of forty-six possibilities although it appears that he has a choice of any one of five hundred. In the "Color Deck" part of the spirit routine outlined at the end of this chapter the spectator is given a choice of six colored cards although the impression that he will carry away with him is that he was asked to "think of any color."

### Pocket Index

This useful device is of particular importance in connection with the limited choice idea. First the performer arranges matters so that the spectator's choice must be limited to one of a relatively few objects. Then the performer arranges some way that he can produce the correct answer no matter which one of the possible choices the spectator makes.

The pocket index is the answer to the second half of the performer's problem. The device is nothing but a means whereby the performer can have in his pocket a large number of slips of paper, each, for example, with the name of a card on it. The problem of the index is to keep the papers separated and in order so that the proper one can be instantly found and withdrawn.

Thus, the spectator is asked to name any one of the cards in the deck out of thin air, so to speak. No matter which card the spectator chooses, the performer is set to come up instantly with a slip of paper with the name of that card written on it. The ruse succeeds for the simple reason that the spectators understandably feel that it is difficult if not impossible to have fifty-two slips of paper handy in a pocket and then find the right one without the audience seeing the search.

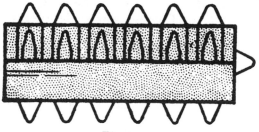

Figure 79

One answer to the problem is illustrated diagrammatically in Figure 79, although there are several other variations on the magic market and in magic literature. The device shown is nothing but a strip of heavy cardboard or light wood on each side of which are fastened six very small wire paper clips. The clips are glued or stapled six to each side of the strip, their business ends protruding slightly over opposite edges of the strip. The inside ends of the clips are then covered with narrower strips of cardboard glued into place to help hold the clips more firmly in position. A thirteenth clip is fastened to protrude from one end.

Two such devices will contain, then, twenty-six paper clips. The name of each of the fifty-two cards of the deck is written on a slip of paper about two by three inches in size and the papers are folded in quarters. Two slips of paper are then stuck in each clip of the index—all the red cards in one index and all the black cards in the other. The papers are arranged in order around the index.

Thus, considering the index as it is shown in Figure 79, the slips bearing the names of the spades and the clubs from ace to six are placed in the clips at the top side in the drawing, the ace of spades and ace of clubs in the first clip, the deuce of spades and deuce of clubs slips in the second, etc. The two "seven" slips go in the end clip and the rest, two by two, in the bottom clips. A short piece of sewing needle is forced into the top cardboard strip to form a bump that the fingers can feel to tell which side of the index is which.

This index fully loaded with slips is placed in the right trousers pocket and one similarly loaded with the red cards is in the left. If the performer wants the five of clubs, for example, he reaches into the proper pocket and, by feeling for the needle bump and the end of the index that has no clip protruding from it, knows in what position the index is lying in his pocket. He then counts around it until he comes to the clip with the two "five" slips of paper. He knows that he put the slips in the index with the clubs next to his body and the spades toward the outside. So he removes both slips from the fifth clip, drops the "spades" slip in his pocket and brings forth the slip he knows bears the name of the five of clubs.

PRESENTATION: Obviously the performer is not going to use the device just to pull the proper slip from his pocket after the spectator has called out a card. The usual presentation is as follows.

The performer asks a spectator to think of any card in the deck. With much frowning and effort, the performer "reads" the spectator's mind. The performer, however, does not immediately announce his impression. Rather he writes it down on a slip of paper which he folds and, holding it at his finger tips, pretends to drop into an upturned hat. Actually he draws the folded paper back into his hand under cover of the pretended dropping movement as indicated by Figure 80A and B.

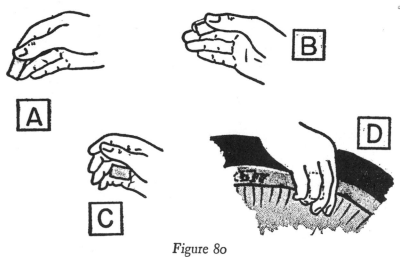

Figure 80

If he were to announce his impression of the spectator's thought, the magician says, the spectator might try to betray him by denying that he was right. This way there can be no doubt. The magician has written his impression and put it in the hat. The spectator will now announce his choice of card and the audience will then see what the magician has written.

As soon as the spectator announces his card, the magician selects the proper slip from the index in his trousers pocket. He holds it at the bend of his third finger as in Figure 80C and secretly drops it into the hat as he picks up the hat as in Figure 80D. He hands the hat to the spectator to remove the slip, which all believe has been there since before the spectator announced his choice.

It is obvious that this same index idea can be applied to any subject matter so long as the spectator's choice can be limited to some convenient number of possibilities (certainly not many more than fifty and preferably less). Thus the index device could be used with the "Book Test" given below instead of the presentation described here, or for an effect involving various colors, brands of cigarettes, and the like, all in the same general manner.

The performer covers his search for the proper slip by chatting with the spectators, recapitulating what has happened, etc., while his hand rests casually in his trousers pocket. It should be noted, however, that the wise performer will arrange matters so that there is something important going on (such as the next step in the mental routine) between the time that the spectator announces his choice and the time the slip of paper must be shown. Thus, not only will the performer have plenty of time to procure the proper slip, but the audience will have something else to look at while he is feeling his way around the index in his pocket.

The same index idea can, of course, be used as a demonstration of the performer's power to predict the thoughts of the spectator as well as to read them by simply writing his "prediction" before the choice is made. Otherwise the presentation would be the same.

## BOOK TEST

The multiplicity of book tests that have been devised by magical inventors makes any consideration of this type of effect very difficult within a short space. The universal effect is that the spectator apparently selects any page of a book and any word on that page and yet the magician is able either to predict or to discover by "mental telepathy" what word the spectator selected.

By far the greatest number of such effects depend on the use of a stacked or prepared deck of cards, dice, or some other counters with which the spectator "freely" selects the page. It is believed that such methods greatly diminish the value of the effect. After all, the idea is that the spectator is picking any word in the book on which to concentrate for a demonstration of the performer's mentalistic powers. The use of cards, etc., to select that page (actually to force it) seems to emphasize the existence of the control the performer must exercise over the "free choice."

Another large category of book tests utilizes two identical books with different covers. One is handed to the spectator with the request that he choose any page. Under the guise of demonstrating just how the spectator is to open his book and select his word, the magician simply opens his own book and finds the word almost as soon as the spectator does. Variations of this idea have included using a regular and a pocket-sized edition of the same book (with a different cover) so as to eliminate the possibility of the books resembling each other.

A further refinement is to use a book such as a large city telephone directory. The spectator thrusts a playing card into the telephone book at any spot. The book is then opened apparently at the page marked by the card and a name is thought of. A duplicate card is placed in the book beforehand and it is to this card that the book is opened. By utilizing a page in the directory on which all the names are the same (but a name not quite as obvious as Smith or Jones) the spectator can then be allowed to select any name on the page in a completely random fashion. The rest of the audience, of course, is ignorant of the fact that all the names on that page are the same. A similar effect has been used for some time by Dunninger and was recently much improved by Dr. F. V. Taylor.

Some day the author hopes to find a book in which the same word appears at the same position on every page (a book of poems by a poet-magician was once printed in this fashion but is now unavailable) but until that happy day arrives, the following book test is recommended.

### 500 Unlimited

EFFECT: One of three books is selected. Then each of three spectators calls out a number and the three numbers are combined to give a page number. The spectator looks at a word on that page and the performer succeeds in reading his mind.

PREPARATION: Three books and a clipboard or pad of paper are needed. The books should be of different sizes. One of them must have a little over five hundred pages.

On the top sheet of the pad or clipboard (or on a piece of paper that will be pasted inside the cover of one of the books) the performer writes (or types) the first word (or the first line or the main idea of the first sentence) that appears on the following forty-six pages of the 500-page book:

| | | | | | |
|---|---|---|---|---|---|
| 234 | 247 | 268 | 348 | 369 | 467 |
| 235 | 248 | 269 | 349 | 378 | 468 |
| 236 | 249 | 278 | 356 | 379 | 469 |
| 237 | 256 | 279 | 357 | 389 | 478 |
| 238 | 257 | 289 | 358 | 456 | 479 |
| 239 | 258 | 345 | 359 | 457 | 489 |
| 245 | 259 | 346 | 367 | 458 | |
| 246 | 267 | 347 | 368 | 459 | |

With the three books on his table and the above list of words handy, the performer is ready for his miracle.

PRESENTATION: First of all, the performer must force the spectator to select the 500-page book from among the three books. To accomplish this, he offers the three books to the spectator in a sort of fan with the 500-page book in the middle, saying that he wants to "eliminate a couple of these books." Would the spectator point to two, please?

If the spectator points to the two outside books, the magician "eliminates" these two by laying them aside and hands the spectator the 500 book. If, on the other hand, the spectator points to the 500 book and one other one, the magician lays the *third book* aside then asks the spectator to point to one of the remaining two. If the spectator points to the 500 book, the magician hands it to him, saying "You want that one?" If, on the other hand, the spectator points to the remaining indifferent book, the magician lays it aside, saying, "All right, we'll eliminate that one too," and hands the 500 book to the spectator.

Now, says the performer, he wants to have one page of that book selected, but selected in such a way that as many persons as possible participate in the selection so as to insure that it is free, fair, and without the possibility of the spectator's being a confederate. To that end the performer will ask three persons at random to call out numbers and then the numbers will be put together to form a page number.

Of course, he admits, using a three-digit number will eliminate all pages less than one hundred. Even so, there still remain—he asks the spectator how many pages there are in the book—four-hundred-some-odd, which ought to be enough to eliminate any chance of coincidence.

Now the performer points to some spectator at random and says the following, almost verbatim: "Will you please give me a number—just one digit—the first number between one and ten that pops into your head. Don't think! Just call out the first number between one and ten that you think of!" The spectator will not say anything until the performer finishes talking. This part of the presentation should be executed in rather breathless haste as if it were really important that the spectators call out the first number that comes into their heads. "And now you, sir," pointing to another spectator, "quickly give me another number between one and ten."

If either of these two spectators have called out *two, three,* or *four,* the performer goes on to a third spectator in the same way, demanding "another number between one and ten—the first one that pops into your head." If, on the other hand, neither of the first two spectators calls out two, three, or four, the performer says to the third spectator: "Since there are only five hundred pages, we need a low number for the first digit. Will you give me a number between one and five?"

The performer then takes the numbers that have been called out and repeats them, *arranging them in ascending order.* Thus, if the spectators called out eight, two, and six, in that order, the magician would say: "Two, six, and eight have been selected. Would you, sir [to the spectator holding the book] look at page 268 and concentrate on the first word [or the first line or sentence] on that page?"

If the above presentation is followed, it will be seen that the magician has limited the spectators to a choice of only the forty-six pages listed above. By asking for a *number,* the magician has eliminated all page numbers containing zero. By asking hurriedly for a number *between* one and ten (instead of "from one to ten") he has eliminated all page numbers containing the digit one. By asking each spectator for *another* number, he has eliminated all page numbers with repeating digits (such as 332 or 252). And finally, by arranging the given digits into *ascending* order, he has cut the possibilities down from five hundred to the described forty-six, although apparently any one of the five hundred pages might have been chosen.

The magician pauses to recapitulate what has happened: how the spectator selected one of several books, how three other members of the audience called out numbers that formed the page number; and how the spectator is now concentrating on just one word (or one line or one sentence) in the entire book of five hundred pages. He then picks up the pad (or whatever item he has the list of words written on) and starts concentrating, making numerous notes on the pad while he finds the proper word in the list. Apparently he is having trouble getting an impression of the spectator's thoughts.

Finally he discards the pad in disgust and gradually discloses the word. (If the spectator is concentrating on a whole line or sentence, the magician is careful only to disclose the sense or principal thought of the sentence or line and then ask the spectator to read the line for confirmation.)

If the magician chooses, he can have the forty-six words written on individual slips of paper in a pocket index as described above and present the effect in that way as either a prediction or a mind-reading demonstration.

NOTE: 1. If one of the number-calling spectators calls a wrong number—that is, one that has already been called, or a zero—the performer merely repeats his demands in a voice that indicates polite condescension toward the spectator's apparent stupidity. The spectator will quickly correct himself without any suspicions being aroused because the audience does not yet know how the performer is going to use the numbers to decide on the proper page.

2. If the performer finds it more convenient he can further reduce the range of possibilities from forty-six to thirty-one by eliminating all page numbers containing the digit *nine*. To accomplish this, he asks each spectator for a number "between one and nine" instead of "between one and ten." This demand sounds fair enough, and in the haste of the moment the spectators will rarely call out the number nine since it has apparently been eliminated by the performer's request. Such a procedure is not recommended unless it is absolutely

necessary to use the smaller list of words because, if a spectator does accidentally call out nine, the performer has no "out" to correct the situation.

## TWO-IN-ONE ROUTINE

The following routine attempts to take the best features of the foregoing effects and to organize them in a simple combination that should fill the reader's requirements for spirit and mental tricks. The effect of the routine (as disclosed in the outline below) is predicated on the simple device of having first the spirits look into the past, present, and future and then having the magician himself demonstrate his own ability to "read" the past, present, and future.

### Outline of Effect and Methods

#### PART I. "THE SPIRITS"

*Past:* "Your Wife's Hair": limited choice plus index idea.
*Present:* "Clipboard Addition": described above, page 283.
*Future:* "Color Prediction": free but limited choice.
Spirit writing materializes on a blank slate.

#### PART II. "MIND READING"

*Past:* "Subconscious Memory": one-ahead system.
*Present:* "500 Unlimited": as described above.
*Future:* "Pretty Name": a picture card force with a prepared deck.

#### LIST OF ITEMS REQUIRED (in the order used)

1. One or two spirit slates with flap (and wrapper if used).
2. Clipboard prepared for "Clipboard Addition."
3. Blank five-by-seven-inch card.
4. Pencil or crayon.
5. Two special "Color Decks" as described below.
6. Three books for "500 Unlimited."

7. List of words for "500 Unlimited" (on clipboard).

8. One special "Pretty Name Deck" as described below.

9. Blank sheets of paper for clipboard.

## Preparation of Items as Listed

As with other effects in this book, the preparation may seem tedious; most of it, however, is necessary only once, no matter how many times the routine is performed.

1. A slate (or slates, depending on which of the several methods given at the beginning of this chapter the performer decides to use) and a flap to fit it are required. Also, a cloth or newspaper wrapper is needed if the performer so desires. "LOOK TO THE FUTURE" is written in chalk on the slate and covered with the flap.

2. A clipboard is prepared for "Clipboard Addition" as described under that effect on page 283.

3. The two special "Color Decks" are made as follows: Forty-eight cards (three by five inches is a sufficient size although five by seven inches will probably be found more convenient for a larger audience) are colored on one side only, eight in each of these colors: red, orange, yellow, green, blue, purple.

Four cards of each color are coated on their *faces* (colored sides) with roughing fluid as described under "Rough-Smooth Deck" on page 186. The other twenty-four cards have lettered on their *backs* (white sides) the total which will result when the figures written on the clipboard (for "Clipboard Addition") are added. Also these same twenty-four cards have lettered on their backs (in addition to the clipboard total) the color of a girl's hair as follows: one card of each color is lettered with the word "BLONDE," one of each color with "REDHEAD," one of each color with "BRU-NETTE," and one of each color with "BROWNETTE." These twenty-four lettered cards then have their *backs* (lettered side) covered with roughing fluid.

Two decks of cards are now made up from the forty-eight cards as follows: Deck One consists of twelve unlettered cards (two of each color), the six "BLONDE" cards, and the six "BRUNETTE" cards. Deck Two consists of the other twelve unlettered cards (two of each color), the six "REDHEAD" cards, and the six "BROWNETTE" cards.

The cards are arranged in each deck with the lettered and the unlettered cards alternating, an unlettered card on top and a lettered one on the face. The colors are not arranged in any special order, but the magician is careful to make sure that he knows which cards are lettered with which hair color. Thus, the *first* red, blue, green, etc., card from the top of Deck One should be the "BLONDE" cards, whereas the *second* red, blue, green, etc., card from the top of the same deck should be the "BRUNETTE," and so on. The unlet-

**CARDS STICK TOGETHER IN PAIRS IN FAN**

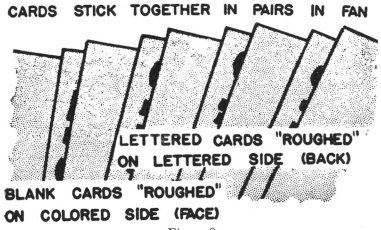

LETTERED CARDS "ROUGHED"
ON LETTERED SIDE (BACK)

**BLANK CARDS "ROUGHED"
ON COLORED SIDE (FACE)**

Figure 81

tered cards should not be paired with lettered cards of the same color. Once the decks are assembled, the *backs* of the unlettered cards and the *faces* (colored sides) of the *lettered cards* should be powdered with zinc stearate powder (see Figure 81.)

It will be apparent that the reader now has two decks of the rough-smooth idea as described on page 186. If either deck is fanned, it will appear to be made up of cards with colored faces and plain white backs. If, however, any of the exposed colored cards is removed, it will bear, lettered on its back, the color of a girl's hair and the total to be arrived at in the "Clipboard Addition."

4. The three books required are of different sizes with one containing a little over five hundred pages as indicated in the description of "500 Unlimited" above.

5. The list of the forty-six words needed for "500 Unlimited" (see page 297) is typed or written on one of the sheets of paper that fits the clipboard and is placed in the clipboard, the second sheet below the prepared flap sheet used in the addition trick.

6. The "Pretty Name" deck is merely a pack of about thirty cards of any size, each bearing a different girl's picture. The pictures should not be of any real person. Magazine advertisements are the best source for such pictures. Each picture is lettered somewhere on its face with a girl's name. One half of the pictures (although all of different girls) bear the same name—for example, "Jeanette"—whereas the other half of the pictures each bears a different girl's name. The names are not lettered in the same spot on every picture but take their location from the pose the girl assumes in the picture. Care must be taken to place the names so that when the deck is fanned to show the girls' faces most of the names are hidden from view in the fan. (For example, many of the names are lettered in the lower right-hand corner.)

The deck is arranged with the "JEANETTE" pictures alternating with the differently named pictures, a "JEANETTE" picture on top, an indifferent picture second, another "JEANETTE" third, and so forth.

7. Several blank sheets of paper are added to the clipboard under the word list for "500 Unlimited." From the top down

the clipboard is set: prepared flap sheet for "Addition," blank sheet, word list for the book test, five or six blank sheets.

## Presentation of the Routine

PART ONE—THE SPIRIT ROUTINE: The magician explains the confusion that rests in the minds of so many persons about mental and spirit magic. The spirits, he says, are very phenomenal sprites. Without any help from the performer, they can look into the past, present, and future. Mind reading, however, is something else again since with that art, the performer does all the work. The magician will try to give a demonstration of each variety of these psychic phenomena.

Although the spirits are very capricious fellows whom the performer is not sure he can completely control, he will try to get them to demonstrate for the audience their ability to see the past, present, and future. Afterward the performer himself will try his hand at seeing beyond the reality of this world. But first, the spirits.

The performer explains that he has concocted a number of test demonstrations for the spirits. He will ask them questions regarding the past, present, and future, and the spirits will answer. Of course, the spirits find it difficult to communicate with human beings. The performer has, however, usually been able to get the spirits to communicate with him by writing on a slate.

He shows the slate (or slates), with flap in place, to be perfectly blank. He then lays it aside (or puts the two together), disposing of the flap in any of the ways listed under "Spirit Slates" on page 275. The spirits, he explains, will write all the answers to the questions on the slate—if, that is, he can get them to work for him now. Since the performer is not an adept spirit medium, he must work within very narrow limits, using nothing but very common objects in order to contact the spirits at all.

First of all, to propound a question relative to the past for the spirits to answer, the performer asks a gentleman in the audience if he remembers the first girl with whom he ever had a date. Does he remember the color of her hair? Was she a blonde, brunette, redhead, or brownette? Very well, that will be the question for the past. The performer speaks very casually and jokingly about the gentleman's first date, asking him if the girl's hair is still that color or did he marry the girl, etc., giving the impression that the conversation is merely for entertainment rather than to find out information. When the spectator tells the color of the girl's hair, the magician asks the entire audience to remember that for future reference.

Picking up the clipboard, the magician proceeds to perform "Clipboard Addition" exactly as described above (page 283) as the test for the spirits' ability to read the present, pointing out (after the addition) that this test is especially appropriate since no one knows until the final addition just what the proper answer is and thus the spirits have not only to see the present but also to add up the figures all by themselves. The blank five-by-seven card is given to the adding spectator on which to write the total and is then stood near the slate so all can see the total.

There only remains the future, says the magician. He picks out a spectator for the future test and asks him to stand. Then he goes to the slate and, handling it very gingerly with just two fingers to obviate the possibility that he is accomplishing any magical duplicity, he turns it over so that the writing is upside-down and flashes it briefly to the audience— just enough so that the spectators can see that something is on the slate but not enough so that they can see *what* is written. He replaces the slate so the writing cannot be seen.

So far the spirits are with us, says the performer. Presumably they have written the past, present, and future answers down already. However, so as not to spoil the demonstration by showing the "future" spectator what has been predicted for him, the performer will not show what has been written until later.

Picking up one of the two "Color Decks" which have been lying on his table out of sight behind some object, the performer fans the deck toward the spectator. The spectator is asked to call out his favorite of the six colors shown. The performer removes the card of whatever color is called (being careful not to show its lettered back) and stands it alongside the card bearing the addition total beside the slate. After the card has been removed from the deck, the magician turns the fan around, showing the white backs of the cards, and remarking that these are just some blank cards colored on one side to help the spectator pick his favorite color quickly, thereby emphasizing (and allowing the audience to see and digest) the fact that the cards all appear to have blank backs.

It should be apparent that the magician picked up the proper deck and removed the proper card *so that the colored card now standing beside the slate bears on its back not only the total from the addition but the proper color of the girl's hair mentioned by the first (the "past") spectator.* Thus if the first spectator had said his first date was a blonde, the magician would have picked up the deck containing the "BLONDE" cards for the "future" spectator's choice. If the "future" spectator had chosen blue as his favorite color, the magician would have removed the blue card which had "BLONDE" on it from the deck, leaving the blue card with "BRUNETTE" on it in the deck.

Now, announces the magician, he will see if the spirits have been with him. Theoretically, he says, the slate should tell the color of the girl's hair, the total of the addition, and the color selected by the third spectator. Very dramatically he turns the slate so that the audience can see it (but does not look at it himself). "There!" he says in a voice implying supreme confidence.

Only when the audience does not break into spontaneous

applause does the magician look at the slate. He is disappointed that the spirits have let him down, but they will have their little jokes, he explains. The only solution is to follow their advice and look to the future.

The magician turns the colored card around, showing the two answers lettered on its back. Obviously the spirits were just being obtuse, he decides, since they answered on the card instead of on the slate. But they did get the answers to the past and the present tests and they wrote them on the back of the "future" card, thereby predicting which of all the otherwise blank colored cards the "future" spectator would pick!

PART TWO—MIND READING: The performer will now let the spirits go their spritely way and attempt to look into the past, present, and future himself, unaided by any departed souls.

Once again, however, the performer must emphasize that he is able to demonstrate his power only within certain narrow limits. Although he hopes some day to improve, he is now unable to read everything in the past, present, and future but must limit himself to certain common objects, etc.

Picking up the clipboard, he tears off the prepared flap sheet used in the addition trick, crumples it up and tosses it aside (where the audience cannot reach it). He approaches one of the spectators for his "past" test.

It is very difficult, the performer points out, to read a spectator's mind with regard to something in the past. Anything that the spectator is thinking of is, of course, a "present" reading. For this reason the magician has developed a test that may seem rather astounding. He asks the spectator if he has a dollar bill in his pocket. When the spectator acquired this dollar bill, his subconscious mind looked at it and remembered certain details about it that even the spectator himself cannot now recall to mind. It is the spectator's subconscious memory, then, that the performer will read for the past test.

Asking the spectator to remove the dollar bill from his pocket without looking at it (just to make sure that he had a dollar and, if not, the performer moves on to a spectator who does have), the performer writes something on the top sheet of the clipboard, folds it in quarters, and places it aside in view of the audience. He explains that he will do the three tests and then at the finale, all the answers will be checked. He leaves the "past" spectator holding his bill, asking him not to put it away.

Actually what the performer wrote on the top sheet of the clipboard was the word "JEANETTE." He folded it so that no one could see what was written and laid it aside.

Momentarily laying aside his clipboard, he picks up the three books used for "500 Unlimited." Now for the present, he says. In order for the thought he is to read to be really in the present, it must be something that the spectator discovers right now. The magician then performs "500 Unlimited" exactly as described above (at page 297). After the spectator has found his word and is concentrating on it, the magician starts to write his "impression" on the clipboard, really looking up the proper word on the list on the board. As soon as he has found the word, he tears the list off the board, crumples it up and tosses it aside as if he had made a mistake. He then writes the proper word on the next sheet, tears it off the board and places it folded along with the first answer.

Telling the spectator to keep his finger on the word, but not to announce it (because the audience may have heard of the "one-ahead" system and think that the performer is using it with the book test), the magician picks a third spectator to act for the future.

Suddenly—as if he had just thought of something he had forgotten—the performer turns to the first spectator and takes his dollar from him, saying he will put the dollar over with the answers "just to keep everything straight." He lays the

bill on the clipboard and asks the spectator to write his initials on it so all will know there was no secret exchange of
the bill. After it is marked, the performer takes the bill and
lays it with the first two folded sheets. Thus, he says, will all
chance of betrayal or confederacy by the spectator be ob-
viated.

As the spectator is initialing the bill, the performer memorizes the serial number on it. This is quite easy. There are
eight digits to the serial number of a dollar bill, preceded
and followed by a letter. The number will be readily memorized and retained for the few seconds necessary if the performer splits the number up, remembering it as if it were two
telephone numbers. Thus, if the number on the bill were
B 17654018 C, the performer would read it to himself as he
handles the bill, Bryant 1765 and then Caledonia 4018. As
soon as he has laid the bill with the two answer sheets, he
writes the serial number he had just memorized on the new
top sheet of the clipboard before he forgets it as if continuing
with the future test. This is why an eight-letter name is used
for the "future" force instead of a shorter one.

Turning to look at the "future" spectator, the performer
apparently decides to change his mind about the prediction
he is writing. He tears the top sheet off the clipboard and
throws it away. After studying the spectator a moment, he
writes the same number again, tears off the top sheet and
places it folded with the other two. This is simply to emphasize that it is the prediction he is writing and not something
to do with the bill.

He has just made a prediction for the third spectator, the
performer explains. Now he will see if this was correct. Since
he can work only within limits, however, the performer cannot predict just anything for the spectator. His prediction
must deal, as he has said before, with common objects.

Just as he says "common objects," the performer picks up
the "Pretty Name" deck of picture cards and fans them so

the audience can see the girls' pictures—and maybe laugh. He explains that he has several dozen pictures of various types of young ladies in various types of costumes and hair-dos. As he speaks he begins spreading out the deck of picture cards between his two hands so that the audience can see they are all different.

To do this, he takes the cards in bunches from his left hand with his right and holds the bunches up for inspection. This is done quite easily as if he were merely picking off random groups of cards to show, but the performer is careful not to get a "JEANETTE" card on the face of any bunch. There is no need to worry about keeping the cards squared up or anything of that sort because the pictures are actually all different. Only the names on the force cards are the same and these names are mostly hidden even when the girl's face is showing from behind another card.

The magician points out that he has given each girl a name, as the audience can see, but he is careful to say no more about the names than that. The audience can see that the girls all apparently have different names. Should the magician make the mistake of stating that each girl has a different name, he would merely arouse the suspicion in the audience's mind that perhaps the names were not all different. Instead he merely calls the names off as he shows the cards in bunches, saying: "We have Jean and Betty and Joan and Mabel . . ." as he goes through the deck.

Addressing himself to the "future" spectator, the performer says that of course the spectator has very definite ideas about the kind of girl he likes. But his ideas are contaminated by custom and the current fashion mode, etc. What the magician has done is to predict the girl that is really the correct type for the spectator, whether the spectator realizes it or not.

Closing the deck, the magician cuts it several times and places it on his outstretched left hand. He asks the spectator to take off a bunch of cards—not to "cut" since "cutting" is for playing cards and indicates that magic is afoot! When the spectator has done this, the magician takes the cut-off cards from him and glances at the face card of the packet. If the face card is *not* a "JEANETTE" card, the magician knows that the *top* card of the *left-hand packet* is and he asks the spectator to remove that card as the type of girl that is really for him. If the face card of the cut-off packet *is* a "JEAN-ETTE" card, the magician shows it with the same announcement.

Taking the "JEANETTE" card from the spectator, the magician stands it along with his three slips of paper and the dollar bill. He then takes a moment out to recapitulate what he has done, pointing out how he read the past by delving into the first spectator's subconscious memory, how he read the present by noting the single word selected by several spectators from all the many words in a book with over five hundred pages (and here, for the first time, he asks the second spectator to read aloud the word he had selected in the book) and how he had predicted, even before the spectator know what was afoot, the very girl which the third spectator would choose from among the many pictured.

Now, says the magician, he will check the answers to see what score he made. He asks another spectator to take the answer sheets and read them aloud in order—past, present, future—checking each with the number on the bill, the word in the book, and the name on the girl's picture. The performer has hit a perfect score by succeeding in all three of his mental test demonstrations!

NOTE: Obviously either of the two parts of this routine—the "Spirit" part or the "Mental" part—can be performed separately or they can be, with increased effect, combined as described. Since both the methods and effects used run the whole gambit of mental and spirit tricks, such a routine might well be used to answer all needs the performer may feel for this type of trick.

When working for a predominantly female audience, the two parts of the routine dealing with girls may be changed accordingly. Thus the first of the spirit routine spectators would be asked if she remembered the color of her first boy friend's hair and a series of male pictures with accompanying masculine names would be substituted for the "Pretty Name" deck of girls' pictures.

Obviously, also, the salesman or public relations expert or television performer might well utilize his client's product in any of the picture decks and forces noted above—either in an impromptu demonstration or in a planned show for a sales meeting or on a television program (or, more emphatically, a television commercial).

# X

## Miscellaneous Tricks

The effects described in this chapter are collected here only because they do not readily fall into any of the categories presented earlier in this volume. Here will be found tricks that may be performed in the living room, on a stage, or at a church or club. All the effects in this section are audience-tested tricks that have been performed not only by the author, but by some of today's most outstanding magicians before all kinds of audiences—both "live" and on television.

A great deal of magical writing and magical thought has been devoted to the search for new effects and new tricks. A newcomer to the magical fraternity may easily get the idea that just because an effect is old, it should be avoided. Generally speaking such an attitude is too extreme.

The professional performer, forced into continual competition with other performers of equal or greater ability, in order to make a living must always be on the lookout for new tricks and effects or at least new ideas for presentation to give him an edge over his competition. The amateur magician does not find himself in this situation, since he does not usually compete with his fellow magicians for the undivided attention of his friends.

Especially is it important for the beginning amateur to direct his attention to the well-known and time-tested effects. First of all he will thus be sure that the trick he is performing is inherently effective, allowing him to concentrate on his own presentation and leaving the trick to take care of itself. Secondly, by performing well-known effects, the amateur will enhance his reputation. When he is asked if he can do the rising card trick like so-and-so or if he can find dollar bills in lemons, etc., the amateur can answer "Yes." He is not relegated to the rather unimpressive "No, that's old stuff, but here's the latest trick on the market!"

A living-room audience is frequently much more impressed by the fact that the performer can actually do a trick that Thurston made famous or even a trick that the "real professional" at the local night spot is currently performing than by the fact that the performer is the first man in the country (or even the best one) to do a certain new effect.

A magical effect is not good just because it is new any more than a play or a musical composition. Just as with a play or a piece of music, it takes a while before one can tell whether a new trick is really effective or not. It would seem, then, that the performer who is just beginning in the field of magic or in a new part of the field of magic should content himself with effects that he knows are good before worrying with new effects that he only thinks may be good.

There is, of course, the other side to the story. Many people in the audience will be the ones to say "That's old stuff! Can't you do anything new?" It is up to the performer, then, to get the most from each of these two different points of view.

He accomplishes the required compromise by adding new twists to tried and true effects and by not being ashamed to utilize old methods and principles to accomplish new effects. If he succeeds in making an old effect take on new interest (regardless of whether he does it differently from the original) he has, to all intents and purposes, a new effect. If he gives a comedy presentation to a well-known effect (such as "Raise You Three" following) or presents an old idea in new garments (such as "Pocket Pastry" following) he has achieved the desired result.

For that reason the tricks that follow in this chapter are well-known effects. The working in some cases is new. New twists have been added to the effect itself or to the presentation. If the reader, then, will take care to follow the detailed explanation and suggestion given here, these tricks will complete for him a varied, workable, effective repertoire.

A few words may here be in point with regard to magic apparatus. If the reader has occasion to visit a magic store, he will see the shelves lined with all sorts of brightly painted and chromed contraptions. It is not here contended that such paraphernalia is not deceptive and effective magic. It is suggested, however, that if the magician is able to entertain his audience with nothing more than drinking glasses, books, handkerchiefs, and such other common, everyday objects, the effect on the audience will be much greater.

After all, the spectators cannot help but believe that there is something fake about a large red and gold box in which the magician causes some magical feat to happen. If the audience sees what appears to be nothing more than a pitcher of milk, however, it will be likely to accept it as such, no matter how "gimmicked" and "faked" the pitcher may actually be.

Therefore, the author has collected here tricks involving nothing but the most common and most innocent-looking of objects. Many of these objects are prepared and "gimmicked" in various ways, but they achieve their eminent deception because they are just things that might be lying around the house.

The professional stage magician is entitled to the flash and spectacle that comes from specially made apparatus and brightly painted scenery. The living-room magician, however faked and prepared his apparatus may be, gains equal value from using objects of the most usual appearance possible.

## LUCKY LEMON

EFFECT: A spectator selects one of several lemons or oranges. Another spectator lends the magician a dollar bill which is caused to vanish and eventually ends up inside the lemon, although the magician never touches the lemon.

This effect is an old one—that is, the idea of a borrowed bill mysteriously passing into a lemon has intrigued magicians for years. The very fact, then, that many of the spectators may be acquainted with the idea necessitates a method of accomplishing the effect that can stand the utmost scrutiny. The following working is suggested, therefore, as one which requires the least effort on the magician's part and offers the least opportunity for detection by the spectator. Although the preparation may seem tedious it is well worthwhile.

PREPARATION: First of all, two one-dollar bills are needed, with consecutive serial numbers. They can be readily obtained at any bank by asking for new bills. Be sure to get bills with serial numbers ending with digits other than 9 and o—that is, two bills with numbers ending in, for instance, -95 and -96, rather than in -99 and -oo. The last digit of the serial number on each bill is now erased.

This is quite simply accomplished by using a typewriter eraser or some other very thin ink eraser, so as to erase only the last digit. The serial numbers are printed on dollar bills after the rest of the bill is printed, and the serial number ink, being applied on top of the other ink, does not soak into the paper and will therefore come off rather easily. The process will be facilitated if a small hole is cut in a strip of thin, stiff cardboard and the erasure is made through this hole so that the eraser cannot come in contact with anything but the desired digit. Crumpling the new bill to remove its "newness" and rubbing the finger over the erased spot will completely disguise the erasure if it was carefully made.

After erasing the last digit of the serial number (in each place that it appears on the face of each bill) the magician will have two one-dollar bills that apparently bear the same serial number. Once two such bills are prepared, the magician is set to do the trick any number of times without further preparation of additional duplicate bills. It is important to notice that the prepared bills never leave the magician's possession.

The next item needed is a man's white handkerchief with a wide double hem. Although any sort of handkerchief may be used, the innocent appearance of an ordinary plain white handkerchief is beneficial. A piece of paper the size of the prepared bill is folded and rolled into a packet just as described below for the bill (see Figure 82B) and is sewed inside the double hem of the handkerchief at one corner, as in Figure 82A. The handkerchief should be of material that is heavy enough to be opaque. If the double hem is wide, the little packet may be hidden there quite invisibly.

Now for the lemon: Selecting a large lemon (or small orange), the pip to which the stem was attached is removed and placed aside for use later. Using the point of a sharp knife, the skin of the lemon is cut in the little indentation under the pip and removed, leaving a circular hole in the skin which is small enough to be covered later by the pip. A pencil is forced into this hole and all the way down into the lemon (being careful not to break the skin at the other

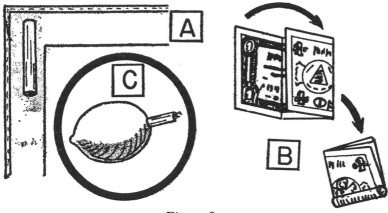

*Figure 82*

side). As much of the juice as possible (without changing the appearance of the lemon) is squeezed out.

One of the duplicate faked bills is now folded in thirds and rolled up tightly, starting with one of the short sides of the folded bill as in Figure 82B. This will give a roll just two inches long and less than a quarter of an inch in diameter. The rolled bill is now rolled in a piece of cellophane several inches long (from the wrapper of a package of cigarettes) and the ends are tightly twisted to make the package as watertight as possible, to keep the bill from getting any wetter than necessary when inside the lemon. There should be three or four thicknesses of cellophane around the bill.

The cellophane-wrapped bill is now slipped into the lemon as in Figure 82C, and the little stem pip is placed over the hole in the lemon and held in place with glue or model airplane cement placed in the hole. To all intents and purposes the lemon should now appear completely unprepared except upon the most minute examination (which it never receives).

The prepared lemon and two regular lemons are placed upon a small plate with the prepared lemon in the middle. A knife and small pad of white paper are placed on the table near the plate of lemons. The duplicate faked bill is folded into quarters (face out so that one of the serial numbers shows) and placed in the *left* jacket pocket or trousers pocket, and a pencil is placed in the corresponding *right-hand* pocket. The prepared handkerchief is in the breast pocket or on the table. The magician is now ready to perform.

PRESENTATION: Without preamble, the magician picks up the plate of lemons and approaches one of the spectators. He must now force the spectator unwittingly to select the prepared lemon from among the three on the plate.

To accomplish this, the magician uses the same procedure as is described on page 298 for forcing one of the three books. The only difference is that when the loaded lemon is finally "selected" it is placed on the floor in plain view of all rather than handed to the spectator.

The magician can speed his demands upon the spectator to the extent that the spectator is so busy choosing which lemon to pick, etc., that he does not have time to look closely at the prepared lemon before the magician takes it from him. Also the spectator does not know what is coming and has no reason to suppose that anything has been done to the lemon. It seems hardly possible to prepare a lemon in any such way as this and not have the preparation show. The thought, then, that the lemon has been tampered with, will not enter the spectator's mind at this point.

After placing the lemon where all can see it well, the magician asks to borrow a bill. For some reason or other, it is usually difficult to get a spectator to lend a magician money. Assurances that it will be returned, plus humorous allusions to the magician's own lack of funds, will finally bring an offer forth. Should a bill of higher denomination be offered, the magician ignores the offer if possible, pretending that he did not hear it, or declines the offer, saying that he would not trust himself with that much money.

Taking the proffered bill from its owner, the magician

folds it into quarters just as the bill in his pocket is folded, and, holding the bill in plain view in his right hand, returns to the table and picks up the pad of paper. He stands facing the spectators with the bill in his right hand and the pad in his left.

"Now we need someone who can write—" he says, and places the pad on top of the bill in his *right* hand, as his *left* hand goes to his left pocket, apparently in search of a pencil. "—and also a pencil," the magician continues, looking rather embarrassed at not being able to find a pencil in his left pocket.

While in the pocket, the left hand grasps the duplicate prepared bill which is there. The left hand is withdrawn from the pocket, holding the duplicate bill. Immediately the left hand takes the pad of paper from the *right* hand, *leaving the spectator's bill in the right hand.* The right hand now goes at once to the right pocket, and, leaving the spectator's bill in that pocket, comes out with the pencil. Apparently the magician has merely searched in one pocket and then another for the pencil, and, in order to do so, shifted the pad and the bill from one hand to the other. The action is diagramed in Figure 83, the arrows indicating the direction of the moving hand in each case.

Since there is at all times a pad and a bill visible to the audience, the fact that it is a different bill after the pad has changed hands will never be noticed or even seen. There is no need to attempt to "palm" the bill. It is merely held well down in the hand. The only time that a bill is actually in either hand when it is not supposed to be is while that hand is moving either to or from a pocket and the presence of the bill will not be noticed.

Effort should be made not to hide the bill, but to execute the exchange as smoothly and as much as possible as though the magician were really just shifting the pad and bill from one hand to the other. The apparent reason for the move is

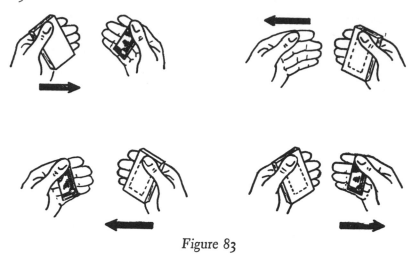

Figure 83

that the magician has forgotten in which pocket he put his pencil, and this fact tends to dissociate the move from the trick in the minds of the spectators. There is no rush and the hands should certainly not move with guilty swiftness.

Having secured the pencil and exchanged the spectator's bill for the prepared bill, the magician advances to some spectator *other than the one who loaned him the bill* and asks him to copy the serial number of the bill onto the pad and to keep the pad for future reference. The magician then takes the bill back and rolls it into a small packet (like the packet sewed in the hem of his handkerchief) which he holds at the tips of his right thumb and index finger as in Figure 84A.

He removes the prepared handkerchief from his pocket and displays it with both hands so that the audience can see both sides. This gives him an opportunity to run his left hand around the hem until his fingers find the packet sewed into the corner. Grasping the handkerchief by the corner containing the packet, he throws the handkerchief over his right hand, carrying the packet corner up underneath with his left hand. The left thumb and index finger hold the packet sewed in the handkerchief. The left thumb and *second* finger grasp the real bill so that the right hand can emerge from under the handkerchief (Figure 84B). The *right* hand then grasps the packet sewed in the handkerchief through the cloth of the handkerchief from above as in Figure 84C.

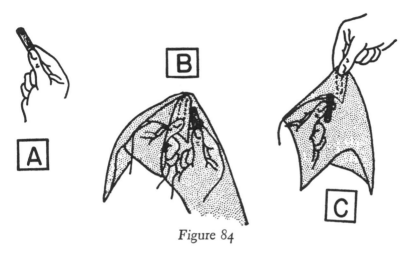

Figure 84

The effect of this move, of course, is that the magician has merely thrown the handkerchief over the bill and is now holding the bill through the cloth of the handkerchief. The left hand hiding the real bill is dropped casually and unhurriedly to the left trousers pocket, where it deposits the bill and where it remains while the magician nonchalantly surveys the audience as if trying to find someone whom he can trust to hold what appears to be the borrowed bill under the handkerchief.

The magician hands the handkerchief he is holding to one of the spectators to hold, just as he did, by pinching the little packet through the handkerchief. The spectator, of course, believes that he is holding the folded dollar bill under the handkerchief. The magician asks him if he can feel the bill there.

Now the magician tells the audience that he intends to make the bill pass invisibly into the lemon. He reminds the audience that he has not touched the lemon since before the bill was borrowed from one of the spectators, and he states that he will not touch the lemon at all. He tells the spectator to let go of the bill and let it drop when the magician counts three. The magician grasps one of the dangling corners of the handkerchief and counts to three. The spectator lets go his hold on the handkerchief and it drops, dangling from the magician's hand. The bill has apparently vanished. The magician shows both sides of the handkerchief, stuffs it into his pocket and points to the lemon. "Watch!" he exclaims.

Taking the knife from the table, he hands it to the spectator who held the handkerchief and asks him to cut open the lemon. Just in case there is something inside, the magician suggests, the spectator is to cut around the lemon rather than trying to slice straight through. The spectator cuts the lemon in half and finds the bill inside.

As the spectator removes the bill, the magician relieves him of the two halves of the lemon. He asks the spectator to unwrap the bill (which is wrapped, he explains jokingly, in accordance with the Pure Food Law) and while the spectator is doing so, the magician offers the unprepared half of the lemon to someone to eat. There will be few takers, so the magician puts the lemon aside.

When the spectator has unwrapped the lemon, the magician asks him to check with the spectator who holds the serial number written on the pad. The magician is very careful to avoid touching the bill. As soon as the spectators have checked the numbers, the magician asks them if the numbers are the same. Of course, they are.

Triumphantly the magician thanks the spectators for their assistance and takes the bill from the spectator, holding it with his right hand. Turning to the audience, the magician asks "Who gave me this bill?" The owner will say that he did. "You gave me this bill? Thank you," says the magician, stuffing the bill into his *right* jacket pocket.

Immediately he withdraws his hand from that pocket, and, smiling at the joke he apparently attempted, returns the bill to its owner. Actually, of course, when he put the bill in his pocket, the magician exchanged it for the original borrowed bill that was previously left in that pocket. After returning the borrowed bill to its owner, the magician reclaims his pencil and the pad with the serial number written on from the spectator who copied the number, thus destroying all evidence of his skulduggery.

NOTE: It will be noticed that at no time did the owner of the bill ever handle or closely examine one of the prepared bills and at no time did any spectator who handled the prepared bills ever handle the original borrowed bill, so the three-way switching of bills will be successful. The magician should, though, take care to crumple his prepared bills so that they do not look too new, and should further refrain from borrowing a very old and dirty bill with which to start the trick.

He should also arrange that at least one more trick follows this one in his program (unless the audience is large) so that the spectator who loaned the bill will not have the chance immediately to start showing the wonderful bill to the other spectators who helped with this trick. The magician need feel no qualms about using a bill with one-too-few digits in the serial number. Who, but perhaps a bank teller, might be expected to know that a bill has eight digits in its number instead of seven? Although the author cannot be certain that he has performed for bank tellers, he has never been called on this point as yet.

## POCKET PASTRY

EFFECT: Starting with milk, flour, and eggs, the magician bakes a cupcake in the spectator's pocket.

The trick is obviously a "switch" on the famous effect of

baking a cake in the spectator's hat. This version is, however, much stronger since the audience can watch and appreciate to the fullest extent the embarrassment and worry of the spectator with a pocketful of gooey flour-egg-milk mixture. It is also easier to perform and entails less fuss and bother on the magician's part.

The comedy inherent in the situation (like that of the audience participation television shows) is hard to equal, because it is spontaneous. The spectator may not be trying to be funny, but his agonized looks as he contemplates a ruined suit of clothes will draw laughs where the best-planned gag will fall flat.

PREPARATION: 1. The one piece of apparatus needed is a gimmicked pitcher. This can be purchased at any magic store but is simple to construct from celluloid and model airplane cement.

Figure 85

The dime stores sell glass pitchers shaped something like that shown in Figure 85A. For this effect the pitcher should not be too large (pint size is plenty). The constriction at the top is, however, essential.

After procuring a pitcher, a celluloid insert (celluloid from the local luggage store or model crafts shop) is fashioned as shown in Figure 85B. The diameter of the top of the insert is the same as the diameter of the inside of the pitcher just below the constriction. There is a bottom on the insert and a small hole (three-eighths of an inch in diameter) near the top of the insert at Point X in Figure 85B.

When the celluloid insert is complete, it is forced into the pitcher by pinching closed the opening at the top. Once inside, the insert will snap back into shape and form an inner wall all around the main part of the pitcher as indicated by the shaded portion of Figure 85A. The hole in the insert should be just under the spout of the pitcher.

With the insert in place, milk is poured around the outside of the insert (that is, between the insert and the glass wall of the pitcher) by forcing one side of the top of the insert inward toward the center of the pitcher enough to allow the milk to get in.

When the space between the insert and the outside of the pitcher is full of milk, the pitcher itself will appear to be full (so long as no one looks in the top). Now when the pitcher is tilted as if pouring the milk out, the milk will merely run through the hole near the top of the insert and back down inside the insert. The level of milk in the pitcher will appear to go down, but actually no milk will pour out of the pitcher. In other words, with the double wall, a few ounces of milk can make a one-pint pitcher look full, and all the milk except an apparent few ounces can seemingly be "poured" out of the pitcher.

2. The second item needed is a plain brown paper grocery sack about ten inches tall or a two-pound paper flour sack. Inside this a smaller sack is glued to the bottom as in Figure 86A. A handful of flour is placed in this small inside sack.

3. The expendable items at each performance include: a cupcake or roll or small Danish pastry or what have you. The only requirement is that there be no frosting or stickiness that might harm the spectator's pocket. The cupcake is

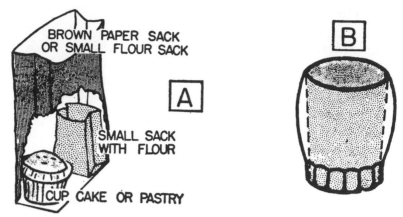

Figure 86

placed inside the large paper sack right beside the small sack of flour as in Figure 86A. A small bottle (resembling a flavoring bottle) filled with cigarette lighter fluid and some matches will be needed.

4. The final requirement is what is known as a "blown" egg, that is, an egg shell from which the contents have been removed. To blow an egg, a small hole is carefully punched in each end with some sharply pointed instrument (an ice pick is fine). One hole should be about a quarter of an inch in diameter; the other hole can be smaller.

As the name implies, the contents of the egg are removed from the shell by placing the small hole to the mouth and blowing. The yolk, white, and everything will eventually (though not immediately) emerge through the quarter-inch hole at the other end of the shell. After the contents are blown out, the inside of the shell should be washed with water out of respect for the spectator's pocket. The result is an empty egg shell which resembles a real egg in all respects when displayed with the thumb and forefinger covering the holes at either end.

PRESENTATION: This effect can be worked using either a

gentleman's jacket pocket or a lady's handbag as a receptacle. Although only the working with a pocket is described, the handbag presentation is identical.

The magician invites a spectator to assist him. He asks the gentleman to remove the contents of his right-hand jacket pocket. Then, displaying the blown egg between his thumb and forefinger, the magician announces that he has a new trick in which an egg is made to vanish. He asks if it is all right to use the spectator's pocket for the trick, pointing out that he would rather not use his own pocket.

Placing the blown egg carefully into the spectator's pocket and standing the spectator just barely to his left (the table holding all the required items is to the right), the magician cautions the audience to watch him very closely. He shows his right hand to be empty by displaying it to the audience palm up about waist high. With his left hand, he pulls his right sleeve back, presumably the better to show his hand empty.

Swinging quickly to the left in order to display his left hand in a similar manner, the performer "inadvertently" hits the spectator's pocket with the back of his left hand and crushes the egg. He is embarrassed beyond measure at this "unexpected" turn of events.

Carefully, the magician reaches into the spectator's pocket and removes the broken egg shell, remembering to shake the "drippings" off the broken shell just as a cook does when she breaks an egg into a dish. The shell is put aside but not before the magician has handled it with many grimaces just as if it were a sticky egg shell.

Should the spectator now attempt to put his hand in his pocket to inspect the damage, the magician stops him with: "Don't put your hand in there! You'll get it all dirty!" Assuming that the performer has been a good enough actor to convince the spectator that something really did go wrong, a muttered assurance to the spectator that all will end well might not be amiss at this point.

The only solution, the magician decides, for the pocketful of egg yolk is to absorb the mess before it has time to soak through the cloth. As he proposes this happy thought, the magician picks up the paper sack and plunges his right hand into it coming up with the handful of flour from the little sack inside. This flour the magician allows to dribble back into the sack being sure that the audience has time to see that he apparently has a sack full of flour and being sure also to get plenty of flour on his right hand.

The right hand dips a second time into the sack, but on this trip it merely twists shut the mouth of the small sack inside so no flour can escape. Immediately the right hand takes the sack by the bottom as the left hand holds open the spectator's pocket. With the bottom of the sack toward the audience, the cupcake is simply poured from the sack into the spectator's pocket. If the spectator is asked to hold his right arm up out of the way, that arm will be in his line of vision and even he will be unable to see the loading of the cupcake into his own pocket.

After the cupcake is loaded into the pocket, the flour sack is withdrawn and imaginary bits of flour are brushed off the edges of the pocket. Since this brushing is done with the right hand (which is covered with flour), the white flour will actually be brushed on rather than off the gentleman's clothes. This evidence of a little flour dust around the pocket will complete the flour-pouring illusion.

The flour will absorb the egg yolk, the magician explains, but he is at somewhat of a loss to know just how to get the flour-and-egg mixture out of the pocket. Perhaps some milk would help. He seizes the milk pitcher and displays it holding it aloft (so the assisting spectator cannot see in the top). The lip of the pitcher is now inserted into the pocket (with the spectator's own right arm and the magician's left hand to obscure the spectator's view of the proceedings) and the milk apparently is poured into the pocket.

With a little practice, the magician can manage to slosh a little of the milk remaining in the pitcher out as he sets it aside after pouring, thus lending mightily to the milk-pouring illusion. The magician now asks the gentleman for his handkerchief, and, while he is getting it, asks him to name his favorite flavor.

Whatever flavor the spectator suggests, the magician says that is just what he has and, picking up the "flavoring" bottle, pours a liberal dose of lighter fluid onto the handkerchief. Striking a match, the magician sets the fluid afire. He allows the flames to shoot up for but a moment before he smothers them in stuffing the handkerchief very hurriedly into the spectator's pocket.

Neither the handkerchief nor the magician's hands will get burned during this procedure. Lighter fluid burns at a very low temperature and the flames do not have time to do any damage in the few seconds that they are allowed to burn. Although the flames are immediately smothered by bunching up the handkerchief, the effect to the audience is that the handkerchief went into the pocket flaming.

The magician now steps back to let the mess cook for a few minutes while he apologizes to the spectator for getting him into this dilemma. The magician also hopes that everything will come out all right.

After a moment of such build-up, the spectator is asked to remove his handkerchief. It is not even singed.

Next he is asked to remove the mess from his pocket. He reaches into his pocket and finds instead the cupcake. As the magician sends the spectator back to his seat he thanks him and whispers to him to take a bite of the cupcake to show that it is the real product.

NOTE: The trick of picking the most staid person present in the audience with whom to do this effect seems hardly to need mention. Ministers, club presidents, school principals, and factory managers seem to provide the best comic situations. Sometimes the performer is lucky in obtaining a spectator who tries to help build up the comedy situation. But even the most passive assistant will provide plenty of laughs.

If the lady's purse presentation is used, the lady's escort should be asked to bring the purse to the front and should be kept on hand (ostensibly to take care of the contents of the purse that are removed at the beginning of the trick) so that his reactions to what goes on will be visible to the audience. He, of course, should be the one to remove the handkerchief and cupcake from the purse at the finale.

If the pitcher is washed out with soap chips and water (particularly the double wall) as soon after the performance as possible, the best results will be obtained. Otherwise the celluloid insert will get rather badly stained (and odorous) from dried milk.

Instead of the pitcher suggested a glass tumbler of the shape shown in Figure 86B prepared with a celluloid insert can be used. The working is the same and some performers feel the tumbler appears to hold a more logical quantity of milk. Such a glass can also be found for sale in the magic shops. The bulbous shape of the tumbler with a constricted top, of course, is necessary.

## RAISE YOU THREE

EFFECT: Three playing cards selected by the spectators rise from the pack despite the fact that the deck is completely surrounded with glass. Without attempting to trace the magician who first conceived the rising card effect, it will be sufficient to credit some of the ideas in this method to Mr. Jean Hugard.

Although this is an effect using playing cards, it is placed in this chapter for the simple reason that its use is limited exclusively to a planned magic program and that it is more an apparatus trick than a card trick, both in the size and appeal of its effect on the audience.

Magicians and audiences alike have always been intrigued with the idea of a selected card rising mysteriously and inexplicably from the deck. Various methods have been devised to accomplish this feat in impossible abundance—all the way from sleight-of-hand impromptu methods to spring reels, clockwork motors, electrical contraptions, and Howard Thurston's full stage presentations involving several assistants. Of all the variations on this same theme to be found in magical literature, however, the one given here combines a simplicity and directness of method with a mystifying and comic effect hard to equal.

PREPARATION: Three playing cards that are easily recognized at a distance are decided upon—usually a low spot card, a high spot card, and a face card. It will be assumed for purposes of explanation that the effect is to be performed with the five of spades, nine of diamonds, and king of spades (for no other reason than that those are the cards the artist used in the drawings).

A full-length picture (about eight by ten inches) of a nude or scantily clad young lady is needed. The young lady's proportions should be such that her entire torso from bust to hips can be modestly covered with the king of spades. Care should also be taken to find a picture of such proportions that, when the king is covering the lady's torso, the card will be in the center of the picture. If whatever garments the young lady has on are completely hidden by the king of spades (so that she appears to be completely nude except for the king) so much the better. Since the picture must be folded and unfolded many times, it should be a picture from a magazine rather than a photograph.

The king of spades is pasted on the picture so that the final

result resembles Figure 87. The picture is then folded backward along the edges of the card so that it is completely
hidden behind the card. If the sides are folded back first along
the dotted lines in the drawing and then the top and bottom,
it will be easier to open out quickly without fumbling.

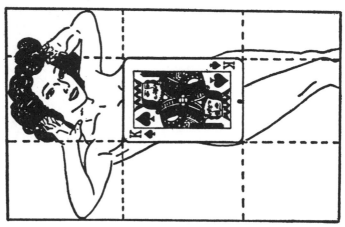

Figure 87

A playing card with a blank face is needed. This can be
made by splitting the back layer off one of the cards in the
deck (see page 193) and pasting it onto a piece of white
cardboard cut to the exact shape and size of a playing card.

Furthermore, two fives of spades, three nines of diamonds,
and a second king of spades are needed, as well as five indifferent cards with matching backs.

At the center of one end of each of the five indifferent
cards, a quarter-inch hole is punched as indicated in Figure
88A.

At the center of one end of two of the nines of diamonds,
one of the fives of spades, and the blank face card, a small
V-shaped notch is cut as in Figure 88B. At the center of one
end of the prepared king of spades (the end toward the bot-

tom of the picture) a slit about a quarter inch long is made.
Just one cut with a pair of scissors through the card and the
folded picture will do the trick, as in Figure 88C.

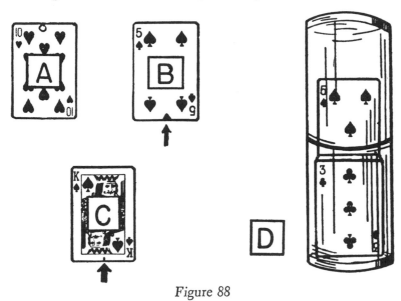

*Figure 88*

The most difficult part of the preparation is to find two
glass tumblers that will hold a deck of cards loosely. Of necessity the sides of the tumblers must be almost straight so
that the cards will not become wedged into the tumbler.
They should be tall enough so that the top of the deck, when
resting loosely in the tumbler, is about even with the top of
the tumbler. Also, the glasses should be of such design that
they will rest one on top of the other mouth to mouth as in
Figure 88D.

The final requirements are several feet of twisted black silk
thread (twisted thread is stronger for its thickness than is
braided thread) and a thumb tip, Figure 89B.

For this trick, however, a large thimble will work as well.

The thimble must be large enough to fit well (and loosely) onto the thumb. A plastic thimble should be used, with the ridges and bumps sanded smooth and the whole thing painted flesh color. One side should be flattened slightly so that the thimble will resemble the thumb when viewed only from the small end (see page 107).

TO PREPARE FOR PERFORMANCE: A knot is tied in the end of the piece of thread. The thread is then slipped into the slit at the bottom of the prepared king of spades, with the knot on the face side of the king. The slit will hold the thread securely. The knot should be large enough so that it will not pull through the slit.

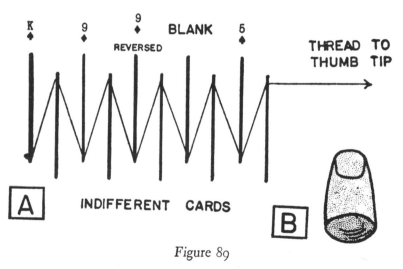

Figure 89

The king is then laid face down on the table and the five indifferent cards (the ones with the holes in them) are threaded onto the thread and laid face downward on top of the prepared king. Notice that whereas the slit is at the bottom end of the king, the five indifferent cards are arranged so that the holes are at the top.

One of the notched nines of diamonds is slipped face down

between the bottom two indifferent cards, the notch (at the bottom of the nine) engaging the thread between the two indifferent cards and forcing it downward. The second notched nine of diamonds is forced between the second and third indifferent cards but this time the nine is reversed so that it is face up. The blank-faced card is forced between the third and fourth indifferent cards, face downward. Finally the notched five of spades is forced face downward between the top two indifferent cards.

The setup is diagramed in Figure 89A. It will be seen that, if the packet of cards is stood upright in a glass and the thread pulled, first the five, then the blank, then the two nines (one reversed) and finally the king will be forced upward by the thread in that order, the five indifferent cards merely acting as pulleys in the process.

With the threaded packet all set and squared up so that none of the cards is protruding, the thread is cut about a foot beyond the packet and the end fastened with a bit of glue or scotch tape to the inside of the thumb tip or thimble. (The way to ascertain the exact length of the thread will be described below.)

The threaded packet (with the thumb tip beside it) is laid face up on the table out of sight behind some object. The two tumblers are also placed on the table. The remaining five of spades, nine of diamonds, and king of spades are placed on top of the deck of cards (in that order, five of spades on top). The deck of cards, of course, being unprepared, can be used for any card effect earlier in the program so long as the required three cards are got to the top before starting the rising card effect.

PRESENTATION: The magician riffle-shuffles the deck of cards (being careful always to allow the top three cards to fall last in the shuffle so that they remain on top) and announces that he is going to test the spectators' powers of concentration.

He advances toward one of the spectators, proffering the deck in his left hand, and asks the spectator to cut off about half the deck. Handing the spectator the bottom half of the deck, he says: "Here, you hold the cards to which you cut." The magician then takes the top half of the deck from the spectator and proffers it to another spectator, saying, "Of these cards that the gentleman cut, will you take one for just a minute?" and points to the top card of the pack. The next card is offered to the next spectator and the third to a third.

Although this seems to be a very blatant force of the three cards, the spectators will not consider it so. The magician has created the impression that the spectator who did the cutting is the one who selected the card and that the other three are merely holding cards for some ancillary purpose. The spectators who were not parties to the selection probably are unaware (because of the exchange of packets with the first spectator) from which packet the three cards came and if someone does realize that the three cards actually came from the top of the deck, he will forget it during the excitement to come.

Of course the performer may use any sort of force that he chooses in order to get the proper three cards in the spectators' hands—any sort, that is, so longs as it is fast, simple, and sure-fire.

The three spectators are asked to memorize their cards, show them to their neighbors, etc. Handing the remainder of the deck to the spectator who did the cutting (and who holds the bottom half of the deck) the magician asks him to collect the three cards and to shuffle them into the deck.

As the spectator is collecting the cards, the magician hands out the two glass tumblers for inspection, cautioning the spectators to be certain that the tumblers are completely ordinary in every way. While the tumblers are being inspected, the magician takes the shuffled deck from the spectator and lays it face up on the threaded packet on his table. If one of the force cards accidentally ended upon the face of the deck, the magician buries it with a cut before laying the deck on the threaded packet. He then goes back to the audience for the two tumblers.

Placing the tumblers side by side near the rear edge of the table, the magician picks up the pack plus the added threaded packet. As he picks up the cards (using both hands if necessary) he slips his right thumb into the thumb tip or thimble. He holds the deck upright facing the audience with his right

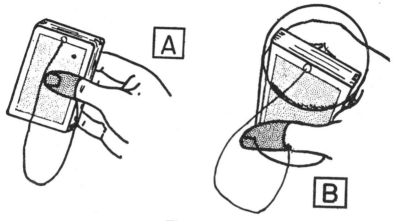

Figure 90

fingers on the face and his thumb (with the tip on it) behind the deck as in Figure 90A.

Explaining that the spectators' powers of concentration are to be tested, the magician drops the deck openly into one of the tumblers and picks it up with his right hand, still keeping the thumb in the rear (and being careful not to clink the thumb tip against the glass) as in Figure 90B. "Let's see," says the performer to the three spectators who removed the cards from the deck, "if you can concentrate enough to cause your card to rise right up out of the deck."

After a moment of concentration, nothing happens. The

magician replaces the tumbler near the rear edge of the table and rests his right finger tips on the table top at the rear edge, the thumb hanging below the edge. He requests the first spectator to name his card. The spectator, of course, names the five of spades.

Perhaps a little "whoofle dust" would help, suggests the magician, and he sticks his right thumb and forefinger into the watch pocket of his trousers (or the lower vest pocket if wearing a vest) and emerges with an imaginary pinch of imaginary whoofle dust which he sprinkles jokingly over the tumbler. Whoofle dust always seems to help, the magician smilingly explains. When the right thumb went into the watch pocket, it left the thumb tip or thimble behind, retained by the tightness of the pocket. The move is apparently mere innocent byplay, but it is really the crux of the trick. Now the magician's hands are both free, but the thread is fastened to his body by means of the thumb tip in his watch or vest pocket. During its trip to the pocket, the thumb tip was hidden behind the relaxed fingers of the right hand as it moved in a natural fashion from the table to the pocket.

Once more the first spectator is asked to concentrate on his card. The magician leans backward slightly (and very slightly) thereby pulling on the thread. The feet should not be moved and the movement of the upper part of the body should be kept to a minimum. The hips alone move backward. The hands should make gestures at the tumbler coaxing the card to rise, but these gestures should not be all related to the card's motion, their main function being to cover any movement of the body.

When the card has risen into view, the magician picks it out of the glass and commends the first spectator on his powers of concentration. The five of spades is laid aside.

The second spectator will now be asked to concentrate, but his job is harder, says the magician. He moves the tumbler a little away from the rear edge of the table (to take up the slack in the thread present after the first card was removed). Taking the empty tumbler, the magician inverts it mouth downward over the glass in which the cards are resting as in Figure 88D, pointing out that now the deck is completely surrounded by solid glass, just to make it more difficult.

The presence of the top tumbler will in no way affect the efficiency of the thread in causing the remaining cards to rise. It may be necessary (if the tumblers have thin edges or the table is wobbly) for the magician to rest one finger of his left hand lightly on top of the top tumbler to keep it from falling off when the thread is pulled. If the tumblers are heavy, this should not be necessary.

Calling on the second spectator to name his card, concentrate on it, and perhaps coax it upward with some foolish pet name, the magician once more pulls on the thread by moving his body backward. The blank-faced card rises. Removing the top tumbler, the magician shows the blank and makes some joking remark about the spectator's blank mind and power of concentration. The blank card is laid aside as the same spectator is asked to try again.

Once more moving the bottom tumbler forward to take up the slack and replacing the top tumbler, the reversed nine of diamonds is caused to rise back toward the audience on the spectator's second try. The spectator has got the right card, but it came up backward, the magician points out. Now the spectator must cause the nine to turn itself around in the deck by concentration alone.

The magician pushes the nine of diamonds (back toward the audience), down into the regular or unthreaded portion of the deck. Once again the top tumbler is replaced and the thread pulled as before. The nine of diamonds rises, this time facing the audience, having apparently accomplished the impossible feat of reversing itself while in the deck.

The third spectator is asked to concentrate on his card (the king of spades) but to no avail. Even removal of the top tumbler and repeated sprinklings of whoofle dust do not seem to aid his powers of concentration. Finally the top of a card does appear, but it disappears immediately. Then a little more comes up, but the spectator does not seem to be able to concentrate enough to get his card all the way up.

Since the king (by virtue of the picture pasted on its back) is heavier than the other cards and since it is the last card in the setup, it is fairly easy to acquire the ability to make it come part way up and then slide back down again. Several such false starts will have the whole audience grunting to help the poor spectator get his card all the way up.

Finally the king rises all the way. The magician's right hand takes the king and, while his left thumb holds the five indifferent threaded cards in the glass, the magician pulls the king free of the thread with a slight tug to cause the thread to slide out of the slit in the card. As he backs away from the table, the thread is pulled through the holes in the indifferent cards and falls unnoticed against the magician's trousers.

Walking toward the audience, the magician says he now knows why the spectator had so much trouble. He was not concentrating fully on getting the king of spades to rise, because his mind was on other things. With that, the magician suddenly unfolds the picture of the nude young lady for his laugh at the spectator's expense.

NOTE: 1. Another face card can be made up with a picture of some currently popular (but not nude) male movie star for use with predominantly female audiences. Also, Mr. Audley Walsh put on the market some time ago an effect called the "Al Jolson Card" for just such a use as this.

2. A great deal of magical thought has gone into the problem of creating a method whereby any card called for by the audience can be made to rise from the deck. It is believed, however, that the reader's own experience will eventually lead to the conclusion that the audience is not so much impressed with what card rises as it is with the fact that any

card rises. How the magician knew what cards to make rise seems always to be lost in the question of how he made any cards rise when completely surrounded with glass, etc.

For that reason it seems more important to have a fast and sure-fire force at the beginning than a deceptive one. Unless the spectators are exceedingly stupid, they are not laboring under the delusion that the foregoing shenanigans occurred with the help of any magical power. Quite obviously this effect is calculated to amuse rather than to mystify, emphasizing comedy as above mystery.

It seems, therefore, unnecessary to belabor the audience with a complicated though mystifying force of three cards. It is sufficient for the effect that the cards were made to rise without any apparent explanation and that an element of comedy was introduced. Audiences would be more receptive to magic if such circumstances occurred more often!

3. Each performer must adjust the length of the thread to his own individual requirements. Since the thread lengthens several inches each time a card is made to rise, the length at the start should be as short as possible. With the tumbler standing at the very rear of the table, the thread should be just long enough to allow the thumb tip to reach the watch pocket. Each time the performer moves the tumbler forward, he should stand as close to the table as possible.

Too long a thread will mean that the last raising can only be accomplished if the performer stands way back from the table and is more than an arm's length from the glass. Such a situation is likely to lead to an awkwardness in the presentation that belies the inherent freedom and simplicity of the effect.

4. Some performers may feel that they would rather have the threaded packet in the right jacket pocket with the thread permanently attached to the belt, adding the packet to the deck by placing the deck in the jacket pocket while handing the glasses out to be inspected.

Naturally such a method could be used. It would, of course, eliminate the need for the thumb tip entirely. If the threaded packet were kept in the little change pocket inside the right jacket pocket, it would be kept in order and readily accessible. It is suggested, however, that during a performance the performer's pockets are likely to be full of a great many necessary items and any items that can conveniently be kept on the table rather than in the pockets should be kept there.

## LINKING RINGS

EFFECT: Solid steel rings are made to link and unlink with each other, metal passing through solid metal, despite the fact that each ring has been inspected by the spectators.

The "Chinese Linking Rings" in one form or another have been in evidence in the magic programs for over a hundred years. One version of the effect is usually included in the toy magic sets that seem always to make their appearance around Christmas time.

Yet despite its age and frequency of performance, the linking ring effect continues to be one of the most successful of the magician's repertoire. If one may judge from personal experience alone, audiences in all parts of the country, when discussing the programs of various magicians they have seen, seem always to mention two tricks above all others. Those are a sleight-of-hand endless production of lit cigarettes from the air and the linking rings. It seems unfortunate, then, that many magicians have discarded the linking rings in the search for newer tricks.

Even reference to the long-enduring success of the various forms of this trick seems unnecessary as an endorsement of the effect achieved. The utter simplicity and yet impossibility of causing two solid steel rings to link one into the other after each has been inspected by the audience cannot help but be a startling effect.

The classical linking ring routine utilized eight rings. That number was essential for the working of the trick. If the magician were really endowed with magic power, however, he would need but two rings in order to perform the demonstration. Lacking such true magic, the magician must use more than two rings, but it seems to be desirable to keep the number of rings as small as possible. The fewer rings used, the more startling the effect seems to be because the fewer are the opportunities for duplicity on the performer's part. Hence this routine utilizes (from the audience's point of view) but four rings.

The basic method can, of course, be expanded to the performer's desire. The presentation here is calculated to emphasize the sheer mystery and impossibility of the trick. Many performers achieve a really beautiful effect by emphasizing the comedy or intricacy of the effect with ten or twenty rings almost in the manner of a ballet.

PREPARATION: Traditionally the effect is presented with steel rings or hoops. Perhaps the most useful size for all occasions is ten inches in diameter. Smaller rings may be used but the effectiveness is somewhat diminished if the rings are small enough to admit the possibility of sleight of hand or the use of the magician's pockets.

Metal (quarter-inch rod bent into the shape of a ring and welded) seems to be the best material for the effect because of its inherent solidity and the hearty-sounding tone emitted when the rings are struck together. There is no good reason, however, why plastic rings or even wooden embroidery hoops (from the dime store) should not be used, especially for an informal demonstration before a small audience.

REQUIRED FOR THE EFFECT: Two rings inextricably linked one through the other, a single ring of the same size, another single ring of the same size in which a gap one-half inch long has been cut, a third single ring sufficiently larger than the others to slip easily over, and lie concentrically around, the ring with the gap are required as shown in Figure 91A.

In addition a round tray (just large enough to accommodate the largest of the rings) is needed. It should be made of light (and noisy) metal and not cloth-covered. If desired a silver circle may be painted around the inside to help disguise the fact that there will always be one ring lying in the tray. The edge of the tray should be turned up to help hide the single ring it will hold. Also an eighteen-inch square of silk will be needed with a small grommeted hole at one corner.

Rings of the types necessary may be purchased at any magic store. Most regular linking rings sets, however, comprise eight rings rather than the five necessary for this effect and usually do not include as a matter of course the larger single ring. The local blacksmith will be able to shape, weld, and chromium plate the rings to the performer's order at little more expense than the cost of the usual set of eight and the larger extra ring.

TO PREPARE FOR PERFORMANCE: The metal tray is on the performer's table. On it is placed the ring with the gap in it (hereafter referred to as the key ring) carefully arranged so that it is in the center of the tray, and so that the oversize ring will fit over and around it when dropped onto the tray.

The other four rings are piled slightly off center on the tray so that they can be picked up in a bunch without disturbing the key ring as in Figure 91B. From the top of the pile downward, the rings are arranged single, two linked, and finally the oversize ring.

The silk is in the performer's hip or trousers pocket. Tied securely to the corner of the silk diagonally opposite from the corner with the grommet is a piece of strong (twisted silk) black thread which goes through the grommet and is then fastened to the performer's belt. The thread should be of such length that it is taut when the tied corner of the silk is held shoulder-high in the right hand with the arm almost fully extended in front of the performer.

PRESENTATION: The performer picks up the bunch of four rings in his right hand as he announces the ancient mystery of the Chinese Linking Rings. A chain of four solid steel

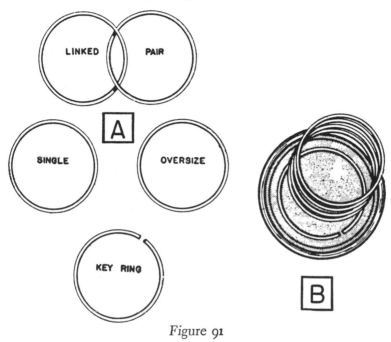

Figure 91

rings with very miraculous powers, says the magician, displaying the four rings as if they were all linked into a chain by holding the two singles onto the ends of the linked chain of two as in Figure 92A.

Four rings linked together, says the magician, but not for long. So saying, the performer gathers the four rings into his left hand, and, with a semblance of effort, pulls one of the singles away from the others and hands it to a spectator at the right to inspect. The spectator is admonished to make sure the ring is solid in all respects.

Turning to the left away from the first spectator, the magician shifts the rings to his right hand and pulls the other

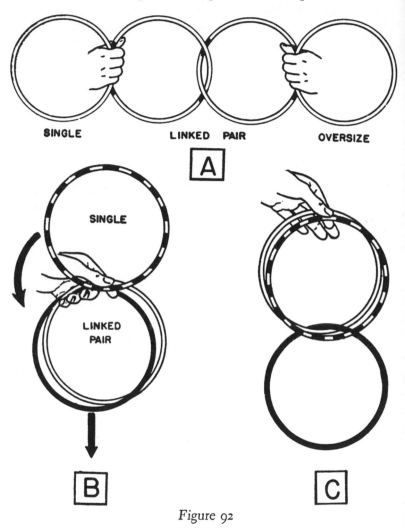

*Figure 92*

single ring away just as if he were unlinking it from the chain with some effort. This he hands to a spectator on his left.

Going back immediately to the spectator on the right (with the remaining two rings in his right hand) the magician, after asking the spectator if he is sure that the ring is solid, takes it with his left hand and adds it to the left side of the linked two he is holding. Shifting all the rings (without changing their order) across to his left hand, the magician moves over to his left, and, with his right hand, takes the ring from the spectator on his left.

While taking the ring from the left spectator, the magician inserts the first finger of the left hand above the right-hand ring of the linked pair—that is, the single ring (farthest to the left) and the first ring of the linked pair are hanging on the first finger of his left hand, while the second, third, and fourth fingers hold the second (outside or farthest right) ring of the linked pair.

The magician announces that he will make the two solid single rings that have just been inspected by the two spectators link together. So saying, he takes the single ring from the second spectator in his right hand and bangs it down against the rings in his left hand. As the bottom of the ring (the dotted ring in Figure 92B) hits the left first finger, the left thumb clamps down on it as in Figure 92B and the right hand releases its hold, allowing the single ring to fall down (in the direction of the curved arrow in Figure 92B) so that it is hanging on the left first finger and is aligned with the rest of the rings in the left hand.

Just as the single ring clashes down against the rest of the rings in the left hand, the left second, third, and fourth fingers allow the one ring of the linked pair (the black ring in the drawing) to slip off and drop so that it is dangling below the rest of the rings as in Figure 92C. Immediately the right hand seizes this lower ring and pulls the linked pair free of the left hand, the left thumb retaining the two singles in the left hand. The right hand holds the linked pair aloft. (Note that one of the single rings has been omitted from the drawing for clarity since it plays no part in the move.)

The effect of this move if properly executed is that the right hand took a ring and linked it into a single ring in the left hand. The noise of the clashing of the rings—once when the right hand hits the rings over the left first finger and again when the linked ring is allowed to drop—seems to aid the effect perfectly. If the rings are turned with the left side to the audience as the two linked are pulled away from the left hand, the illusion will be complete.

Immediately the magician hands the linked pair to a spectator with the suggestion that he try to take the two rings apart as easily as the magician got them together. Pausing just long enough to let the rest of the audience see that the spectator will have little success in that direction, the magician remarks that there are still two rings of the chain left. Taking the two single rings in his left hand, the magician pretends to pull them apart as if he were unlinking them with some effort and hands the two rings out to left and right for inspection.

He allows just enough time for the two spectators to acknowledge that the two single rings are completely solid and unprepared and to emphasize that all the rings are now in the spectator's hands. Then the magician takes them back—one in each hand with the oversize single in his right hand. The table with the tray on it is to the magician's right.

The peculiar linking and unlinking powers of the rings, the magician explains, are due exclusively to the peculiar properties of the special alloy from which they are made. Just placing two rings together and rubbing causes the one ring to penetrate the metal of the other. The magician holds the two rings as in Figure 94A and starts to rub them together just as he will later when doing the linking move described in connection with Figure 94.

As a matter of fact, the magician says, stopping his work

with the rings as he talks, the metal of the rings will allow anything to penetrate it. He starts once more to do the linking moves described below and then stops as if struck by a sudden thought.

"Here, I'll show you," he says, "anything will go through the rings." He lays the oversize ring in his right hand on the tray ostensibly to get rid of it temporarily. Naturally it goes around the key ring already lying on the tray. He puts the left-hand ring in his mouth as he removes the silk from his pocket with his right hand and displays it momentarily with both hands as in Figure 93A. Note that the right hand holds the grommet corner of the silk (Y in the drawing) between the index and second finger.

The left hand thrusts its corner (X in the drawing) through the ring toward the magician's body as indicated by the arrow in Figure 93A and the right hand takes it between the thumb and index finger. The left hand now removes the ring from the mouth. The silk is around the ring like a sling. "Watch!" says the magician.

The performer lets go the ring so that it hangs in its silk sling as in Figure 93B, the thread passing over his right hand. He raises and lowers the silk several times. Finally he lowers the silk, moving his hand in toward the body and letting go of the tied corner (X) with his right thumb and first finger while still holding the grommet corner (Y) between his index and second fingers.

The weight of the ring and the fact that the thread is slackened by the hand being lowered allows the ring to slide off the silk onto the floor. Immediately the performer raises his right hand again and moves it away from his body. The move is just as if he were playing with a yo-yo. Raising the hand and extending it tightens the thread, pulling the tied end (X) free of the ring and right back up to the right thumb where it started. The motion of the hand (which does not need to be fast once the proper adjustment is dis-

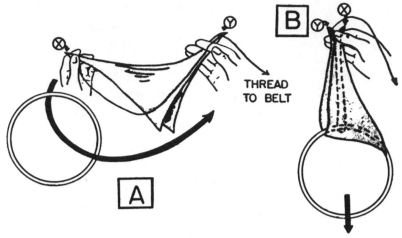

THREAD
TO BELT

*Figure 93*

covered) and the clang as the ring hits the floor after "pene-trating" the silk are perfect cover for the silk business. The fact that the right hand began and ended holding opposite corners of the silk is enough to complete the illusion.

Obviously, says the magician, anything will penetrate the very special metal of the rings. He replaces the silk in his pocket and reaches over to the tray to pick up the ring he laid there a moment before. Instead of picking up the over-size single ring, however, he picks up the key ring nestling inside the oversize single.

It is little wonder then, the performer points out, that the rings may be linked together by just rubbing them gently. Holding the two rings as in Figure 94A, with the key ring in his right hand, the thumb and forefinger covering the open-ing in the ring, the magician prepares to do the slow-motion linking move that is the high spot of the linking ring routine.

With the rings as in Figure 94A, the performer rubs them gently against each other at the same time rotating the two rings as indicated by the arrows and bringing his hands closer

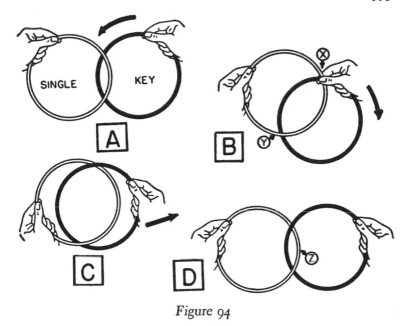

Figure 94

together. The right hand is lowered slightly so that the position of Figure 94B is reached when the right thumb and fingers can slip the single ring through the opening in the key ring at Point X while the hands are oscillating up and down. The performer, however, keeps his gaze fixed on the spot where the two rings cross each other at the bottom (Y in Figure 94B) as if that were the place where the penetration were going to take place.

As soon as the single has slipped through the opening in the key, the right hand is revolved clockwise as in Figure 94C and the hands begin to separate. The performer, still concentrating on the bottom of the rings, follows the movement of the key ring until the position of Figure 94D is reached. Then he blows at Point Z and clicks the two rings together to show that they are linked.

It must be remembered that the audience cannot tell

whether the rings are really linked or just overlapping until the position of Figure 94D is reached. That is when the linking occurs as far as the spectators are concerned—just as the magician blows on the rings. Also, although the linking move is here broken up into steps for purposes of explanation, it is performed as one continuous movement. Apparently the magician merely overlapped the two separated rings, rubbing them against each other, and, when he separated his hands, they linked together. The motion is smooth and without hesitation.

Especially should there be no hesitation when the opening in the key is slipped over the single ring. The fact that the performer keeps gazing at the bottom of the rings and immediately rotates the right ring so that his right hand gets away from the single as soon as possible will give the impression that the right hand never touched the single ring at all. Since the audience cannot tell exactly when the rings did link together, the effect is that the penetration occurred in the Figure 94D position when the hands were widely separated—that is, that the penetration occurred at a spot on the rings that was in plain view and not covered by the fingers.

Immediately the left hand drops its ring and gives it a spin. The left hand then reaches over and takes the key ring from the right hand, being sure to hide the opening with the left fingers. While the bottom ring is spinning, the right hand reaches up through the bottom ring and once more takes the key ring back, tossing the other linked ring off over the right wrist to dangle once more from the key.

However meaningless that last series of moves may seem upon reading, they give the audience the impression (if performed briskly) that the two linked rings have each been allowed to dangle and spin from the other and they help to emphasize that the two linked rings are just alike and that there is nothing special about either.

The rings are now unlinked in slow motion by the same

linking moves. The rings are held as in Figure 95. The hands rotate and come together just as with the linking move described above. As soon as the key is revolved to where the opening is as in Figure 94B, the left ring is slipped out of

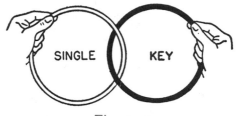

*Figure 95*

the key. The two rings are still held together, however, as the right hand rotates back to its far right position. Only when the rings reach a position similar to Figure 94D are they slowly slid apart, the magician stopping and blowing just before the rings finally separate and then pulling them apart very slowly just as if he were really pulling one through the other at Point Z.

The illusion of the rings separating is startling, since the audience cannot tell whether the rings are really linked or merely overlapped. Apparently the two rings that the audience has just seen linked together simply melt apart when the magician blows on them.

Handing the left-hand ring to a spectator, the magician asks him to select the most solid spot on that ring and to hold the ring up in front of him with the selected spot on top. The magician takes the key ring in his right hand, holding it with the whole fist, the little finger being curled around the opening (as at Y in Figure 96A). Holding the key ring at right angles to the spectator's ring as in Figure 96A, the magician strikes the top of the spectator's ring several times with the bottom of the key ring (Point X in the drawing).

On the third stroke the magician bends his right wrist upward so that his little finger is now at the bottom of the key ring as in Figure 96B. As the key hits the spectator's ring, he lets the spectator's ring slip through the opening by relaxing and then replacing his little finger, immediately rotating the

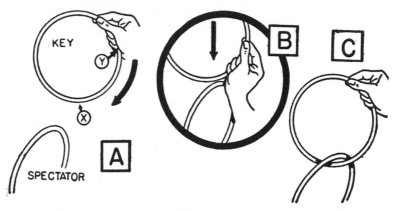

Figure 96

key ring so that his hand is once more at the top as in Figure 96C. This motion of the right wrist is covered by the larger motion of the whole arm in striking the spectator's ring with the key ring. The effect, of course, is that the two rings were linked together at Point X on the key ring right before the spectator's very eyes while he held one of the rings.

Taking the two rings immediately from the spectator, the performer shows them linked as before and then unlinks the two as described above.

Taking both the single rings in his left hand (key ring outermost with his thumb covering the opening) the magician retrieves the permanently linked two from the spectator who has been holding them for the last several minutes.

Now he will try to link three rings together, says the magician, and, as he returns to his position, he quietly links the key through one of the two linked rings. No particular secret move is needed. The magician merely slips the key into position in handling the rings, covering the opening with his fingers.

Three rings for purity, body, and flavor, says the performer, holding the three rings up so that they resemble the famous

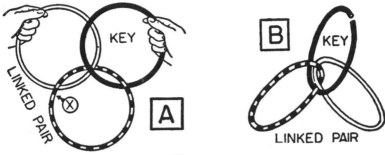

Figure 97

Ballantine trade mark for beer as in Figure 97A. His right thumb and forefinger cover the opening in the key and the left thumb similarly holds another of the rings, the third ring dangling below.

Or, if the spectators prefer, suggests the performer, the trade mark of Mission Bell Wine, and he links the key through the other side of the ring in the left hand at Point X in Figure 97A and then releases the left hand and allows the two solid rings both to swing bell-like from the key ring as in Figure 97B.

And now, announces the magician, the most difficult feat of all—putting all four rings together again. With a great deal of clatter, clash, and haste (since he is building for his finale), the magician unlinks the key from only one side of one of the linked pair (so the three are now in a straight chain) and links the last single into the key. Then, grasping the single ring with his left hand, he allows the entire chain to hang therefrom, still keeping the thumb and forefinger of his right hand over the opening in the key ring (now second from the top of the chain).

He displays the chain of rings, holding them against his body as one might display a necklace or new tie. All four of the solid steel rings once more linked into a chain just as they were at the beginning, he exclaims as if he had just turned the world upside down, and that is the Chinese Linking Rings!

NOTE: 1. In lieu of the thread device to cause the "penetration" of the silk through one of the rings, a magical device called the Petrie Utility Reel can be used. In that case the silk would be made apparently to penetrate the ring with the usual moves for that device.

2. The performer may, of course, want to change this routine according to ideas of his own. It does not seem advisable, however, to try to eliminate any of the routine as given. Despite the necessarily long description, the routine takes but three or four minutes to perform and is thought to be as concise as practicable.

It must be remembered that the high spots of the effect are the slow-motion linking moves with two rings and the linking while the spectator holds one ring. Ideally, the magician should stop after performing these moves since nothing can validly surpass them. All that precedes the two-ring moves is calculated merely to get the key ring into circulation after the audience is completely convinced that all the rings are solid.

Should the performer stop after the two-ring moves, however, he would have no good reason for not handing the rings out for immediate examination and no good excuse for appearing on stage with four rings in the first place (as he must do) instead of only two. The latter part of the routine, therefore, is calculated to correct this situation.

It is not pretended that the beer trade mark and the bell business are awe-inspiring. These two moves provide a use for three rings together and act as an acceptable "cute" pause to allow some contrast just before the performer links all four rings together. Obviously the real climax is seeing two solid steel rings melt slowly through each other, but the magician cannot stop there and still maintain his effect. So he must build a fake climax (but one that is logically acceptable) by convincing the audience that linking three and then four rings together is more startling than linking only two. Also he must have a fast, almost hectic, finale which, because of the well-recognized customs of showmen, will lead the audience to believe that the performer will bow over the rings and walk off. Thus the spectators will not be surprised that the magician does not end his trick in the casual manner in which it began and pass all the rings out for examination again.

Some performers may, however, want to eliminate the silk penetration business. Merely picking up a silk with which to wipe off the rings could be used as an excuse for laying the oversize ring in the tray. Since that notion seems to be less logical (and hence, less effective) as an excuse, it is not recommended.

3. There is no need to worry about the ring that is in the tray being seen. It is, of course, completely visible should anyone look for it. The attention of the audience is, however, adequately directed elsewhere. Incidentally, the reason for using a metal tray is simply that the rings will clank as the oversize is slipped over the key ring lying in the tray. If a metal tray is used, some clanking is expected as the ring hits the tray and so the presence of the extra ring is not disclosed.

## BATHTUB GIN

EFFECT: A glass of perfectly clear liquid instantly changes to inky black while the magician holds it in his hand.

The basis of this effect is a classical chemistry demonstration illustrating the progress of two concurrent reactions with varying reaction rates. This product of the classroom can well be adapted into a mystifying interlude for the magic stage.

Some years ago, chemical tricks were very popular among magic audiences. Most of them revolved around the theme of changing water into wine and were based on the fact that the chemical indicator phenolphthalein changes from colorless to bright pink, depending upon whether it is in an acidic or alkaline solution.

As a matter of fact, the story is told that it was a magician who discovered the physiological properties of phenolphthalein when he gulped down his glass of "wine" in a fit of excessive realism and was unable to finish his show. Phenolphthalein is the active ingredient in such preparations as Ex-Lax, Pheno-Lax, and Feen-A-Mint.

The principal disadvantages of chemical magic today are twofold. First, the tricks are likely very literally to smell. Secondly, somewhere in almost every chemical trick comes the necessity of pouring one solution into another. It is rather difficult today to elicit much wonderment at causing a solution to change color by pouring something into it. The present effect, however, eliminates both of these difficulties.

The primary difficulty with the effect as given here is the inconvenience of procuring and mixing the chemicals. There are for sale, however, by the magic dealers, the necessary chemicals in powder form with which to perform this same effect (athough they may not adhere to the same formula as given here). The reader who is a student or who has other access to the chemical supply of a school or commercial laboratory will have little difficulty in procuring the necessary ingredients. A good drugstore should be able to supply them.

The chief magical attribute of the effect stems from the fact that the magician is holding a glass of water when suddenly and all at once, without any move on the magician's part, the entire content of the glass turns inky black—just like that!

Chemistry students will be further interested in the possibility of fooling learned chemists with such a well-known chemical demonstration by virtue of the interpolated magic technique in the form of the prepared pitcher described below.

PREPARATION: The formula as given here makes 1,000 cc (a little over a quart) of each of two solutions, which are mixed fifty-fifty. This should be enough for four performances as described. Since neither of the solutions will keep very well, attempting to perform the effect with old solutions should be avoided.

SOLUTION A.

Dissolve one gram of potassium iodate ($KIO_3$) in a little distilled water and dilute the solution to 1,000 cc with distilled water.

SOLUTION B.

1. Dissolve four-tenths of a gram (0.4 gm) of sodium bisulfite ($NaHSO_3$) in 900 cc of distilled water.

2. Add to this solution one-fourth cc (0.25 cc) of concentrated sulfuric acid ($H_2SO_4$) and five grams (5.0) of starch in suspension.

The starch suspension is made by dissolving ten grams (10 gm) of starch in as little as possible cold distilled water and then adding an equal quantity of boiling distilled water. One half of this solution when cool (comprising, of course, five grams of starch) is added to solution *B*. (The standard starch indicator for iodometric analysis may be used if available instead of the suggested starch suspension.)

In addition to the two solutions, a prepared glass pitcher is needed. For convenience in handling the pitcher should have a large top as indicated in Figure 98, and should be able to hold between a half-pint and a pint when only two-thirds full. In addition, the pitcher should have a complicated etched

*Figure 98*

or cut-glass design so that, while it appears to be transparent, the sides cannot be seen through readily. The proper variety can usually be found in a dime store.

A small glass tumbler (or the bottom part of one) large enough to hold five ounces of fluid and yet short enough to be hidden inside the pitcher is cemented to the bottom of the pitcher next to the pouring lip as shown by the shaded area of Figure 98.

To prepare for performance, four ounces of one solution (either one) are poured into the glass insert in the pitcher, taking care not to spill any of the solution into the pitcher proper. Four ounces of the other solution are then poured into the pitcher proper. A ten-ounce glass tumbler or highball glass is placed beside the pitcher on the table.

It will at once be seen that, owing to the construction of the pitcher, the two solutions will be mixed upon being poured together from the pitcher into the glass. As far as the audience is concerned, however, only one fluid is used, there being no apparent pouring of one solution into another.

PRESENTATION: The concentrations of the solutions as given above are calculated to cause the change from colorless solution to inky blackness thirty seconds after the two solutions are mixed at normal room temperature. The speed of the reaction, however, varies considerably according to the temperature. The effect should not be attempted without trying it out just as performed (to get the exact timing) just before starting the program. If the tumbler will be held in the hand during the performance, it should be during the trial in order to include the warming effect of the hand.

With his watch lying where it can be seen readily, the magician picks up the glass tumbler and a handkerchief and begins to wipe the glass, turning it upside down, etc., as a tacit demonstration that it is entirely empty. He relates an experience he remembers hearing his uncle tell about during the Prohibition Era.

It seems that at that time the manufacture of bathtub gin was quite a household industry. The efforts were frequent but the product was pretty awful. The domestic stills apparently turned out nothing but raw alcohol, like this. The magician picks up the pitcher and pours the contents into the glass. He glances at his watch and knows that he must talk for exactly thirty seconds (or whatever time his solutions take) until the climax.

He points out that raw alcohol is colorless, as the audience can see, and looks just like water, although there is considerable diffcrence in the taste. It cannot be called whisky because the bathtub variety was never aged or allowed to mellow in wooden casks as whisky ought to be. Sometimes it was colored with caramel, but the coloring did little to the taste or effect.

The performer goes on talking casually about bathtub gin, either holding the glass in his hand or placing it on the floor or table where all can see. Or he may choose as his topic the frequent use by the soldiers in the last war of 190 proof medical alcohol mixed with canned pineapple juice or powdered lemonade as a beverage. The medical alcohol is colorless, but it still had the teeth in it, especially when many soldiers did not realize that it was about twice as strong as the strongest whisky on the market.

In any event, the magician keeps one eye on his watch from time to time, and, as the moment for the change approaches, he ends up with some such line as: "And they used to drink this stuff! Why, they would have been better off if they'd taken to drinking *INK!!*" As he says the last word, he gestures toward the glass that he has been casually holding and the entire contents instantly change to ink.

NOTE: If the performer prefers, he may, of course, make up some other sort of patter story involving a clear liquid and ink. The story could be so constructed that the performer would not have to worry about the exact timing. He would say a sentence, and, if the change did not occur, he would say another short sentence—and so on until the change did occur, each sentence being a logical predecessor of the color change.

Such a presentation is not as strong as the one described, for there is something completely impossible about the effect of what appears to be a glass of water changing instantly into a glass of ink without any mixing or any more provocation than the performer's casual gesture toward the glass.

## A WORD ABOUT SUCKER TRICKS

The four tricks next following are all different in effect and method but they have one thing in common: they all depend for their success upon the fact that the magician apparently blunders but finally succeeds in accomplishing the trick.

The addition of this "sucker" climax to any trick will immeasurably enhance the effect of that trick on the audience. It can probably be analyzed to be akin to the "audience participation" appeal of the current television programs. With "sucker" effects the magician plays a trick on the audience as well as for the audience. The spectators laugh not only at the magician's patter but at their own gullibility. Each spectator is sure that the other spectators have been just as baffled as he, since each spectator is led to make as much of a fool of himself as the others.

"Sucker effects" are as useful with adults as with children (contrary to a popular misconception). The difference is that the younger spectators shout and scream when they think they have caught the magician in some misstep whereas the more adult (and more polite) spectators will smile derisively and sit in embarrassed silence. But the adults are thinking the same things the children are shouting. With younger audiences, the magician pretends not to understand the shouting and "milks" the audience for all the excitement he can work up. With adults, he simply pauses long enough for each spectator to say to himself, "What an easy trick to see through!" and then he vindicates himself with the final move.

The comments and reactions of audiences of all types indicate that even a performer who is unable to put across "straight" tricks can get a good effect with a sucker trick. And the cynical spectator who refuses to be impressed with a performer's prize trick will "bite" just as hard as the next man on a well-presented sucker effect.

The sucker idea can be utilized in several ways and for several purposes. For instance, in "Stung Again" (as well as "Sucker Trick" on page 198) the main point of the effect is to get the audience to "bite" on the sucker idea. In "Read to Shreds" the sucker notion is used, under the guise of "explaining" the trick to the audience, to put new life in an old standby. The device can also be used for some ancillary purpose such as in "20th Century" on page 239, where it aided in causing a silk to vanish.

In addition to the three effects here described, there are numerous other sucker tricks on the market. The apparatus used in such effects is, however, too complicated to warrant description here. Of such tricks the one most to be recommended is the "Sucker Die Box." The effect to be obtained with this trick—especially on child audiences—is usually sufficient to override the objection to magical-looking apparatus expressed in the first chapter of this volume.

The reader is also recommended to an effect called "Soft Soap" wherein ink spots are mysteriously removed from several handkerchiefs while inside a box of soap chips, accompanied by an extremely strong sucker climax.

## STUNG AGAIN

EFFECT: The magician attempts to make one of three large pictures vanish but his efforts are so fumbling that the audience is far from deceived until the end, when there is a double sucker climax. So far as can be determined, this is an original adaptation of a classic effect the inventor of which it is impossible to trace.

PREPARATION: Three pictures are needed for the effect and five pieces of thin white cardboard on which to paste the pictures. The contents of the pictures and the size are both up to the performer's fancy and requirements. For even intimate work, it would seem best to have the cards at least four by six inches to help eliminate thoughts of possible sleight of hand. The theater performer would probably want cards of eleven by fourteen inches. A happy medium seems to be eight by ten inches.

Probably the most readily adaptable presentation (the one given here) is based upon three pictures of bathing girls (as might be found in "Esquire" magazine)—a blonde, a brunette, and a redhead (with the redhead the least attractive of the three). For children's shows three animated cartoon or comic strip characters might be more to the point, with a suitable patter story built around them. This sort of trick lends itself well, also, to the salesman who uses magic with his customers and to the magician who performs frequently before trade groups and business conventions in that the three pictures might be of various brands of cigarettes, whisky, automobiles, etc.

Whatever pictures and sizes are decided upon, the three pictures are pasted on three of the pieces of cardboard. On the fourth piece of cardboard the legend "STUNG" is lettered on one side and "STUNG AGAIN" on the other (or "FOOLED" and "FOOLED AGAIN" or such other similar legend as may suit the performer's fancy).

The edges of the three pictures and the "STUNG" card are all bound with colored scotch tape to give the effect of a frame. The fifth (blank) card is similarly bound with colored scotch tape and is then hinged to one long edge of the redhead card with the same scotch tape, making a folder with the redhead picture on the front. One of the other cards should be inserted between the blank and the redhead card while the tape hinge is being fashioned so as to make the hinge loose enough to carry one of the other cards unnoticed in the folder. Figure 99A indicates the required cards.

The only further requirement is some sort of screen or cover. The best thing for this purpose is a colored decorative mat made of tiny wooden slats and painted with a picture of a Chinese pagoda. These mats were popular as wall decorations at one time and may still be found in some out-of-the-way stores. Their virtue is that they are completely flexible and can be rolled up (see Figure 99B).

In lieu of such a mat, a piece of stiff paper or opaque cloth (perhaps colored to look like a bath towel or beach robe, or some such article) stiffened at the ends with pieces of wood or wire will serve. This cover is rectangular, its dimensions depending upon the size of the pictures. The cover should be a couple of inches wider than the pictures are long and two and one-half times as long as the pictures are wide.

To prepare for performance, the "STUNG" card is placed

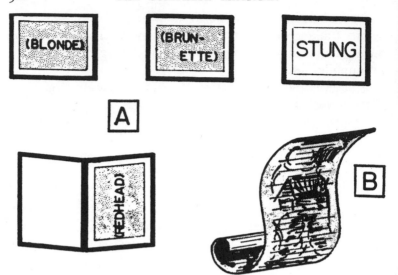

*Figure 99*

inside the redhead folder. The blonde and brunette cards are placed above and below the redhead card and put on the table. The cover is rolled up (a tacit demonstration that it contains no hidden cards) and is placed beside them.

PRESENTATION: Picking up the three picture cards, the magician displays them in a fan. He relates that these are pictures of three girls he encountered recently on the beach.

Extending the three pictures toward one of the spectators, the magician asks which one he finds most attractive, the blonde, the brunette, or the redhead. If the spectator picks either the blonde or the brunette, the magician says, "Fine. We'll use the girl you selected." If, on the other hand, the spectator picks the redhead, the magician acts as if his question were purely incidental and had nothing to do with the trick, saying: "That's what everybody says—and I always thought gentlemen preferred blondes!" or some other such bit of inanity. In any case either the blonde or brunette will be used. We shall assume the spectator selected the blonde.

While on the beach, the magician says, he ran across these three girls sunning themselves and, like the spectator, he was greatly attracted to the blonde. While talking to them, the magician discovered that the brunette and redhead both had previous engagements for that evening, but the blonde, much to the magician's delight, was unattached. The magician asked the blonde for a date, to which she agreed rather coolly, saying she would meet him outside her bathhouse when she had changed her clothes.

The magician picks up the cover with his left hand, allows it to unroll, and shows it on both sides. He then holds both the top and bottom of the cover in his left hand so that it forms a sort of sling or folder into which the pictures will

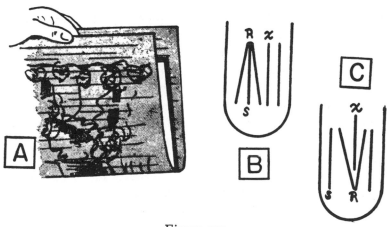

Figure 100

fit as in Figure 100A. The cover is to represent the bathhouse, he explains.

All three girls, the magician relates, then went into the same bathhouse to change their clothes. So saying, the magician places all the pictures inside the fold of the cover, being sure that *the open edge* of the redhead folder is *down-*

ward. Figure 100B diagrams the cards in the folder—X being the blonde picture, S the "STUNG" card, and R the redhead folder. He cautions the audience to remember the situation: there is the redhead, the brunette, and the blonde all in the bathhouse. As he repeats each name, the magician removes that picture from the cover, shows it to the audience, and puts it back.

When the magician removes the redhead picture to show it, he leaves the "STUNG" card behind in the cover (that is, since the redhead folder was originally placed in the cover with the open edge down, the magician merely picks the folder up from around the "STUNG" card). When he replaces the redhead folder after showing it separately, he turns it so that *the open side is uppermost* in the cover as in Figure 100C.

Then the blonde and brunette pictures are separately removed and shown. When the blonde picture is replaced in the cover, it is slid *inside the redhead folder* where the "STUNG" card originally was as in Figure 100C. Since the cards are all completely hidden by the cover, the magician may take his time to make sure that the inserted blonde picture is lined up with the folder so that subsequently the redhead folder can be shown to the audience, completely hiding the blonde card inside.

The trouble was, the magician continues his story, that in a few minutes both the brunette and the redhead came out of the bathhouse without having changed their clothes. So saying, the magician removes the redhead folder from the cover with the blonde card concealed inside, shows it back and front, and lays it aside. (A small point to remember is that when the redhead folder is turned to show the back, the hinged edge rather than the open edge should be turned toward the audience.) The brunette card is also removed, shown back and front, and tossed casually onto the table (to dispel any suspicion of holding two cards as one).

But, says the magician, the blonde never reappeared. The magician's patience was finally exhausted and he looked into the bathhouse (he peers into the cover) but the blonde had vanished. He even looked behind and underneath the bathhouse, but no blonde.

As he says this the magician begins to execute the baiting moves calculated to make the audience "bite." First, the magician drops the end of the cover *nearest* his body as dia-

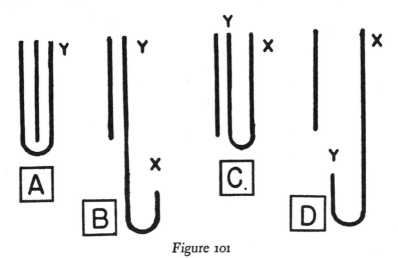

Figure 101

gramed in Figure 101B. Then reaching down with his right hand, he picks this bottom end up and brings it up to his left hand on the side toward the audience as in Figure 101C. As soon as the *bottom* end reaches his left hand, the *top* end is dropped as in Figure 101D. This can be easily accomplished if the "STUNG" card is held between the thumb and first finger of the left hand and the end of the cover is held between the first and second fingers.

The effect of this baiting move is that the magician is trying to show both sides of the cover while still hiding a card behind it. The magician repeats the move of dropping the rear end of the cover and then bringing that end back up in front and dropping the other end. As a result the cover is constantly revolved end-for-end, but it always hides the "STUNG" card (which the audience believes to be the supposedly "vanished" blonde).

Occasionally the magician varies the procedure by bringing the bottom end of the cover up *behind* the "STUNG" card and then turning the whole thing around and continuing the moves with the other side facing the audience. As he "shows the cover empty" the magician keeps repeating that the blonde has completely vanished from the bathhouse.

The length of time consumed in baiting depends upon the audience. With an audience of children, the spectators will be quick to point out that they are not the least convinced that the blonde has vanished. With adults, several of the baiting moves are sufficient. Care must be taken, however, to give the impression that the magician is trying as best he can in all earnestness to convince the audience that the blonde card has vanished. The more seriousness and self-satisfaction that the performer can convey, the harder the audience will bite.

Finally, in the process of showing the cover back and front, the magician allows a corner of the "STUNG" card to slip into view past the edge of the cover. This should be done just as the magician repeats very didactically that the blonde really has vanished. The corner of the card peeking into view after the very clumsy attempts of the magician to hide it forms a complete "clincher" for the notion that the audience is way ahead of the magician in his trick.

The magician pretends to hear someone in the audience make reference to the protruding corner (with children, no pretense is necessary). "Oh that," he says. "That's not the blonde," and he whips away the cover and shows the "STUNG" card. During the laugh which the audience will give at its own expense, the magician gathers up the cover in his left hand to indicate without saying so that there are no cards concealed therein.

At last, pretending to hear someone in the audience suggest that the blonde is on the other side of the "STUNG" card, the magician says, "No, she's not here, either," and turns the card over to expose the "STUNG AGAIN" side to the audience's view for another laugh.

NOTE: The performer will probably want to make up his own patter story to go with this trick. The author wishes to state, however, that he is well aware that the foregoing bit of plot is hardly a thing of dramatic beauty and joy forever. As a matter of fact, such a story would be considered too ridiculous by any sensible audience and it would be a brave magician who attempted to build a "straight" trick on any such plot. The fact, however, that the audience thinks that the plot of this trick is just about as absurd as the magician's attempts to deceive seems to aid materially in the final climax.

The ultimate effect to be achieved with a sucker trick is for each spectator to say to his neighbor (before the climax) not only "Anyone could see how that is done!" but also "How could anyone bother with a stupid trick like that?" Even the loud-mouthed cynic who declaims to all and sundry how silly the trick is will be left open-mouthed and defenseless at the mercy of the audience's laughter.

So long as the effect is not too ridiculous to admit of the possibility that the performer might be serious, no amount of silliness is amiss in a sucker effect of this type.

## READ TO SHREDS

EFFECT: The performer tears a newspaper to shreds and succeeds in restoring the same newspaper to its original condition. In explaining the working of the trick to the audience, the performer succeeds in fooling the spectators a second time with a sucker effect climax.

Although torn and restored paper effects are abundant in the literature of magic, this particular presentation, patterned somewhat after the effect sold by Mr. Jean Hugard, seems to combine the greatest effect with the greatest ease of working.

It is well to note that prepared newspapers with which to perform a similar effect (manufactured by Mr. Hugard) may be purchased ready-made from any magic dealer and the reader will undoubtedly find it more convenient to purchase than to make his own if he performs the effect with any frequency. Since the author's version of the effect differs in a few particulars from the standard method, it is felt that the preparation should be described to complete the explanation of the effect. Also it seems a trifle difficult to convince guests in a living room in Podunk, Iowa, that the magician just happened to pick up a copy of *The New York Times* with which to do this effect and that the paper is really unprepared.

PREPARATION: The main advantage of tearing and restoring a newspaper instead of a paper napkin or something of the sort is its size. Not only can all the spectators be sure to see it, but they are all reasonably convinced that a duplicate paper was not substituted by sleight of hand for the torn pieces since the size seems to prohibit that. For this reason the classical torn and restored effect with a full-size newspaper came into popularity.

The reader will, however, find it more convenient from several aspects to use a smaller newspaper, and no less effective. This description, then, concerns itself with pages from one of the metropolitan tabloid-size newspapers or pages from the half-size Sunday supplements (like the *American Weekly*, etc.). Three copies of the same edition of such a newspaper are needed for the complete effect.

Remove one double sheet (four pages) from one of the newspapers and spread it out. For convenience of explanation. it will be assumed that this double sheet comprises the pages numbered *one*, *two*, *three*, and *four* of the paper. Actually, however, the front page should be avoided since it will have a large headline or easily recognized pictures that will tell the audience immediately that the paper being used is not today's.

The lower right-hand corner of page three is torn off and put aside for the moment. Although the size of the torn piece is hardly critical, it should be about four inches on a side as in Figure 102A. The tearing should be ragged.

The double sheet is now folded in half along its center crease so that pages one and four are face to face on the inside. The resulting folded piece is then folded lengthwise in

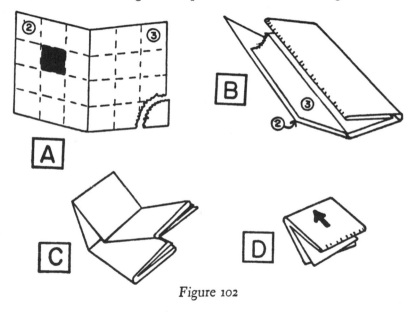

Figure 102

thirds as indicated in Figure 102B. The resulting long narrow strip will have the page number "two" showing on the outside and the torn corner hidden on the inside.

The narrow bundle is then folded crosswise in fourths as indicated in Figure 102C to form the little packet shown in

Figure 102D. The top edges of the pages are the lower edges shown in both Figures 102C and D. The side of the packet with the arrow on it in Figure 102D will later be pasted onto a duplicate page. It is the same portion of page two as the shaded square in Figure 102A. The dotted lines in Figure 102A indicate the creases that are made in the folding just described.

Now the same double sheet is removed from another of the newspapers—that is, also pages one, two, three, and four —and also spread out with pages two and three facing up. The folded packet just made (Figure 102D) is pasted on page two of the duplicate paper at the center of the upper left quarter of the page, as indicated by the darker shaded

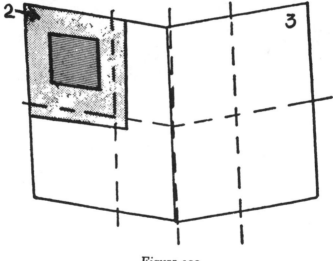

Figure 103

square in Figure 103. The packet is arranged so that the arrow in Figure 102D points toward the bottom of the duplicate page two—that is, so the open edges of the folded packet are toward the top of the duplicate page two. Rubber cement is recommended for the pasting.

A heavy book (or several of them) is now laid on top of the folded packet while the paste dries to compress the packet and set the creases so it will stay folded.

When the cement is dry and the folded packet pressed as flat as possible, the piece torn at the start from the corner of page three is stuck loosely into the folds of the packet. Then from the third of the identical newspapers a large section of page two is cut out and pasted (at the edges only) over the folded packet to hide it as indicated by the large, lightly shaded area on Figure 103. If the right-hand edge of this extra piece is cut right along a column line and the bottom edge rather roughly cut, it will be impossible to tell at a little distance that there is any preparation of page two.

The prepared pages are closed—that is, with the packet on the inside—and the paper folded in half just as it comes from the newsdealer.

Using a different double sheet from the newspapers, another prepared paper is made in exactly the same way except that the corner is not torn from the folded duplicate, and the final extra masking piece (the larger shaded area in Figure 103) is omitted. This prepared paper is also folded just as it comes from the newsstand.

Finally the double sheet that duplicates this second prepared paper is taken and folded just as the little folded packet in Figure 102D (but without tearing off a corner). It is pressed flat so the creases will remain and is then unfolded and refolded in the usual way so that it too is just as it comes from the newsstand.

The three papers are then placed on the magician's table and he is ready to perform. The order of the papers is, from the top down, the prepared paper with the torn corner packet, the unprepared but creased paper, and the second prepared paper without the torn corner.

## Part I

PRESENTATION: Picking up the top prepared paper (the one with the torn corner packet) the magician opens it out and shows it on both sides. Holding it with pages two and three toward himself, he tears the double sheet in half downward along the center fold and places the right-hand half (pages three and four) in front of the left (that is, toward the audience) so that the folded packet hidden by the extra pasted-on piece of paper is toward the magician's body.

So many people have heard about a magician's tearing up newspaper and trying to restore it, the magician explains, that he thought the spectators might like to see the difficult feat accomplished. He tears the two pages again in half downward, again placing the right-hand pieces in front of the left. Then he tears the whole bundle in half crosswise, placing the bottom pieces in front of the top pieces in his left hand.

The dotted lines of Figure 103 indicate where the tears are made. Each of the torn pieces, obviously, is the size of a quarter page of the original paper, the double sheet having been torn into eight pieces. The tearing has loosened the right and bottom edges of the extra pasted-on piece of paper and so, as a final move, the magician grasps this extra piece and tears it off, placing it in front of all the other pieces and thus exposing to his view the folded packet. All the pieces are now held vertically in the left hand, the folded packet hidden from the audience behind them.

Saying that it is really simple to accomplish the trick if all the pieces are carefully folded together, the magician begins to fold the edges of the torn pieces forward (toward the audience) along the sides of the duplicate folded packet. In the process of this folding, the torn corner that has been resting loosely in the folded packet drops to the floor, but the magician is careful not to notice it.

This folding of the torn pieces can be most easily accom-

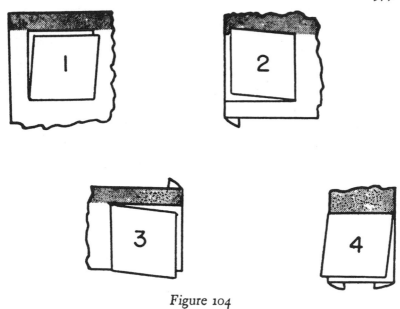

Figure 104

plished if Figure 104 is followed. Thus, first the top edges are folded forward and down. Next the bundle of pieces is turned to bring the former right-hand edges uppermost and these are folded forward and down. Next the original left-hand edges are folded. Finally the bundle is turned so that the original bottom edges of the torn pieces are uppermost and these are folded forward and down.

On this last fold (from Position (4) in Figure 104) the whole packet is turned over under cover of creasing the edges down. That is, the right hand starts to fold the edges forward and down and just keeps right on going so that the whole bundle is turned end-for-end, thus bringing the duplicate packet toward the audience and the torn pieces toward the magician, hidden behind the folded packet.

Giving all the folded pieces a little extra squeeze with his thumbs to make sure they stay in place, the magician blows on the bundle of pieces (or mutters the magic word) and flicks the folded packet with his fingers so that it unfolds downward. Immediately he grasps between each thumb and index finger one of the two corners of the duplicate folded sheet thus exposed and spreads the whole double sheet out by simply separating his hands. The torn pieces remain fastened to the back of the apparently restored sheet.

Only when the "restored" pages are completely expanded will the audience notice that one corner is missing. The magician chuckles at his mistake and, reaching down for the torn corner on the floor, shows that the piece dropped during the tearing actually fits the torn spot on the restored paper. Apparently he got all the pieces "restored" except the one he "accidentally" dropped.

## Part II

There is, of course, no reason why the magician should not stop there, but a second tearing and restoration with the addition of a sucker climax and an apparently unprepared piece of paper enhances the effect materially. This is one of the very few tricks that are better if done twice.

Crumpling the newly "restored" paper and throwing it to one side (out of reach of the audience) the magician suggests that, if the spectators enjoyed the trick, they might like to know how to do it so they too could use it to fool their friends.

Picking up the second paper (the unprepared one) in the pile, the magician shows it openly on both sides and then folds it along the previously made creases so that it looks exactly like the folded duplicate packet pasted on the back of the remaining paper. He explains that the audience did not realize it, but he had such a duplicate secreted in his left armpit. The magician places the folded unprepared paper openly under his left arm or inside his coat in such a way that the audience cannot see it.

Reaching over for the third of the papers, the magician

opens it out (but does not show the back side) and then quickly tears it into pieces just as he did the first time, explaining how to tear the paper, etc., as he goes along. The same movements are used as described above (except for dropping the torn corner). The torn pieces are folded together and the packet is turned over.

Now, the magician says, while he was blowing on the folded bunch of pieces and muttering the magic word before, he actually made a quick turn to the left which the audience does not remember. Under cover of that turn, he explains, the folded pieces were exchanged for the folded duplicate hidden in the armpit. As he says this, the magician does make a slight turn to the left and pretends to exchange the packet he holds in his hand for the duplicate under his arm.

From now on it is easy, says the performer, as he opens out the packet in his hand to show the "restored" paper. The folded pieces are, of course, stuck to the back of this paper, so the magician crumples it and tosses it aside as he did with the first "restored" one.

Of course, there will come a time, he says, when the audience will catch him in the act of exchanging the pieces for the duplicate. That will put him in a tight spot. He takes what the audience thinks to be the torn pieces from under his left arm. The only thing to do in such a case, he says, is really to use magic. Blowing violently on the "pieces," the magician unfolds the unprepared paper and shows it on both sides. The pieces have once more apparently been restored. This unprepared sheet of paper the magician tosses out to the audience to satisfy its curiosity.

NOTE: The working as given above is roughly Mr. Hugard's routine as it is currently sold by magic dealers. Many performers prefer to use the trick as a straight sucker effect. For such a working only Part II of the effect as given is used.

But the patter is as in Part I in that the magician is doing a trick, not "explaining" one to the audience.

The unprepared paper is already folded into a small packet and fastened with a paper clip to the packet pasted on the prepared paper. In the act of showing the prepared paper, the small packet is placed under the left arm, but it is done as though the magician really wanted to do it secretly. While holding the double sheet with the left hand, the right hand reaches up, takes the packet, clip and all, and places it in the left armpit.

After the paper has been torn, the magician goes through the motions of exchanging it under his arm, once again making sure to do it as if he really meant it and not as if he were kidding. As he pretends to do the exchange, he pulls the packet under his arm forward into plain view and then unfolds the prepared paper to show the pieces have been restored. He crumples up the "restored" paper and waits for the audience to call his attention to the packet protruding from his armpit. This packet, of course, he finally shows and tosses out to the spectators.

Such a working eliminates the possibility of using the torn corner idea to its best advantage, since, at the time of the "restoration," the magician wants the audience to think there has really been a substitution. This brings in the torn corner on the wrong beat, so to speak, and diminishes its effect considerably.

For that reason the full effect was given here first. The torn corner idea in "torn and restored" tricks has taken quite a beating lately at the hands of magical writers as being a waste of time and motion. That may be so. The audience, however (contrary to what many magicians seem to think) actually does not believe that the pieces were magically restored. The spectators start out with the assumption that a substitution was made although they could not see how it was made.

One has only to listen to audience comments after the newspaper trick to discover that the spectators are not impressed with the fact that the newspaper was restored. That, they feel, is commonplace for a magician. But the idea of one of the "original" pieces fitting perfectly a torn spot on the "restored" paper piques the fancy of even the most ardent cynic.

## READY MIXED

EFFECT: The performer mixes flour, egg, and milk in a flour box and makes biscuits without the need for heat, but with a very emphatic "sucker" climax.

PREPARATION: An empty box of Bisquick or some other ready-mixed biscuit flour, a prepared paper cup as described below, some flour, two biscuits, a "blown" egg, and a fake glass milk pitcher are needed. The last two items are described in connection with "Pocket Pastry" on page 325 and will not be further explained here.

The Bisquick box is carefully opened at both ends and emptied of its contents. A short piece of scotch tape is affixed as a latch to both the top and bottom so that the box can be opened and closed at will at either end. If about a quarter inch of the scotch tape is turned back on itself (sticky sides together) a little nonadhering tab will form that can easily be grasped to aid in sealing and unsealing the box.

The prepared paper cup is the largest size procurable at the dime store, into which has been glued a curved partition most of the way around the cup and slanting from the top toward the bottom as in Figure 105A. If, after the partition is in place, flour is poured into the cup (so that it falls clear to the bottom through the opening in the partition), the flour will not pour back out of the cup, but will be retained by the partition when the cup is inverted as in Figure 105B. The outside of the cup is marked off to appear like a measuring cup into ounces and fractions of a cup.

The two biscuits or muffins are placed into the bottom of the empty Bisquick box as in Figure 105C. Using a needle and thread, several criss-cross stitches are taken from one side

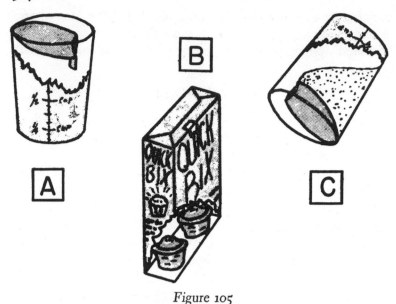

*Figure 105*

of the box to the other, just enough to keep the biscuits from falling out when the box is turned upside down.

As much flour as the prepared cup will accommodate (that is, as much as can be poured into the cup and retained by it without spilling when the cup is inverted) is now poured into the top of the Bisquick box and the top closed. It is well, if convenient, to sift the flour before using to facilitate pouring, and Bisquick itself should be avoided because of the lumps of sticky shortening it contains.

The empty prepared paper cup and loaded flour box are put on the table along with the "blown" egg (empty egg shell) and loaded fake milk pitcher.

PRESENTATION: The magician points out what a boon it is to busy housewives that so many products come in packages ready-mixed. All you have to do, he says, is add water to the right package and heat and you have pancakes, waffles, muffins, rolls, biscuits, or even pie crust. Many people don't know, however, just how really amazing some of these products are.

For instance, says the magician, he has found that he does not even need heat with Bisquick (or whatever brand name is on the box), especially if the cook goes to the trouble of adding other ingredients instead of just water to the ready-mixed flour. The magician will demonstrate.

He opens the box and starts to pour the flour it contains into the paper cup, saying that exactly one cup is needed. He seems a little surprised to find that there is not enough flour in the box to fill the "measuring" cup he is using to the proper level. He is sure that it will be enough, however, and he taps the bottom of the box in order to get the last bit of flour out (and off the biscuits).

One of the conveniences of the ready-mixed foods—or of this particular brand anyway—is that it can be used anywhere. For instance, since he has no biscuit pan or mixing bowl handy, the performer will just use the empty box. So saying, he takes the paper cup and apparently pours the flour he has just "measured" back into the box. Before he "pours" he taps the cup on the table to level the flour (and get it below the partition) and makes a great show of noting exactly how much flour there is in the cup. The partition in the cup, of course, retains the flour so that none goes back into the box.

If the sides of the box are squeezed so that it bulges outward and the top of the cup is placed inside the box as the magician pretends to be very careful not to spill any flour, the pouring illusion will be complete. The cup is placed aside but not until after it has been inverted over the box and the bottom tapped to give the impression that it is completely empty.

Next the "blown" egg is shown and cracked on the edge of the table. The halves of the egg shell are separated inside the box and the magician goes through the motions of shaking the last drippings of egg off the shell into the box. If the egg is opened inside the box and the hands immediately raised in the shaking moves, it will look as if an egg really did go into the box. The magician's acting ability is at a premium here to convince the audience that he really has broken an egg into the box. Care must be taken to crack the egg carefully on a sharp edge for the shell will crush easily since it is empty.

The magician points out that actually only water is needed, but that the egg, etc., give a richer and more wholesome product—at least that is what the directions on the side of the box say. But, he says, you must never put the egg in the box until after the flour is in, for the egg would soak through the box without the flour to absorb it.

Finally the milk is apparently poured into the box from the prepared pitcher. The magician now handles the box with utmost care as if he were afraid to spill some of the contents, just as though he really did have a box of flour-egg mixture.

Closing the top of the box, the magician begins to mix the contents by moving the box slowly from side to side. As the contents get "better mixed," he begins to shake the box more vigorously, finally turning it upside down during the shaking. The magician explains that with this particular brand of flour, just the energy used in shaking the ingredients violently together is sufficient to do the baking; no heat is needed.

To prove his point, the magician opens the box and removes two well-baked biscuits. The audience, of course, will not overlook the fact that the magician is now holding the box upside down and has removed the biscuits from the bottom. Naturally the audience will assume that the ingredients previously poured into the top of the box are still there, hidden in a false bottom of some sort.

The magician looks around as if expecting applause for his feat of making biscuits without heat right in the flour box. If the audience is made up of children, they will clamor to see the box. If the audience is entirely adult, there will probably be an embarrassed silence. The magician builds his effect up as much as he can and then, tearing the box to shreds, he tosses it to the audience saying, like any oven, it is empty when the biscuits are removed.

The little of the original flour that clings to the biscuits will go unnoticed, even if they are given to members of the audience to eat. The threads in the box are destroyed by the tearing and will pass unnoticed with the pieces.

NOTE: The same effect, of course, can be adapted to almost any variety of presentation desired. The magician might make cookies or a cake in a cake flour box or candy (some variety that uses eggs) in a candy box, using sugar instead of flour. With either small cookies or candy, a sufficient quantity could be carried in the box to pass out to the entire audience—a device that can always be used to good effect with children.

The important thing, as with all the other sucker tricks, is to convince the audience up to the last minute that the magician is really trying to receive and that he thinks he is being successful.

# L'Envoi

It is with regret that the author has ended the last chapter of this volume. There is so much of the art of magic that any book—or even many books—seem to be such an inappropriate limit to set about the exposition of magic's many aspects. All that can be hoped is that the foregoing materials may in some measure titillate the reader's interest in magic and then, perhaps, form a representative foundation on which he can build a more complete, more elaborate, more comprehensive structure of magical knowledge.

It cannot be overemphasized, however, that, although the frills and embellishments and ramifications of magic be virtually numberless, the underlying basic principles of deception, misdirection, and entertainment are as few as the performers who thoroughly understand them.

Naturally the reader will at first consider magic solely as a means of entertainment. But it would be (and, as many currently unemployed performers are finding out, it has been) a bitter mistake to limit one's thinking of magic solely to the picture of the bearded Mephisto standing on his gas-lit nineteenth-century stage surrounded by his black art cabinets and incomprehensible apparatus.

The theory of deception, the art of mystification, and the technique of entertainment may run generally hand in hand. But they are not necessary companions. The basic principles underlying why and how the effects presented in this volume succeed are *human* principles, not just magical principles. Hence magic and its rudiments are not only the tools of the entertainer but also the source of ingenious techniques for uses in other fields.

There are such obvious applications of magical knowledge as the use of a magic routine in connection with the salesman's problem of making friends and gaining an audience with his customers. One thinks, too, of using magic in sales promotion work by using the product as an object with which to do a trick. Also, the technique of deception is an important part of the whole theatrical illusion of any stage play or musical show, entirely apart from whether magic is presented as such in the show. For example, when the script of the recent Broadway musical, "Finian's Rainbow," called for a magic spell to turn a white man into a Negro, the change was accomplished by the use of the stage magician's technique although there was no suggestion that the scene was a magic show or magician's trick.

However, there are more subtle applications. One who develops the necessary combination of human understanding, circusy showmanship, and a knowledge of what makes people sit up and take notice should find little trouble in devising new advertising ideas for a brand of soap chips. One who develops the technique of selling his audience on a false premise regarding a pack of playing cards should be that much better able to understand how to emphasize the best features of a contract he is trying to negotiate. One who fully understands how to make people laugh or enjoy themselves and be mystified or entertained should have few lonely moments during his life.

The author may be accused of overextending himself in the above extolling of the utility of magic. Suffice it to say that he believes it . . . and that he hopes most fervently that the tricks and discussions presented in this volume may provide to some extent, at least, a little enjoyment as well as a little profit for the reader.

# Index

Addition Trick, 283
"Al Jolson Card," 342
"All Out—of Nowhere," 257
"Ambitious Card," 86
Aviator Cards, 194

Baker, Al, 61, 76, 283
Baker Spirit Slate, 283
Baking Cupcake in Pocket, 325
Baking Cupcake in Purse, 332
"Backward Glance," 46
"Bathtub Gin," 359
Benson, Roy, 236
Berland, Samuel, 246, 259
"Between the Eyes," 65
Bill in Lemon, 317
Bill Switch, 320, 325
Bill Vanish, 322
Billet Palming, 294
Billet Switches, 286
Billets, 286
Bisquick Trick, 383
"Blackout," 152
Blackstone, Harry, 8, 71
"Blackstone's Penetration," 71
Blank Face Card, 334
"Blendo," 260
Blown Egg, 328, 384

Book Test, 295
Book Force, 298
Bottom Card, 38n
"Brain Wave" Deck, 196, 231
Broken and Restored Watch, 124

Calling Card Trick, 91
Carbon Paper, 290
Card at Any Number, 83
Card Changes in Spectator's Hand, 86
Card Discoveries, 82
Card Escape from Box, 71
Card Fan, 136
Card Flourishes, 136
Card Forces, 95, 175, 186, 189, 198,
   201, 215, 219, 278, 279, 280
Card Penetration, 71
Card Prediction, 65, 215, 227
Card Routines, 80
Card to Pocket, 202
Card to Purse, 204
Card to Spectator's Pocket, 87
Card to Wallet, 204
Card Transposition, 205, 220
Card Vanish, 209
Cardini, 8
Cards, Size of, 155
Changing Water to Ink, 359

Changing Water to Wine, 360
Chapman, Franklin M., 246
Chemical Trick, 359
"Chinese Linking Rings," 344
Cigarette Trick, 107, 127
Cigarette Vanish, 107
Clark, Keith, 245, 246, 260
Clipboard, 282, 283, 290
"Clipboard Addition," 283, 301
Clipboard Forces, 282
"Clipboard Svengali," 282
"Clippo," 115
"Clippo Fix," 115
Collins, Ted, 97
"Color Blinding," 53
Color Changing Silk, 234
Color Decks, 302
Color Prediction, 301
Color Separation, 53
Controlling Selected Cards, 83, 159,
   166, 190
Crushed and Restored Watch, 124
"Crystal Clear," 118
Cupcake Trick, 325, 383
Curry, Paul, 60, 65
Cut and Restored Paper, 112
Cut and Restored Rope, 97
"Cutting Wit," 112

Dagger Trick, 211
"Demi-Tasse," 117
"Die Box," 366
Dinner Table Tricks, 117
"Divining Dagger," 211
Dollar Bill Trick, 317
Double-Backed Cards, 192
Double-Faced Cards, 192, 206
"Double Lift," 171
"Double Trouble," 205
Doyle, Sir Arthur Conan, 273
"Drawn and Quartered," 97
Drinking Glass Penetration, 120
Dubois, Richard, 211
Duke University, 273
Dunninger, 273, 288, 297
Duplicate Card, 198, 202

"Easy To Fool," 141
Egg Trick, 325, 383
Elliott, Bruce, 7

Envelope Trick, 220
Elimination Force, 201, 298, 320

Faked Paper Cup, 383
Faked Pitcher, 326, 361
False Cut, 161
Fan Force, 175
Fancy Cuts, 138
Feather Flowers, 258
Fifteen Card Trick, 220
"Fifteen Miracle," 220
Fish Bowl Production, 258
"Five Hundred Unlimited," 297
Flaming Handkerchief, 331
"Flaming Proof," 127
Flour Trick, 325, 383
"Flying Knot," 146
Forces, 95, 175, 186, 189, 198, 201,
   215, 219, 278, 279, 280, 298, 320
Forcing Decks, 186, 215, 220, 278,
   279, 281, 302, 304
"Four Told," 215
Fox Lake Cards, 194

Glide, 163
Gravity Magic, 85
Grote, Dr. Walter, 91

Handkerchief Ball, 246
Handkerchief Ball Manipulation, 250
Handkerchief Ball Production, 249
Handkerchief for Vanishing Bill, 318
Hat Load, 254, 259
Hat Production, 253, 258, 259
Haunted Pack, 196
Hindu Shuffle, 139, 165
Houdin, Robert, 8
Houdini, 273
Hugard, Jean, 246, 332, 374

Impressions, 290
Injog, 161
Ink Trick, 359
Index, Pocket, 291, 300

Kellar, 8
Key Card, 38
Key Card Location, 42, 48, 61, 64,
   144
Knot Without Letting Go Ends, 102

Lambi, Allan, 206
Lemon Force, 320
Lewis, Petri, 259, 358
Limited Choice, 291, 297, 300
"Linking Rings," 344
Location Using Key Card, 42, 48, 61, 64, 144
Locked-Flap Spirit Slate, 283
"Look, No Hands!" 37
"Lucky Lemon," 317
"Lumpy Legerdemain," 129

Magic Apparatus, 316
"Magic Bow," 151
"Magic Hangman," 149
Marked Cards, 190
"Master Silk Routine," 259
Match to Silk, 259
Match Trick, 152
"Mene Tekel Deck," 189
"Mental Effects," 272, 274, 281, 286, 301, 308
Mental Routine, 301, 308
Milk Glass, 332
Milk Pitcher, 326
Milk Trick, 325, 383
Mind Reading, 272, 274, 281, 301
Mind Reading Routine, 301, 308
Misdirection, 23
Misdirection, Rules of, 25, 26, 27, 28
"Mis-made Flag," 260, 261, 270
"Mistaken," 86
Mulholland, John, 221

Napkin Trick, 120, 121, 124
Neck Penetration, 149
Newspaper Trick, 373

"Old Hat," 253
One-Ahead Principle, 215, 289
One-Out-of-Three Force, 201, 298, 320
Opening Tricks, 146, 236
Outjog, 161
"Out Of This World," 60
"Overhand Shuffle," 158

Palming, Card, 168
Palming, Billet, 294

Paper Flour Cup, 383
Paper Tricks, 112, 118, 373
"Peek Deck," 196
Peeling Cards Apart, 193
Penetration, Handkerchief, 71
Penetration, Table Cloth, 127
Penetration, Table Top, 120
Petrie Utility Reel, 358
Pin-Up Girl Card, 334
Pocket Index, 291, 300
"Pocket Pastry," 325
"Pocket Pickings," 202
"Pocket Slates," 277
Powder for Cards, 187
"Precognition," 227
Predicting Selected Cards, 65, 215, 227, 278
Predictions, Non-Card, 283, 300, 307, 310
Prepared Playing Cards, 186
"Pretty Name" Deck, 301, 304
Producing Single Silk, 249, 256, 259
Pull Vanish, 236
"Pure Luck," 88
Purse Trick, 325

"Raise You Three," 332
"Read to Shreds," 373
"Ready Mixed," 383
Reversed Card, 46, 84, 85, 205
Reversing Top Card, 46
Rhine, Dr., 273
Riffle Shuffle, 156
Ring Penetrating Silk, 351
Ring Switch, 351
Ring Trick, 344
Rising Cards, 332
Rope Trick, 97
Rosebud to Silk, 255
"Rough-Smooth Deck," 186, 227, 302
Roughing Fluid, 187

"Salt and Pepper Cheat," 121
Salt Shaker Vanish, 121
Self-Tying Knot, 146
Set-Up Decks, 53, 194, 215, 278, 279
Set-Up, Stebbins, 194, 215
Short Card, 190
"Should Not Knot," 102

Showmanship, Rules of, 19
Shuffles, 156, 158, 165
Silk, Color Changing, 234
Silk from Matchbox, 259
Silk Loads, 247, 249, 252, 254, 259
Silk Penetration, 149, 351
Silk Production, 243, 246, 255, 257, 259
Silk Production, Bare Handed, 246
Silk Pull, 268
Silk Reel, 358
Silk Routine, 244, 259
Silk Streamers, 254
Silk Tricks, 102, 103, 146, 148, 149, 151, 234, 236, 239, 243, 246, 255, 259, 261, 265, 267
Silk Vanish, 236, 240, 268
Silks, 232
"Silks at the Finger Tips," 259
Silks, Care of, 233
Silks, Size of, 233
"Sleight of Foot," 85
"Sloppy Shuffle," 139
Soap Chip Trick, 366
"Soda Jerk," 118
Soda Straw Wrapper, 118
"Soft Soap," 366
Special Decks, 196, 221, 227, 278, 281, 282, 302, 304
"Spellbound," 48
Spelling Trick, 48
Spirit Addition, 283
"Spirit Calling Card," 91
Spirit Message, 278
Spirit Routine, 301, 305
Spirit Slate, 275
Spirit Slate, Pocket, 277
Spirit Writing, 91, 275
Spring Flowers, 258
Square Knot, 100
Stebbins, Si, 194, 215
Stillwell, George, 245, 246
"Stung Again," 366
"Subconscious Memory," 301
Sucker Die Box, 366
Sucker Effect, 198, 240, 364, 366, 381, 383
"Sucker Trick," 198
Sugar Trick, 118, 129
"Svengali Deck," 189

Switching Decks, 185, 197, 214, 217, 220, 229
Switching Dollar Bill, 320
Switching Envelopes, 225
"Sympathetic Silks," 260, 265, 269
"Sympathetic Student," 60

Table Cloth Penetration, 127
Table Magic, 117
Tarbell, Dr. Harlan, 234
"Tarbell Silk," 234
Taylor, Dr. F. V., 48, 107, 206, 297
Thumb Tip, 107, 335
"That's All," 76
Thurston, Howard, 8, 333
Top Card, 38n
Torn and Restored Paper, 118, 373
Transposition of Cards, 205
Transposition of Sugar Cubes, 129
Trick Knots, 102, 146, 148, 149, 151
"Tumbling Tumbler," 120
"Turnabout," 87
Twentieth-Century Trick, 239, 260, 267, 270
"Two-in-One Routine," 301
"Two to One," 236

"Vanishing Cane," 259
Vanishing Card, 209
Vanishing Deck of Cards, 76
Vanishing Dollar Bill, 322
Vanishing Knot, 148
Vanishing Silk, 236
"Vanishing Wand," 259
Vernon, Dai, 8
Victor, Edward, 97

Walsh, 259, 342
"Watch Out!" 124
Watch Trick, 124
Water-to-Ink Transformation, 359
Water-to-Wine Transformation, 360
"Where There's Smoke . . . ," 107
Writing by Spirits, 91, 275
"You Do as I Do," 64
"Your Number," 83
"Your Wife's Hair," 301

Zens, M. F., 221